Why Do You Need This New Edition?

More and more people get their information from online sources, and they want their information in a clear, to-the-point style of writing. Even as methods of information delivery change, the need for good writing becomes more important. Writers and journalists will be successful only if they can gather information and present it accurately and concisely and in language that appeals to a specific audience—no matter what the medium used to display the information.

In today's media world, students need a book like *Reaching Audiences* to strengthen grammar, spelling, punctuation, and math skills, while at the same time to refine basic writing skills. The basics are often less important or even lost in high school and sometimes in college, but they are essential to clear writing. As more information is loaded online, students need to be able to assess the quality and accuracy of that information. They must be able to discern whether what they are reading and hearing is accurate and important enough to become part of their own writing.

The fifth edition of *Reaching Audiences*

1. Continues to stress the basic writing, editing, and reporting skills essential to all good communication, whether the product is a print or online article, a news release, a broadcast story, or an image-building advertisement.

2. Adds a new chapter on producing online content and strengthens the existing section on online editing.

3. Includes historical context for recent changes in transmission of information.

4. Contains updated examples from newspapers and news sites around the country and exercises to provide practice in writing.

PEARSON

Reaching Audiences

A Guide to Media Writing

FIFTH EDITION

Jan Johnson Yopp

University of North Carolina at Chapel Hill

Katherine C. McAdams

University of Maryland at College Park

Ryan M. Thornburg

University of North Carolina at Chapel Hill

Allyn & Bacon

Boston   New York   San Francisco
Mexico City   Montreal   Toronto   London   Madrid   Munich   Paris
Hong Kong   Singapore   Tokyo   Cape Town   Sydney

Acquisitions Editor:	Jeanne Zalesky
Series Editorial Assistant:	Megan Lentz
Marketing Manager:	Blair Tuckman
Production Editor:	Karen Mason
Editorial Production Service:	Elm Street Publishing Services
Manufacturing Buyer:	Debbie Rossi
Electronic Composition:	Integra Software Services Pvt. Ltd.
Cover Administrator:	Kristina Mose-Libon

Between the time website information is gathered and then published, it is not unusual for some sites to have closed. Also, the transcription of URLs can result in typographical errors. The publisher would appreciate notification where these errors occur so that they may be corrected in subsequent editions.

Library of Congress Cataloging-in-Publication Data

Yopp, Jan Johnson.
    Reaching audiences : a guide to media writing/Jan Johnson Yopp, Katherine C. McAdams, Ryan M. Thornburg.—5th ed.
        p.   cm.
    Includes bibliographical references and index.
    ISBN-13: 978-0-205-69310-8
    ISBN-10: 0-205-69310-5
    1. Mass media—Authorship.   2. Mass media—Audiences.
I. McAdams, Katherine C.   II. Thornburg, Ryan.   III. Title.

P96.A86M38 2010
808'.066302—dc22

                                                            2008048623

10   9   8   7   6   5   4   3   2   1—EB—13   12   11   10   09

Allyn & Bacon
is an imprint of

www.pearsonhighered.com   ISBN-13: 978-0-205-69310-8
                               ISBN-10: 0-205-69310-5

Contents

6 Beyond the Lead: Writing the Message   146

7 Producing Online Content   170

8 Beyond Breaking News   199

PART THREE ▪ *Gathering Information*

Preface

More than 15 years ago, we had a great idea: We wanted to create a book about the core skills needed for all media writing—the skills writers need so they can reach audiences anywhere, in any medium, on any topic. Today, the convergence of media predicted in the early 1990s has become a reality, making our little book more valuable than ever. In editing the fifth edition, we have focused again on teaching writers to reach active audiences in a vibrant, fast-changing world by applying age-old principles of good communication. To keep us on the cutting edge of new technologies, we have added a co-author, Ryan Thornburg, who has extensive experience as an editor in today's online environment.

Information-age media offer a multitude of ways to send and receive information. Audiences are drawn to today's dazzling array of sources for news and entertainment: News reaches audiences now by cable, Web, iPod, and iPhone, as well as by magazines, newspapers, radio, and TV. Wave after wave of invention adds to the growing list of available media. Each new medium invites attention, analysis, and adoption. Developments seem to appear faster than they can be mastered and offer more interactivity for audiences.

Technology allows communicators to produce messages efficiently and quickly, just as it allows users to access information faster, more selectively, and in greater quantities. Technology has also broadened the field for communicators. Students graduating from journalism and mass communication programs have many career possibilities, including but extending far beyond traditional jobs in newspapers, magazines, public relations, advertising, radio, television, and multimedia. Recent graduates have found themselves with such titles as Web developer, Web master, content editor, and media products coordinator.

Professors of journalism and mass communication still teach specific styles of writing. Students interested in journalism first learn the inverted pyramid style of writing, then more complicated formats. Broadcast students follow a shorter and more casual electronic format. Advertising students learn copywriting. Public relations students practice writing news releases and brochures. Photojournalism students write cutlines. Online editors write blurbs. Multimedia producers create multilevel infrastructure. Graphic designers write legends. Each format has its prescribed guidelines, and fields frequently overlap. Some print journalists write versions of their stories for online sites or for distribution via individual email addresses. Advertising and public relations at times blend into integrated marketing. Broadcasters stream video to Web sites and pop stories to podcasts.

Regardless of format or medium, today's students must meet the demand for writing that is clear, accurate, relevant, and appealing. They must think constantly about their audiences. They must know their audiences and their specific language uses and interests. Students need to understand the importance of good writing and be willing to take on the task of reaching audiences.

At the same time, professors must push students harder to pay attention to their writing and editing skills. The key ingredient for success in any communication job is good writing. Today's students are the communicators of tomorrow—regardless of how portable or accessible their writing becomes.

In today's world, writing often suffers. The proliferation of technology has diverted many communicators from their main task: clear, concise, complete writing. Communicators can be charmed by the medium of delivery—so much so that they are distracted from thinking about the content and structure of the message. In the rush to produce and send information, people often overlook the critical need for accuracy and proper spelling and grammar. Too many communicators believe the first draft is good enough and do not spend time editing and rewriting, a critical issue with online postings. Working quick and dirty is a habit that can erode informative, entertaining, accurate, well-crafted writing. Technology allows anyone with information to put it out for public view. As a result, much published information is poorly written and irrelevant to audiences.

Students need to learn the skills required to become exceptional communicators, to rise above the mire of quick-but-sloppy writing so often seen in today's media. Students must be committed to the craft of writing. They cannot rely more on computer spell-checkers and grammar-checkers than on their own knowledge. They must know the basics of proper sentence construction. They must know how to gather information, sort it, and put it in a format audiences will notice. They must be willing to check for accuracy. All along, they must use critical thinking skills to connect the message with their audiences. Otherwise, communication will not happen. Remember: Communication must get through to the audience.

The 14 chapters in this book stress the basic writing skills essential to any student in any mass communication field, including news-editorial, advertising, public relations, strategic communication, broadcast and online communication, photography, graphic design, and multimedia presentation. The essentials of good writing apply to all writers, regardless of format or medium.

Part One of the book presents the basic components of the writing process and the critical role of audiences. Students will learn the fundamentals of print journalism, how to write text for different media, and the value of the inverted pyramid style of writing in all media. Any informative writing must be grounded in the tenets of basic newswriting and reporting, and it must be checked and rechecked for precision and clarity. Chapter 2 speaks to the need for accuracy and provides diagnostic spelling, grammar, and math tests. Specific tips are given to improve writing—from word selection and sentence length to grammar and usage. Students also will learn the steps of editing, a crucial part of the writing process for any delivery system.

Part Two of the book shows students how to write leads and organize different story formats.

Part Three discusses how to gather information through three principal methods: research, observation, and interviewing. Students also are introduced to online searches and resources as well as the dangers of libel and unethical conduct in newsgathering and how to avoid bias in writing.

Part Four discusses other media writing: broadcasting and strategic communication, often referred to as public relations and advertising. These types of messages also must be formatted to reach particular audiences.

The appendices to the text contain the answer keys to the self-guided spelling, grammar, and math tests.

Mass communication at all levels demands writing that is accurate, complete, fair, and concise. Writers must constantly consider their audiences; they must create messages that are well written and that will reach the intended individuals.

We clearly embrace technology with all of its changes and challenges. Without it, we would not have been able to produce our writing in this text efficiently and easily. Technology will not disappear, and no one would wish it away. But technology changes. The importance of good writing does not.

Acknowledgments

Writing a book is never the work of just the individuals whose names are under the title, and so it is with this book and its fifth edition. A number of colleagues and friends have provided invaluable contributions.

The core of the book would not have been done without Kevin Davis of Macmillan, who many years ago saw the potential in our initial concept and encouraged us to write, and Karon Bowers, Jeanne Zalesky, Karen Mason, and Megan Lentz at Allyn and Bacon and Amanda Zagnoli at Elm Street Publishing Services, who guided and assisted on the fifth edition.

For the fifth edition, we thank at the University of North Carolina at Chapel Hill, Associate Professor Rhonda Gibson, Associate Professor Michael Hoefges, Assistant Professor David Cupp, and Assistant Professor Barbara Friedman. We also thank researchers Alissa Weinberger and Meg Elliott. In addition, we gratefully acknowledge the following reviewers of this fifth edition: J. Linn Allen, University of Illinois at Chicago; Scott Brown, California State University at Northridge; Deborah Petersen-Perlman, University of Minnesota; J. Frazier Smith, University of Dayton; and Gale A. Workman, Ph.D., Florida A&M University.

Beyond our professional colleagues, we also acknowledge the contributions of our families and their support.

—J.J.Y.

—K.C.M.

—R.M.T.

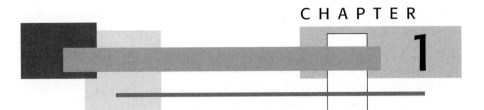

Understanding Today's Audiences

Each morning, Tom Adams rises at 6 a.m. and turns on his TV to check the weather and last night's sport scores. After he showers and dresses, he checks his BlackBerry for e-mail that would alert him to any emergencies he might have to deal with at work or traffic jams on his personalized commute route. At 7 a.m., he pours a traveling cup full to the brim and heads for his car, stooping carefully to pick up *The Washington Post* on his doorstep. Today's *Post*—all 127 pages of it—rides shotgun for the 15-mile trip to the environmental consulting firm where Adams works.

While driving, Adams plugs in his iPod to listen to a podcast of highlights from his favorite sports talk show from the town where he grew up. His phone buzzes with a text message from his friend—their softball game for tonight may be cancelled because of rain.

Once in the office, Adams flips on his computer. He logs in to his account on Facebook to track his friends throughout the day and quickly browses a few blogs that round up the latest news on environmental science and regulation. At lunch, he scans a few national news sites and then sorts through the day's postal mail: two brochures on upcoming seminars, along with current copies of the *Environmental Reporter* and the *Federal Register*.

It is noon in the Washington, D.C., area, and Adams already has processed hundreds of media messages—and ignored or missed thousands more. By the time he returns home at 6:30 p.m., he will have processed hundreds more before he ever sits down to order an "on-demand" movie or play video games online with his brother in Miami.

Several hundred miles away, Lorayne Oglesbee begins her day with a televised morning show, complete with news, weather, and tips for entertainment, cooking, and fashion. As she dresses and packs her briefcase, she pauses from time to time for a look at the TV screen or to attend to one of her two school-aged daughters.

She says her goodbyes when the kids board their bus, then picks up her regional newspaper—*The News & Observer*—from the driveway. She relaxes with the paper over breakfast for a few minutes before her three-mile drive to work. As she drives, she listens to XM Radio, a gift from her husband intended to help with the morning's transition to her hectic life at work. She is an attorney for a large regional hospital.

Oglesbee spends most of her days at work reading, researching, and meeting with legal staff and other attorneys. At the end of a day filled with complex information, she likes to spend leisure time watching television drama or mystery shows with her family. Some evenings, by necessity, are devoted to working on her laptop computer or responding to e-mail messages that arrived late in the day.

Mass communicators have trouble reaching active audiences because of heavy competition from various media and from busy lifestyles. Think about your day so far. How did you get information as you moved through the day? You, like Adams and Oglesbee and other people in the 21st century, are bombarded by an overabundance of media messages. You are faced with many choices about what to read, view, and access.

As a result, only a select few messages actually reach the average person, who is blocking or tossing out messages judged irrelevant, unclear, or uninteresting. Messages must be carefully structured to reach an intended audience. The fate of any message lies in good writing that is streamlined to reach a busy and active person. This chapter discusses

- a historical context to understand the evolution of today's media and audiences,
- how writers can understand and serve audiences,
- how writers can overcome roadblocks to reaching audiences, and
- why the writing process is important for communicators.

Reaching Audiences

Heavy competition from various media and from busy lifestyles vie for people's attention today. Children and adults—including you—have developed the skills to sort constantly what will and will not be read, watched, or heard in the limited time available.

People today have a nearly insatiable desire to be informed about breaking news, such as devastating floods in the Midwest, entertainment figures, or how athletes fared in the Olympic Games. How people sought information was clearly evident in the terrorist attacks on the United States in September 2001, in the aftermath of Hurricane Katrina in 2005, and in the presidential elections of 2008. They went to live audio and video on television and online news services and used e-mail and text messages to connect with relatives and friends. Newspapers—even if they were morning newspapers—rushed to put out special editions or updated their news sites.

People in an uncertain and changing world are looking for information that keeps them safe and saves them money. Today's audiences also seek relief from economic and military tensions around the world, turning to media for entertainment and information about leisure activities. Some people enjoy the analysis and discussion of events found on online independent sites and blogs. Overall, audiences want and need information that will help them cope with—or escape from—everyday life.

How do writers get through the clutter of today's lifestyles and multimedia? How do they reach waiting audiences? They can do it with good writing. They write messages that are simple, clear, and accurate. Audiences will not stick with messages that are confusing, incoherent, or unbelievable. Writers today must craft messages that attract and hold people with their content and structure and that are relevant and emotionally compelling.

Most writers today have a purpose in writing. They want to tell of a family's trauma after massive earthquakes or other natural disasters. They want to inform voters about candidates. They want to entertain viewers of a late-night talk show. They want to highlight a product's usefulness. They want to sell a client's services. These writers want their messages to reach a destination, and they want audiences to pay attention.

Writing Is the Basic Task

Before they are printed, broadcast, aired, or distributed, messages are written. Communicators have to write first, regardless of what medium or technology they use. Consider these examples:

- A school principal writes the monthly calendar of activities before posting it on the school's Web page.
- A radio reporter types stories before she reads them on the 6 a.m. news show.

- A working mother sends her teenage son a text message, asking him to prepare dinner.
- An advertising copywriter creates a direct mail letter for customers of a sporting goods company.
- Three television journalists write their scripts before the weekly Sunday morning news program.
- The editor of the campus newspaper writes two editorials for each edition.
- An advocate of stringent controls on auto emissions adds his opinion to a clean-air blog.
- A student carefully words the subject line of an e-mail to a state senator.
- A Web site developer maps the story flow for an animated guide to holiday performances.

All communicators—whether journalism or mass communication students, newspaper reporters, advertising copywriters, school principals, or even colleagues—must write a message before it is sent to its intended audience. Once writers let go of the message, that is, after the message is aired or distributed, they have little control over whether the audience absorbs the message. Although the message might have arrived, it might be crowded out, deleted, or ignored.

For audiences to pay attention, writers must create messages that are accurate, appealing, organized, readable, relevant, compelling, clear, complete, and simple. Audiences today require good writing.

Roadblocks to Reaching Audiences

A variety of obstacles exist between writers and their audiences:

- **Media and information glut.**   More kinds of information delivery systems become available almost daily. Each memo, article, text message, or news brief has infinitely more competition for an individual's attention than could have been imagined a decade ago. People use interactive and on-demand media in addition to traditional magazines and newspapers. They are hungry for information of all kinds and can choose from an array of media most relevant to their lifestyles.

- **Taxing lifestyles.**   Despite labor-saving devices, audiences today are busier than ever with multiple commitments to work, family, and recreation. People are spending more of their leisure time on family activities and household chores and less on media consumption.

- **Diversity of audiences.**   U.S. society and the media are becoming increasingly diverse in many ways: racial, ethnic, sexual orientation, family structure, and so on. Media writers constantly must work to keep up with changes in audience makeup as well as audience needs and interests. No longer is the average media consumer a white, middle-class man.

- **Unfriendly messages.**   Poor writing interferes with message comprehension, just as commuting, working, children, and too many media choices do. A message that bores or taxes or takes too long to understand can be the greatest roadblock to complete communication.

Media Glut

Writers must remember that today's world offers more to read, watch, and listen to than anyone could possibly consume. In the early 1960s, Marshall McLuhan predicted today's trends, suggesting that new media would alter society in dramatic, unanticipated ways:

> *Electronic technology is reshaping and restructuring social patterns of interdependence and every aspect of our personal life. It is forcing us to reconsider and reevaluate practically every thought, every action and every institution formerly taken for granted. Everything is changing—you, your family, your neighborhood, your education, your government, your relation to "the others."*

He was right: Society has changed. McLuhan could hardly have envisioned the information explosion today. Blog search engine Technorati reported that between 2003 and 2007 more than 72 million blogs were created, and that the blogosphere continued to grow at a rate of 1.4 new blogs every second.

No one can possibly read or see the tiniest fraction of information available today. Media pervade daily life. Technology has overcome the barriers of geography and cost—almost anyone can buy the equipment to be in touch with anyone anywhere in the world. People in remote areas can tune in to events via satellite dishes; a sailboat captain in the Caribbean can view an online copy of the latest *Wall Street Journal*; a vacationing executive can send or receive messages via a BlackBerry or iPod; viewers can watch live Web cam broadcasts from Iraq.

Changes in Media and Audiences

Although the preferred media have changed, the need for information and entertainment is constant. The changes, however, have not been so good for traditional media, such as newspapers. Research has shown that fickle audiences may not return to a medium once they have abandoned it for another.

Newspapers have been hard hit by change as audiences have moved to other technologies to get information and entertainment faster. Since the 1980s, the circulation of daily newspapers has dropped, and hundreds of daily newspapers have closed. Critics of the newspaper industry have said that newspapers have not kept up with technology and have not changed enough to attract readers. Some newspapers have taken steps to reach out to readers by distributing news via online social networks or encouraging the creation of "user-generated content." Others have launched special reporting projects targeted to community interests.

Watching television news is still a daily activity for most Americans. Although television still appears to be the main source of news, it also has dealt with declining ratings and increased competition from other news sources. ComScore, a company that tracks and analyzes media usage, reports that 11 billion online videos are viewed each month in the United States. Apple's iTunes Store has more than "100,000 podcast episodes from independent creators and big names like HBO, NPR, ESPN, *The Onion*, CBS Sports, and *The New York Times*." Awards that traditionally recognize excellence in broadcast news are now awarded to newspapers like *The Washington Post*.

Media forms continue to evolve, taking audiences on a rollercoaster ride into an unimagined future of interactive and virtual reality. More specialized media, more ethnic media, and more electronic media—in fact, more media of all kinds—are on the market. And all these media, old and new, compete fiercely for audience share and attention.

You saw in the Adams and Oglesbee examples that people do not accept or assimilate every message that comes their way. They sift through messages and choose which ones they will hear and read. Successful communicators know they must compete for audience attention. Writers must understand an audience's lifestyles, media preferences, interests, and languages. That knowledge will aid in selecting topics and polishing any message so that it fits an audience's needs and interests. Audiences change, just as society changes, and successful communicators take into account the impact of these changes on their audiences.

The latest census shows that most people in the United States live in households but less than half of those household groups are what was once considered a stereotypical family. Single-occupant, single-parent, and blended families are more common than the so-called typical family household. Neighborhoods and communities that were once homogeneous are now home to many racial and cultural groups.

New media directly affect audiences. New technologies give them greater access to information, entertainment, shopping, bill paying, and even online dating and meditation.

Today's media audiences are filled with people accustomed to fast food, fast travel, and fast information. Today, hundreds of millions of people worldwide have Internet access via desktop PCs and an ever-increasing array of mobile phones, and many of them regularly use the Internet for daily tasks such as banking and shopping. Increasingly sophisticated audiences expect immediate, accurate, high-quality information.

Lifestyles and Diversity

Life today is complex with more sources of news from all directions. Media have proliferated, but no new hours have been added in the day to give audiences more time to use more media. So media choices change and shift.

Even though some audience members use new media to search for information, others are more resistant. Caught in the demands of daily living, they still rely on the more traditional media for information. Perhaps they do not have the financial means to buy computers and software to go online. Writers must be aware, therefore, of how to communicate in both old and new media.

At the same time, people's lifestyles are changing in the United States, and the country is witnessing another trend affecting media use: cultural diversity. Demographic experts predict increasing shifts. The latest U.S. Census data show that minorities make up the fastest-growing one-third of the U.S. population. The traditional categories—African Americans, Asian Americans, Hispanic Americans, and Native Americans—lose meaning as new groups, such as Caribbean and Pacific Islanders, immigrate and as intercultural families become commonplace. Some young people of mixed heritage will no longer classify themselves in a single ethnic category.

Although ethnic- and gender-specific media have long had a role in this country, the changing complexion of the United States has meant an increase in media that address specific groups and individuals. The changes have meant new topics, new discussions, new themes, and new services. Media, particularly general-interest newspapers, cover issues that for many years were carried only in specialized media, such as the black or Hispanic press.

Changing diversity means media are also working to hire employees who represent different groups so that newsrooms will more accurately reflect the makeup of the population in general. This evolution has not been easy. African American, Asian American, and Hispanic American reporters, for example, are still few in number. They are not represented in newsrooms in the same percentages as they are in the population overall.

To attract and retain audiences, media executives consider constraints such as money, lifestyles, increasing demands on time, and the lure of other media. Smart media managers realize they must adjust and be flexible to reach specific audiences. They recognize that often they need to create a profile of their audience members, by research and other means, to find out exactly who they are and what they need. Armed with knowledge about audiences, media leaders—and writers—can aim messages more specifically at their targeted destinations.

Knowing Audiences

People who write tend to read more than the average person. They are likely more educated, have a larger vocabulary, and exhibit a greater interest in various topics. They may write to please themselves or to satisfy what they think audiences want to know. As lifestyles and diversity change, these writers might be out of touch with their audiences and not know who their audiences truly are.

Such ignorance is dangerous. Writers are at risk if they do not know their audiences or if they assume they know their audiences. They also cannot assume that all audiences can grasp complicated, technical messages. Successful writers make an effort to know and get in touch with their audiences.

Identifying Audiences

This explosion of media choices means it is more important than ever to know your audience. A survey of online journalists indicates that analysis of how people are using their Web sites is one of the most common and time consuming parts of their job.

Few writers have a single audience, although many mistakenly write for what they call a mass audience. In today's world, mass audience is only a rough term used to describe a conglomeration of many smaller, specific audiences. Some may consider CNN, for example, to have a mass viewing audience. But even its audience can be broken into subgroups.

Members of small audiences have much in common. Some typical smaller audiences are veterans, working mothers, union members, and power company customers. An audience may be tiny (members of Temple Sinai) or huge (Americans interested in better health care).

Regardless of size, every audience may be subdivided. For example, members of the congregation at Temple Sinai will include smaller audiences of children, teens, young adults, singles, marrieds, new parents, empty nesters, maintenance staff, grounds workers, and so on. Even a smaller audience in the congregation, such as immigrants from other countries, could be further divided into those from specific countries, such as Poland, Germany, or Israel.

Breaking an audience into its composite groups is an important activity for people who need to communicate essential messages. Each subgroup may have specific needs for information and a particular way of getting it. A university, for example, has many audiences, including students, faculty, staff, alumni, potential students, governing bodies, the press, and potential donors. No single message will effectively reach all of these audiences. Most universities spend a great deal of time and money developing specific messages targeted to their many audiences, such as the alumni newsletter for alumni, direct mail for potential donors, and news conferences for the media.

Writers must identify their audiences. A shortcut is to ask the question, "Who cares?" The answer will be a list of groups or audiences that are potential consumers of the message.

Let's try the "Who cares?" method for listing audiences for a message. You are writing an article for your company newsletter on a new policy that provides preventive health care benefits to employees with children. "Who cares?" yields this list:

- married employees with children,
- single employees with children,
- employees thinking about having or adopting children, and
- part-time employees who have no children but wish they had health care benefits.

Listing audiences is important because once writers have at least listed them, they may change their writing approach. For the employee newsletter, your initial attempt at an introduction might have read:

A new company policy will provide health care benefits for preventive medicine.

But after you list audiences, your introduction becomes more personal:

As a single parent, staff geologist John Payne has worried about the extra expense of annual medical exams for his three children and a doctor's visit if the children were only mildly ill.

But Mega Oil's new health benefits program will ease those worries. The plan will reimburse employees with children for preventive health expenses such as well-child checkups.

As audiences are subdivided and defined, so are writing tasks. When writers take time to identify specific audiences, such as single parents, messages can be targeted for those audiences. The approach, structure, and language can be chosen to suit the audience, and communication becomes possible—and even likely.

The Writing Process Explained

E. B. White, in the introduction to *The Elements of Style*, explains that good writing is a writer's responsibility to the audience. He tells how his professor and coauthor, William "Will" Strunk, taught rules to writers out of sympathy for readers:

All through The Elements of Style *one finds evidences of the author's deep sympathy for the reader. Will felt that the reader was in serious trouble most of the time, a man floundering in a swamp, and that it was the duty of anyone attempting to write English to drain this swamp quickly and get this man up on dry ground or at least throw him a rope....I have tried to hold steadily in mind this belief of his, this concern for the bewildered reader.*

It is time to return to Strunk's wisdom. As a teacher in the early 20th century, Strunk knew that audiences were hindered by poor type quality and low levels of literacy. Today, writers contend with new distractions Strunk could never have imagined. But the remedy in either era is the same: clear messages that show consideration for audiences.

Many people believe that good, skillful writing springs not from teaching and learning but from inborn talent that eludes most ordinary people.

Nonsense.

Writing a straightforward message requires no more inherent talent than following a road map. Author Joel Saltzman compares learning to write with learning to make salad dressing:

> *This is the only way I know to make a terrific salad dressing: Mix up a batch. Taste it. Mix again.*
>
> *The secret ingredient is the patience to keep trying—to keep working at it till you get it just right.*
>
> *Do most people have the talent to make a terrific salad dressing? Absolutely.*
>
> *Are they willing to make the effort to develop that skill? That's a different question.*

Good writing, like good salad dressing, can make even dry material palatable and can make good subject matter great. Like ingredients in a recipe, each word, sentence, and paragraph is selected carefully with one goal in mind: pleasing the consumer. The first bite will determine whether the diner eats more; good writing will sell a piece beyond the first paragraph. Like cooking, not every writing session will produce a masterpiece, but the end product must be palatable.

Writers today work in the same way as writers have worked throughout time—by following a regimen called the writing process. Once writers have identified their topics, they follow seven stages of the writing process presented here: information gathering, thinking and planning, listing, drafting, rewriting, sharing, and polishing.

All writers—whether producing a dissertation or a birth announcement— follow these steps. Even students writing under deadline pressure in class can go through the process in an abbreviated way: thinking, organizing, drafting, and revising.

Stages of the Writing Process

The same sequence of steps outlined here occurs in good writing of all kinds. Once they have a topic, all communicators must gather information, think about and plan the message, list key information, draft the message, rewrite the draft, share the message, and polish by checking and editing. Together, these separate stages of activity form the writing process: a set of behaviors common to all writers. The order of stages may vary, and some stages may be repeated, but each stage is essential to producing a good message.

Critical thinking is essential at each stage as well. In selecting a topic, writers have to assess the value of the idea, whether it will appeal to audiences, whether information is available, and how to approach the research and information gathering. At the actual writing stages, writers again think carefully about how to communicate the information clearly in such a way that the audience gets the message. If readers or listeners cannot understand the relevance of the message because the language is convoluted, full of jargon, or unappealing, then the writer has failed. For communication to be successful, audiences have to understand and react or act. Often for inexperienced reporters or writers, knowing the broader context within which an event or situation lives is the greatest challenge to understanding and presenting information to audiences.

Each stage in the writing process is briefly explained here. As you read through them, consider the critical thinking skills needed in each. Later chapters in this book will explain writing tasks in greater detail. You will be referred to relevant chapters as each stage is discussed. Following these stages will produce successful writing in business, education, advertising, public relations, the new media and news media, and daily life. Throughout this text, you will learn what professional writers know: Writing is a skill that can be learned like other skills, one stage at a time. And the first stage is to go beyond yourself to gather information. Good writers are seekers.

Stage One: Information Gathering. Gathering information or reporting on your topic is the first stage of the writing process. To begin the search for information, you must answer questions that all people are prone to ask: Who? What? When? Where? Why? How? How much? Then what?

New technologies put many answers at our fingertips. Basic facts and figures are easy to obtain online, but every writer needs to go beyond superficial statistics. The Internet is just one tool.

Never begin to write without talking to other people or reading their work. Good writing requires basic external information or reporting. Once you know the questions, go beyond your own knowledge to find the answers. Even if you are an expert on the topic, you must find other reliable authorities as quotable sources.

In writing an announcement of an art exhibit at a local art gallery, for example, a writer might begin the questioning by talking with obvious experts—perhaps the curator and an art professor—who can provide answers and lead the writer to additional sources. For the exhibit announcement, aside from the basic *when* and *where* questions, the audience still needs to know the following: What types of artwork will be shown? Will prizes be awarded? Will any special guests appear at a reception? The additional questions will guide the next steps in the information-gathering search:

1. **Interviews.**   Writers talk, in person or by phone or e-mail, to authorities or to people when initial sources suggest. (Interviewing is discussed in Chapter 10.)

2. **Library and online research.**   Any kind of writing can require research in libraries, Web sites, or databases. For example, if the art on display at the art gallery celebrates Impressionism, the writer needs to find out about the Impressionists and their art. (Basic research skills are included in Chapter 9.)

3. **Other sources.**   Brochures, publications, or archives can provide helpful information. For example, an article or brochure about last year's art exhibit could be located through a newspaper index or online archive. (Chapter 9 explains how to use traditional and innovative reference sources.)

It is important to gather information from a variety of sources. Ideally, a writer compiles more information than actually needed so that he or she can be selective about which information to use.

A writer takes notes on every source used in the information-gathering stage. He or she never knows when an important fact or statistic will emerge or when a quotable statement will be uttered. It is best to have a notepad always ready. In addition, careful notes enable writers to attribute interesting or unusual information to sources and to be accurate in what they have written.

Some writers refer to the information-gathering stage as "immersion" in the topic or reporting. Whatever it is called, this first stage of writing turns the writer into an informal expert on the subject matter.

Stage Two: Thinking and Planning.   Once information is gathered, the writer studies the notes taken in Stage One, scanning the material for what information that seems most important and most interesting, and then determines the angle and focus.

A good writer always makes decisions about priorities, keeping in mind the audience that will receive the message. Successful writers actually picture the probable audience, hold that image in mind, and plan the message for that imaginary group. Some writers say they write for a specific person, such as a truck driver in Toledo or Aunt Mary in Hartford. Sometimes the thinking stage will allow the writer to see possibilities for creative approaches to writing.

In this stage of the writing process, the writer may realize that more reporting is needed before listing and writing can begin. Once the writer has gathered enough information, he or she will begin to evaluate and set priorities, asking, "What does my audience need to know first? What next?" and so on. If no further gaps in information become apparent at this stage, the writer takes pen and notepad in hand and moves on to Stage Three.

Stage Three: Listing.   Listing requires writers to list the facts and ideas that must be included in the message. Some writers note key words; others write detailed outlines. Initial lists should be made by brainstorming, jotting down each important message element, and perhaps scratching out, adding, or combining items in the lists. The lists incorporate the decisions the writer made in Stage Two.

Once lists are committed to paper, the writer reviews them and attempts to rank the information. Imagine, for example, the top priority item on the list is "student art in the show." Another item is "students outside the arts," and another is "Impressionism is the theme." Isolating these items guides the writer to structure a message that will feature student art, mention Impressionism, and appeal to students in majors other than the arts.

In this stage, the writer imposes order and organization on the information, and the text begins to take shape.

Stage Four: Drafting the Message—As You Would Tell It.   For most people, even experienced writers, writing seems somewhat unnatural. In contrast, conversational speech always seems to flow. So the efficient writer drafts a message by writing it as it might be told to a friend, thinking about the language that will appeal and resonate.

Checking the lists made in Stage Three, the writer would begin by "talking" about the first and most important element in the message, perhaps like this:

> A student art show that displays the talents of 27 of the University's young Impressionists will open at 7 p.m. Wednesday in the Parents' Association Gallery in Stamp Student Union.

Once this telling process has begun, it continues easily. The writer will move smoothly through interesting aspects of the message to a stopping point after the listed priorities have been included.

By the end of this stage, the writer has created a draft, rather than a message. The term *draft* distinguishes this version from a finished product. It is different from a polished message, and purposely so. Think of the draft as a raw lump of clay, in which substance is what counts. The stages that follow will shape the clay, giving form to the finished message. Drafting messages is discussed in Chapters 5, 6, 7, and 8.

Stage Five: Rewriting.   In this stage, conventions of the written language are imposed on the draft. Writers must look at their work with the eye of an editor, critically assessing how to improve the earlier draft. Sentences are checked for completeness and coherence, paragraphs are formed and organized, and transitions and stylistic flourishes are added.

A good portion of this book is devoted to the skills involved in rewriting or content editing. Only through rewriting—sometimes repeated rewriting—can a message be streamlined to reach its intended audience. All good writers rewrite; great writers pride themselves on the painstaking reworking of their original phrases. Author E. B. White labored for three years over his slim classic *Charlotte's Web*, and he willingly revised much of his other work as many as 14 times.

Of course, writers on deadline cannot afford the luxury of spending years, or even hours, rewriting a draft. But they can carefully edit the content and check the accuracy of their work even in a few minutes, determining if all facts are included and supported in effectively organized language. At this stage, every writer is a tough editor of his or her work.

Writers develop shortcuts to rewriting as they become familiar with print formats, as described in Chapters 6 and 8. But no good writer ever skips the rewriting or content editing stage.

Rewriting is separate from polishing (Stage Seven), in which fine points of style, such as capitalization, are debated. If a writer stops in mid-draft to debate a style point, the train of thought is interrupted, and the writing process stops. Small decisions are left for the last stage—a stage that may be conducted by someone other than the writer.

Rewriting or content editing a draft is the bulk of the writing process. It is hard, time-consuming work; factors to consider in the process are discussed in Chapters 2 and 3. A rewritten draft is far from a finished work, however.

Stage Six: Sharing.   The revised draft should go to another reader—almost any other reader. By this stage, most writers have lost perspective on the message. They have become knowledgeable about the topic, and they may no longer be able to judge how the message would be received by an average member of the audience.

Sharing your work at this stage gives you a much better idea of how an audience member may react. Outside readers will quickly let you know whether the information is confusing or unclear or whether any important details are missing.

It is a good idea to share your work with a naive reader—someone who knows far less about your topic than you. Sometimes a colleague at work or a family member is an excellent choice for sharing because of that person's distance from your topic. In class, your instructor might allow peer editing of stories.

In large offices, outside review of your revised draft might be built in. For example, in big companies, drafts usually are reviewed by one or more editors and often by top management. Such an editing process is helpful in many ways, and certainly it saves the time and trouble of finding someone with whom to share your writing.

Regardless of who is sharing and commenting on your work, you as a writer must never forget that you did the initial research. You have expertise on your topic that your colleagues, family members, or even top managers may not have. Be sure to get feedback from your outside readers in a setting where you both can talk. You may need to explain why certain parts of your message are written as they are. Good editing is negotiation; no editor is an absolute dictator. You as a writer need to work with, and not for, editors and outside reviewers. Together, you can produce clear, correct writing.

Stage Seven: Polishing. The final stage in the writing process is one that many people ignore or abhor. This stage ensures the mechanical aspects are accurate and clear. A misplaced comma can confuse a reader.

Here's where writers consider: Is there an apostrophe after "Parents"? Is the "the" capitalized in "The Parents Gallery"? Finding the answers to such polishing questions is an essential and critical part of the writing process, and it is appropriately the last stage. Many young writers feel that all capitalization, punctuation, grammar, usage, and spelling must be perfect, even in an initial draft. Concentrating on perfection in all those areas is unimportant in the early stages of writing. You might spend 10 minutes looking in the dictionary for a word you eventually decide not to use!

Working on word-by-word perfection at the early stages of writing is wasteful and even paralyzing. Writers who worry about every comma will find it difficult to get through the stages of drafting and revising. Writing becomes a much more comfortable and speedy task when polishing is put off until its proper place at the end of the process. After the important substance and form of the message have been established, writers should spend time with style books, dictionaries, and thesauruses.

All writers should polish their work, even when they pass the message to someone else to edit. An editor or editorial assistant may make the final checks for correctness and consistency and put a message in final form. Confident writers welcome assistance with this final, cosmetic touch, knowing that letter-perfect writing will add to the credibility and clarity of their message.

Getting across messages to people in today's society is an unparalleled challenge. Writers have to accept that they cannot do much to change an individual consumer's lifestyle. They cannot reduce the number of media.

They cannot modify society's diversity. They cannot alter the fact that audiences pay attention to only a few messages amid the daily clutter.

But they can control one aspect: the structure of the message. Good writers have context for today's media world. They know which techniques and which structures best fit their audiences. They use their critical thinking skills to select topics and the approach to developing a story, and they follow the stages of writing to ensure messages are concise, complete, and correct.

Exercises

1. Keep a media log for a 24-hour period between today and the next class. Make a chart showing how you got information, how you communicated information, and which media you used. Indicate how long you viewed or read, a summary of messages, and what else you were doing while using each medium. Indicate whether you had interferences or distractions. Be prepared to compare your media-use patterns with those of others in the class.

2. Interview a relative about his or her media use, formulating questions based on your log. Explore how his or her media use has changed during the last five years, 10 years. Where does the person get most news? entertainment? information that is dependable? in-depth information? Does your relative use new media or more traditional media? What is his or her age?

3. Write a few paragraphs describing the characteristics of the audience for your student newspaper. Then explain how you could follow Strunk and White's advice to help the audience use and better understand the student paper.

4. Choose a news event that occurred today. Select several sources from different media that reported the event. Compare the way each introduced and developed the story. Look at writing style, language, length of story, anecdotes, and quotations. Does the format for presenting the news fit the medium's audiences? How?

5. Interview a classmate. Follow the stages of writing in producing a 30-line story about the person. Explain what you did in each stage. For example, in listing, you might list the person's accomplishments or extracurricular activities. In sharing, you might have another classmate read your draft.

References

Apples iTunes homepage, accessed at http://www.apple.com/itunes/store/podcasts.html.

Associated Press Managing Editors Home Page. Available: www.apme.org.

"11 Billion Videos Viewed Online in the U.S. in April 2008," comScore, accessed at http://www.comscore.com/press/release.asp?press=2268.

Marshall McLuhan and Q. Fiore, *The Medium Is the Message: An Inventory of Effects*. New York: Bantam Books, 1967.

The Poynter Institute Media Diversity Beyond 2000 Home Page. Available: www.poynter.org/dsurvey.

Joel Saltzman, *If You Can Talk, You Can Write*. New York: Ballantine Books, 1993.

William Strunk, Jr., and E. B. White, *The Elements of Style*. New York: Macmillan, 1979.

"The State of the Blogosphere," Sifry's Alerts, April 5, 2007, accessed at http://www.sifry.com/alerts/archives/000"493.html.

U.S. Census Bureau Home Page. Available: www.census.gov/population.

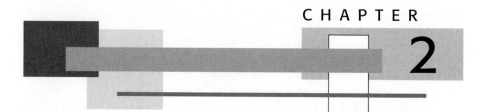

Tools for Writers
Spelling, Grammar, and Math

An ad for used cars states that many more comparible cars are available.

A morning television news show posts a headline that the U.S. secretary of state is meeting with NATO officials in Brussles.

A company's annual report notes that revenues rose from 80 million to 90 million, or a 10 percent increase.

A student blog says, "John Peter Zinger established free speech in America."

A close check of all the above statements shows that more *comparable* cars are available; the meeting is in *Brussels*; the revenues actually rose 12 percent; and it was *John Peter Zenger* who made his mark as a Colonial journalist.

Writers can take care as they gather information and write stories. But if they are not careful in checking their grammar, punctuation, spelling, numbers, or facts, they can damage their credibility—as well as their company's credibility. With the Internet, inaccuracies can be captured and spread indefinitely. Readers might not see posted corrections.

Errors need not be dramatic to cause audiences pause or dismay. In announcing the university's hiring of a prominent journalist, a campus newspaper headline billed him as a "Pultizer Prize winner." Did you catch the typo? CBS reported on shark attacks along the North Carolina coast, and the map identified the location as Monteo, rather than Manteo. Often, such errors are caused by haste or carelessness.

Research has shown that when messages are perceived to be error free, they also are thought to be credible and well written. The perception of quality carries over to the writer and to the medium, be it newspaper, television, or online. In other words, messages free of errors are perceived to be of high quality and produced by professionals.

Students often argue that they do not need spelling, grammar, or punctuation skills. They believe an editor—somewhere—will fix any errors or errors will be caught by spell-checkers or grammar-checkers. Wrong. As a communicator, you must be both writer and editor, particularly if you are writing for an online site or blog. Spell-checkers don't always catch the difference between *principal* and *principle*. Any number of synonyms and homonyms can present problems, so it's up to you to know the difference.

Communicators who pay attention to their audiences know they must also pay attention to detail. That means attending to spelling, grammar, punctuation, and style. Most media have style rules. They follow Associated Press style, or they have developed style guidelines of their own. Adopting a specific style ensures consistency in all articles, regardless of who writes them or where they appear. Even in short text messages, writers follow a certain style of known abbreviations; otherwise, recipients would have difficulty translating the meaning. (Style is covered in Chapter 3.)

Writers today are expected to know basic math and elementary statistics. They need to know how to compute percentages, figure out square footage, determine whether poll data are representative, and analyze budget figures.

In this chapter, you will learn

- typical spelling errors to watch for,
- common adult grammar problems, and
- bottom-line math skills.

Spelling in the Computer Age

Writers, BEWARE: Spelling skills are essential in the computer age. This warning might sound exaggerated because, as we all know, computers can check spellings of thousands of words in minutes. But take heed.

What Spell-Checkers Will (and Won't) Do

Checking systems embedded in computers are a great invention, virtually eliminating senseless typographical errors, such as "scuh" and "typograpical," as well as common spelling problems such as "seperate" and "mispell." Unfortunately, however, spell-checkers merely highlight many potential problems without correcting them. You, the writer, are expected to check the highlighted words or phrases and to approve them or provide correction.

Here's an example: If a computer merely finds a word in its dictionary, it "checks" that word, assuring the writer that the spelling is correct. Say, for example, the computer encounters this sentence: "Robin was going too the fare." The sentence checks. The words "too" and "fare" exist in the dictionary, so they pass muster. And if "Robin" happens to be spelled correctly as "Robyn," that error will go unchecked because "robin" would be found in the computer's dictionary. Or perhaps the typo is an actual word, such as "count" instead of "court." The error would slip by as correct, and the writer would have created an immediate audience-stopper and confusion.

So spell-checkers aid writers in only some spelling instances, not all of them. Some of the most challenging spelling tasks (listed in the next section) are still the writer's responsibility.

A Do-It-Yourself List.   By now, it should be clear that spell-checkers will not do everything. The writer has the hands-on, do-it-yourself responsibility of checking the following problems that spell-checkers do not correct.

Homonyms.   Writers must distinguish among homonyms, or words that sound alike but have different meanings and are spelled differently. Any writer's credibility would drop if his or her readers saw these sentences:

Mrs. Margolis consulted two professional piers before suspending the student.
(Readers will see Mrs. Margolis conferring in a lakeside setting.)

Barnes said he didn't want to altar his plans.
(Will Barnes offer his plan during religious services?)

All navel movements will be approved by the commanding officer.
(Whose belly buttons?)

Investigators found millions of land mines sewn into the earth.
(Did someone use a needle and thread?)

Such homonyms as "pier" and "peer," "alter" and "altar," and "sewn" and "sown" escape highlighting by the spell-checker, which recognizes each as a dictionary word. Writers overconfident in the ability of spell-checkers will undoubtedly leave simple errors in their writing. Some words writers should watch for include the following:

to, two, too   aid, aide

their, they're, there   it's, its

no, know   whose, who's

Some subtle and damaging errors are made when writers confuse other commonly occurring homonyms, such as those listed below. Good writers distinguish between or among homonyms.

affect (verb)

effect (noun, meaning result, verb meaning bring about)

a lot (colloquial expression substituted for "many" or "much")

allot (to distribute)

allude (refer to)

elude (escape)

altar (in a church)

alter (change)

altogether (adverb meaning entirely)

all together (adjective meaning in a group)

bare (naked, uncovered)

bear (animal, to support)

baring (showing)

bearing (supporting)

bore (to drill, to be dull)

boar (pig)

canvas (cloth)

canvass (to poll)

capitol (building)

capital (city)

compliment (flattering statement)

complement (fills up or completes)

counsel (to advise, legal adviser)

council (assembly)

consul (diplomatic officer)

dual (two)

duel (combat between two people)

flair (style; panache)

flare (torch)

guerrilla (person who engages
  in warfare)
gorilla (ape)

immigrate (come to a new
  country)
emigrate (leave one's country)

legislature (body)
legislator (individual official)

miner (in a mine)
minor (under age)

naval (of the navy)
navel (belly button)

pore (small opening; to
  examine closely)
pour (to cause to flow)

pier (water walkway)
peer (social equal)

principal (head, first)
principle (lesson,
  belief)

role (in a play)
roll (list)

stare (regard intensely)
stair (step in a staircase)

stationery (paper)
stationary (permanent)

vein (blood vessel)
vain (conceited)
vane (wind detector)

Similar Words with Different Uses.   Spell-checkers will highlight commonly confused pairs of words, such as "conscience" and "conscious," "affect" and "effect," "flout" and "flaunt," "loose" and "lose," "lead" and "led," "read" and "red," "border" and "boarder," or "populace" and "populous." Keeping a good dictionary, stylebook, or grammar guide on your desk is the best way to make distinctions between similar words. Again, the writer or editor must catch the error, even though his or her computer includes a spell-checker.

Compound Words.   Some compound words, such as "speedboat" and "bookkeeper," will pass spell-checkers as two words, even though they are correctly spelled as single words. The reason? The spell-checker recognizes the separate words—"speed," "boat," "book," and "keeper"—as valid entries, leaving the writer appearing not to know the correct spelling.

Proper Names.   As noted earlier, proper names—unlike most units of language—may be spelled any way an individual desires. The infinite variety of name spellings makes it essential to check and doublecheck all names, regardless of what spell-checking approves. Many names, such as Robin and Lily, are also common nouns listed in computer dictionaries. Often the correct spelling for the proper name is different from that offered by a spell-checker. For example, Robin may be "Robyn," and Lily may spell her name "Lillie." Double-check names in any document.

Both spell-checking and manual, word-by-word editing are essential parts of the writing process. No software can replace the complex decision-making an editor provides. In the information age, good writers and editors ensure accurate writing.

BOX 2.1   Useful Tools for Writers

Professional writers and editors have their favorite resources. Despite their age, some reference books have timeless value vis-a-vis more modern Web sites.

Books

Theodore M. Bernstein, *Dos, Don'ts and Maybes of the English Language*. New York: The Times Book Co., 1977.

John Bremner, *Words on Words*. New York: Columbia University Press, 1980.

Claire Kehrwald Cook, *Line by Line: How to Improve Your Own Writing*. Boston: Houghton Mifflin, 1985.

Norm Goldstein, ed., *The Associated Press Stylebook 2005 and Briefing on Media Law*. New York: The Associated Press, 2005.

Lauren Kessler and Duncan McDonald, *When Words Collide*. Belmont, CA: Wadsworth, 2004.

Purdue University's Online Writing Lab. Available: http://owl.english.purdue.edu/handouts/grammar/index.html.

William Strunk, Jr., and E. B. White, *The Elements of Style*, 3rd ed. New York: Macmillan, 1979.

Kathleen Woodruff Wickham, *Math Tools for Journalists*. Oak Park, IL: Marion Street Press, January 2002.

Web Sites

www.editteach.org, with resources for language, editing, teaching.
www.newsu.org, the site for News University with access to a range of reporting and writing courses that require user registration.
www.poynter.org, the site for the Poynter Institute.

Grammar to the Rescue

Our world is fast-paced and fast-changing—hardly the kind of place you would expect to need something as tedious as a lesson on grammar. But today's communicator cannot afford to slow down audiences, and faulty grammar does just that. Just as writers are cautioned about relying too much on spell-checking systems in computers, they should be aware that grammar-checking programs also have flaws.

Consider the reader who encounters "its" where "it's" should be. For a split second, the reader will pause and wonder about the error, the writer, and the site. Sometimes the musing reader will stop reading entirely because of the slowdown or because of the reduced credibility or appeal of the flawed message.

People do not have to be grammar experts to stop and wonder about correctness. For example, any unusual use of "whom" or "who" may cause a reader to reflect rather than read on. "Now, what was it I learned about whom?" the reader muses, and the tempo of reading is lost.

Television viewers may cringe when the news announcer says, "The committee will reconvene their meeting tomorrow morning." They know a committee is referred to with an "its," not a "their." As they pause to correct the sentence, they lose the remainder of the announcer's message.

But My Grammar Is Good...

Most of us who pursue writing as a career consider ourselves to be language experts, and in general, our grammar and language use are far above average. Even educated people have problems, however. Evidence of grammar problems is found in mistakes made daily by adults in business letters, memos, and reports, as well as in newspapers and on the airways. An ad proclaims, "There's no down payment and no service charge!" To be grammatically correct, it should say, "There are no down payment and no service charge." A newsletter states, "Children will be grouped by age, irregardless of grade in school." There is no such word as "irregardless"—it simply is an aberration of "regardless."

Educated people regularly make grammar mistakes that other educated people will recognize. Writers need to identify their most frequent grammar errors and learn how to correct them. A first step in checking your grammar is to know what errors you are most likely to make.

Grammar Problems

Author Katherine C. McAdams, associate professor at the University of Maryland, developed "The Grammar Slammer," a workshop on grammar problems that identifies five areas in which real-life errors are most likely to occur:

- punctuation, especially commas, semicolons, colons, apostrophes, dashes, and hyphens
- subject and verb agreement
- correct pronoun choices that provide agreement and avoid gender bias, such as "Each student has his or her book" rather than the more common and erroneous "Each student has their book"
- correct sentence structures, especially when sentences use modifiers or require parallel structure
- word use—that is, using words (such as "regardless") correctly; this area often involves spelling problems and confusing words that sound alike (such as "affect" and "effect," or "vain" and "vein").

This section follows the format of the Grammar Slammer workshop, giving a short lesson on each of the problem areas and following that lesson with some exercises. The approach is designed for writers who are bright, motivated, and capable of learning quickly.

The lessons provide a quick fix rather than an in-depth lecture. They are designed to refresh and renew rather than to re-educate. Going through the grammar lessons will help you identify your grammar deficiencies. You can then be on guard for your particular problems when writing and editing. You may find you have many weaknesses in language skills and understanding. If so, you will want to study the books recommended at the end of this chapter or take a grammar course.

Test Yourself

To determine your grammar problem areas, take the following diagnostic quiz. Record your answers on a sheet of paper.

Grammar Slammer Diagnostic Quiz

The following sentences contain errors in grammar and punctuation. No sentence contains more than one error. Read each sentence. Circle the error, and in the margin note how the sentence should be written correctly. Sentence 1 is corrected for you as an example.

1. If past performance is any indication, Maryland should be considered a top challenger for the championship; having downed defending regional champion Duke twice in the regular season. (*Correction*: Use a comma in place of the semicolon because the second half of the sentence is not an independent clause.)

2. The list of candidates being considered as successors for the university chancellor have been trimmed to approximately 50 names, including four university officials.

3. The computer did not seem to be working today, it kept rejecting the operator's instructions.

4. The following afternoon, Wednesday, October 25 a Royal Indian Air Force DC-3 landed in the abandoned dirt strip of Srinagar Airport.

5. Traditionally expected to be in control of their surroundings, the insecurity makes students uncomfortable in their new situation.

6. The president's body will lay in state until services are held at the chapel.

7. Hopefully, the council will pass a new noise ordinance before the students return to campus in September.

8. Among those who attended services for the coach were Ralph Brooks, head football coach at Eastern, Mary Barnes, chancellor; Michael Thomas, former chancellor; and Paul Wells, former athletic director.

9. She predicted that neither the speaker or the minority whip would receive the Republican nomination.

10. In its advertising, the Acme Company claims that they are in business only to do good works for the community.

11. Millie Rosefield, chair of the Cityville Historic Preservation Committee ran fifth in the Nov. 6 race for four council seats.

12. One of every five of the state's residents live in the sort of poverty that drove Erskine Caldwell to write.

13. Three-fourths of the business district in Long Beach, N.C. was destroyed by Hurricane Hugo, which struck the coast in 1989.

14. Many a boy use to believe that he could acquire practically super human strength by eating the right cereal.

15. The mayor said the parade would feature the homecoming queen, the marching band will play, and as many floats as possible.

16. Several people, all of them eager to give their opinions and all of them pressing forward to meet the governor, who was conducting interviews with voters in the area.

17. I like ice cream and cookies, I don't like cakes with icing.

18. Rosalie complained, and she had no heat.

19. Being a weight lifter, his muscles were well developed.

20. The alligator is hunted for their skin.

Several of the following words are misspelled. Circle the misspelled words and write the correct spelling for each in the space provided.

1. principal (of a school) ————————————————

2. waiver (permission slip) ————————————————

3. bore (a wild pig) ————————————————

4. naval (belly button) ————————————————

5. stationery (you write on it) ————————————————

6. role (a list) ————————————————

7. roommate ————————————————

8. canvass (cloth) ————————————————

9. complement (flattering statement) ————————————————

10. cite (reference or footnote) ————————————————

Answers for the diagnostic quiz are included in Appendix A at the end of the book.

Grammar Problems Up Close

Examine the items you missed on the diagnostic quiz. You should have an idea of which grammar problems you need to review. The discussion of each problem is presented here, followed by exercises. Test your proficiency and move on. Record your answers on a sheet of paper. To check your work, look at the answers in Appendix A.

Problem 1: Punctuation

Perhaps no problem looms larger than punctuation. Few people actually know the rules and regulations of punctuation use. Most of us, much of the time, use the "feel good" school of punctuation, saying, "I just feel like I need a comma here" or "A semicolon just felt right."

Professional communicators must give up their "feel good" philosophy of punctuating. The first rule of punctuating professionally is this: **Do not punctuate unless you know a rule.** When you even think of adding a mark of punctuation, stop and think about whether it is justified by the rules in this chapter. If not, you probably do not need to punctuate at all.

If you find you are punctuating excessively—that is, using more than three punctuation marks within any given sentence—it is probably time to rewrite that sentence. Sentences requiring many punctuation marks, even if they are all correct, usually are too long and complex to be easily understood. So another rule of punctuating professionally is this: Less is better. Less punctuation leads to clearer, more readable copy. When in doubt, leave the comma out.

Commas.   Literally hundreds of comma rules exist. But the nine listed here, distilled by high school English teacher Mary Penny in the 1940s, have been found over the years to take care of most everyday comma problems.

Rule 1.   Use commas in compound sentences when clauses are separated by a conjunction such as "and," "but," "for," "nor," or "yet."

- She managed the restaurant, but he did the cooking.

Note: In such sentences, leaving out the conjunction leads to an error known as a comma splice, whereby a comma is left to do the work of joining two sentences: "She managed the restaurant, he did the cooking." Like weak splices in a rope, commas are not strong enough for this task. A period or semicolon is needed to make a correct sentence:

- She managed the restaurant. He did the cooking.
- She managed the restaurant; he did the cooking.

Rule 2.　Use commas to separate elements in a series. Such elements usually are adjectives, verbs, or nouns.

Note: Journalism departs from traditional rules of punctuation by leaving the comma out before a conjunction in a series of elements, following this rule in *The Associated Press Stylebook*. The text in this book follows the comma in a series rule, but the journalism examples do not—as you may have already noticed in reading this text.

English composition version:
- The tall, dark, handsome man hailed, lauded, and applauded Ben, George, Maude, and Rebecca.

Journalism version:
- The tall, dark, handsome man hailed, lauded and applauded Ben, George, Maude and Rebecca.

Rule 3.　Use commas when attributing from quoted material. Commas set off words of attribution from the words of a one-sentence quotation unless a question mark or exclamation mark is preferred. Use them also in greetings:

- He said, "Hello." "Good-bye," she replied. "The fair has been canceled," she said.

Rule 4.　Commas follow introductory matter, such as after an introductory adverbial clause:

- When the team was forced to kick, the coach sent in his best players.

Commas also follow two or more introductory prepositional phrases:

- In the spring she returned to College Park. (no comma)
- In the spring of 2008, she returned to College Park. (comma needed because "in" and "of" are two prepositional phrases)

Also use a comma with a phrase that contains a verbal (i.e., a verb form used as a modifier):

- Singing as she worked, Mary answered her phone.
- Kicked by a horse, Don was more than stunned.
- To cure hiccups, drink from the far side of a glass.

Rule 5. Commas follow the salutation of a friendly letter and capitalized elements, such as the complimentary close (e.g., Sincerely, Very truly yours). A colon follows the salutation of a business letter:

- Dear James,
- Dear Dean Smith:
- Sincerely, Dean Smith

Rule 6. Commas follow all items in a date or full address:

- July 16, 1992, is his date of birth.
- She has lived in Lake City, Fla., all her life.

Rule 7. Commas surround nonessential words or phrases:

- Well, we will just have to walk home.

Commas also set off appositives, which are words or phrases that rename a noun. Appositives amplify a subject:

- Betty Brown, his mother-in-law, has been married four times.

Also use a comma to set off nonessential modifying clauses and phrases:

- The president-elect, suffering from laryngitis, canceled his speech.

Rule 8. Commas surround words of direct address:

- Maria, please pass the butter.
- I can see, Fred, that you are lazy.

Rule 9. Commas indicate omitted verbs, usually expressed in another part of the sentence:

- Talent often is inherited; genius, never.

This rule is an old one and is rarely used today except in headlines. It would be rare to find a comma indicating an omitted verb in contemporary writing, but far from surprising to see such headlines as:

- Pilots Ask for Guns; Airlines, for Marshals
- Coach Smith Has Much to Gain This Season; His Team, Even More

Semicolons and Colons. Miss Penny added three more rules to her list to take care of another widespread punctuation problem: the correct use of semicolons and colons. Miss Penny's rules 10 and 11 explain the two uses of the semicolon—the only two uses. Rule 12 explains the use of colons.

Rule 10. Semicolons connect two complete sentences if sentences have a related thought. Use of a semicolon usually creates a sense of drama:

- The brown-eyed, dark-haired, vivacious model, at age 18, seemed destined for quick success; on Sept. 11, 2001, her apparent destiny was altered.

Rule 11. Semicolons are used in a list separating items that require significant internal punctuation:

- He lived six years in Richmond, Va.; four years in Raleigh, N.C.; one year in Greenville, S.C.; and six months in Baton Rouge, La.

Rule 12. Colons precede formal lists, illustrations, multisentence quotes, and enumerations:

- The following students received scholarships: Jim Johnson, Juanita Lopez, Martha Taylor, Tiffany Eldridge, and Courtney Sampson.
- He answered her with a parable: "A man once had six sons. Five of them...."

- The senator listed the steps in her economic recovery program: first, to raise interest rates; second, to reduce spending....

Do not use a colon after "include" or forms of "to be," such as "was" or "were." Example: Her best friends were Sally, Marisa, and Claire.

Slammer for Commas, Semicolons, and Colons

Now, using Miss Penny's list of 12 rules as your reference, complete the following exercise. Remember, the most important rule is that you do not punctuate unless you know a rule. Defend each mark of punctuation you use by citing one of the Penny rules on a sheet of paper and listing the rule next to the sentence.

Rule or Rules

1. Although we watched the Super Bowl we don't know who won.
2. John Blimpo an egocentric man dropped his hat in the fruit salad.
3. Guitars have six strings basses four.
4. The tall dark handsome man listed his hobbies as reading fishing painting and writing.
5. To Whom It May Concern:

   The spelling and grammar test will be given on March 2 3 and 4 2009 in Room 502 of Knight Hall.

   Grammatically yours

   Dean Sarah Jones

6. Dad go ahead and send the money now.
7. The women's basketball team was down by four points at halftime however it came back to crush the opponent.
8. Congress passed the bill but the debate took several weeks.
9. Well just be in by daybreak.
10. Her blind date was a real disappointment he talked loudly and constantly about his pet snake.

11. She was elected on Nov. 4, 2008, in Baltimore, Md., the city of her birth.
12. She named her courses for the fall semester, journalism, English, political science, history, and French.

Check your answers by looking at the answers in Appendix A. Then go on to tackle some other troublesome marks of punctuation.

Hyphens and Dashes. Remember that hyphens and dashes, although often confused, are different. The hyphen differs from a dash in both use and appearance. The hyphen is shorter (- as opposed to —), and it comes, without additional spaces, between two words combined to express some new concept, such as polka-dot and part-time. Hyphens are useful joiners that bring some creativity to language.

Rather than joining phrases, dashes are useful in separating them—usually where that separation can be heard. Dashes are sometimes used to replace commas to ensure that a pause is audible and even dramatic (e.g., "Although charming, he was—on the other hand—a thief").

Here is a list of guidelines for using hyphens and dashes correctly:

1. Never use a hyphen after a word ending in "ly."
   - The newly elected president stepped to the podium.
2. Use a hyphen to connect two or more related modifying words that do not function independently.
   - Kim always ordered the blue-plate special.
   - Todd dreaded any face-to-face confrontations.
3. The dash is a punctuation mark one "hears." It is a noticeable pause. Choose a dash instead of a comma so the audience can "hear" the pause.
4. Dashes work where commas would also work. The only difference is the dash adds drama—and an audible break in the text. Because dashes may substitute for commas, they are used to set off nonessential material.
   - The murderer was—if you can believe it—a priest.
5. Too many dashes in any text may be distracting and even irritating to readers. Limit dashes to only the most dramatic of pauses. In most cases, such as this example, commas will suffice.
   - She is—as most of you know—a punctuation expert.

Other marks of punctuation, especially apostrophes, can be troublesome. Correct use may vary from time to time and publication to publication. Always check your stylebook, and keep a current grammar reference book handy.

Problem 2: Subject and Verb Agreement

Few writers make obvious errors in subject and verb agreement, such as "I is interested in cars" or "The class know it's time to go to lunch." But most people struggle with the following subject–verb agreement problems:

1. Collective subjects can be confusing. Some nouns that appear to be plural are treated as singular units:
   - The *Girl Scouts* is a fine organization.
   - *Checkers* is an ancient game.
   - *Economics* is a difficult subject.

   Some collective subjects, however, have Latinate endings and remain plural, although spoken language tends to make them singular. In formal writing, these plurals require plural verbs:
   - The *media* have raised the issue of the senator's competency.
   - The *alumni* are funding a new building.

2. The pronouns "each," "either," "neither," "anyone," "everyone," and "anybody" are always singular, regardless of what follows them in a phrase. Take, for example, this sentence:
   - Either of the girls is an excellent choice for president.

   The phrase "of the girls" does not change the singular number of the true subject of this sentence: the pronoun "either." Following are some other examples of correct usage:
   - Neither has my vote.
   - Either is fine with me.
   - Each has an excellent option.
   - Anyone is capable of helping the homeless.
   - Everyone is fond of Jerry.

3. A fraction or percentage of a whole is considered a singular subject.
   - Three-quarters of the pie is gone.
   - Sixty-seven percent of the voters is needed to withhold a veto.

4. Compound subjects, in which two or more nouns function as the subject of a sentence, can lead to agreement problems. To solve such problems, substitute a single pronoun, such as "they" or "it," for the sentence's subject or subjects. For example, transform this problem sentence: "The students and the teacher is/are waiting for the bus." By substituting, the subject becomes "they": They are waiting for the bus. The following are some other examples:

   ▪ The opening number and the grand finale thrill the audience. (they thrill)
   ▪ There are no down payment and no service charge. (they are not charged)
   ▪ The Eagles, a classic rock band, is my dad's favorite group. (it is favorite)

5. When subjects are structured with either/or and neither/nor, use the verb tense that corresponds to the subject closest to the verb, as in the following cases:

   ▪ Either the leader or the scouts pitch the tent.
   ▪ Either the scouts or the leader pitches the tent.
   ▪ Neither the parents nor the students win when rules are broken.

Slammer for Subject–Verb Agreement

Check your knowledge of subject–verb agreement by taking the following quiz. Select the verb that agrees.

1. He did say he would look at the sheet of names, which includes/include the owners of two apartment buildings.
2. Their number and influence appears/appear greatest in West Germany.
3. Experience in the backfield and the line gives/give the coach a good feeling on the eve of any opening game.
4. A first offense for having fewer than 25 cartons of untaxed cigarettes results/result in a $500 fine.
5. Before you make a final judgment on this student's story, consider the time and effort that has/have gone into it.

6. Who does the teaching? Full professors. But so does/do associates, assistants, and instructors.

7. She said they would visit Peaks of Otter, which is/are near Lynchburg, Va.

8. The news media is/are calling for a peace treaty that is fair to everyone.

9. The United Mine Workers exhibit/exhibits solidarity during elections.

10. There is/are 10 million bricks in this building.

11. The president said that students today are too job-oriented and neglect the broader areas of study that constitutes/constitute a true education.

12. Five fire companies fought the blaze, which the firefighters said was/were the longest this year.

13. Each of the 100 people believes/believe in God.

14. It is/are the boats, not the swimmers, that stir up the dirt in the lake.

15. The editor told the staff there was a shortage of money for the newsroom, a shortage she said she would explain to the board of directors, which decides/decide all matters on the budget.

16. One of my classmates typifies/typify student apathy.

17. Drinking beer and sleeping is/are the most important things in my life.

18. Dillon said he has insurance for everything except the buildings, which is/are owned by Thomas F. Williams.

19. Approximately 51 percent of the U.S. population is/are female.

20. There is/are only one way to beat taxes.

21. Neither the professor nor her two assistants teaches/teach this course in a style students like.

22. Each student is/are responsible for getting the work done on time.

23. All students considers/consider that an imposition.

24. The General Assembly and the governor disagrees/disagree on the solution.

Check your answers against those in Appendix A.

Problem 3: Correct Use of Pronouns

Pronouns are little words—"he," "she," "you," "they," "I," "it"—that stand for proper nouns. Look at this sentence:

- International Trucking is hiring 20 new drivers because it is expanding in the Southeast.

In this sentence, the word "it" is used to substitute for International Trucking. Pronouns help avoid needless repetition in language by doing the work of the larger nouns, called antecedents. In the previous example, "International Trucking" is the antecedent for the pronoun "it."

Pronouns must agree with their antecedents, as in the following examples:

- Marianne said she (Marianne) would never color her (Marianne's) hair.
- Baltimore became a model city after it (Baltimore) successfully restored the waterfront.
- Journalism is a popular major, and now it (journalism) prepares students for many careers.

Following are guidelines to ensure correct pronoun choices:

1. Watch for collective subjects—groups treated as single units—and use the correct pronoun.
   - The committee gave its report.
   - The United Mine Workers gave out a list of its legislative goals.
2. When using singular pronouns, use singular verbs.
   - Each of the rose bushes was at its peak.
   - Everyone in the audience rose to his or her feet and chanted.
3. Use correct pronouns to handle issues of sexism in language. The generic person is no longer "he."
   - Each of the students had his or her book.
   - The students had their books.
4. Be attentive to stray phrases or clauses that come between pronouns and antecedents and cause agreement problems.

- He presented the list of candidates being considered for the office and told the committee members to choose from it. (antecedent agreement; it refers to the list)
- He posted the list of candidates for the position and read it aloud. (antecedent agreement; "it" refers to the list)

5. Use reflexive pronouns, such as himself or herself, only when a subject is doing something to herself or himself or themselves.
   - Jan introduced herself to the new chancellor.
   - Henry never could forgive himself.
   - The relatives had the chalet to themselves.

Slammer for Pronouns

To ensure you understand agreement of pronoun and antecedent, select the appropriate pronoun for each of the following sentences.

1. Each student had (his or her/their) assignment completed before class.
2. General Foods plans to change (its/their) approach to marketing baked goods.
3. Larry introduced me and (him/himself) to the governor.
4. The jury took (their/its) deliberations seriously.
5. The board of directors set a date for (their/its) annual retreat.
6. The Orioles (is/are) my favorite team.
7. Neither the Terps nor the Crimson Tide (was/were) having a winning season.
8. Neither of the teams (was/were) victorious.
9. The alumni voted to charge $1 an issue for (their/its) magazine.
10. Any of the three finalists (is/are) an excellent choice.
11. The six-member committee voted to reverse (its/their) decision.
12. The librarian's collection fascinated him, and he asked to borrow from (her/it).
13. The media (is/are) ignoring the mayor's speeches.
14. Each of the students could handle the job by (himself or herself/ themselves).
15. Everyone in the audience rose to (his or her/their) feet for the ovation.

Check your work against the answers in Appendix A, and prepare to tackle the biggest pronoun problem of all: the *who/whom* dilemma.

Who and Whom.   The word "whom" has all but disappeared from spoken English, so it is little wonder that few of us know how to use it correctly. Even though usage is changing, writers of published materials still need to know the rules that govern the distinction between "who" and "whom":

1. "Who" is a substitute for subjects referring to "he," "we," or "she," or the nominative pronoun.

    ■ Who saw the meteor?

    The statement, "He saw the meteor," as a question becomes, "Who saw the meteor?" "Who" is substituted for the subject "he." Relative clauses work the same way when "who" is substituted for a subject. In the sentence, "He questioned the man who saw the meteor," "who" substitutes for the subject of the clause, "He saw the meteor." The entire clause serves as an object of the verb "questioned." But the function of the clause does not change the role of a pronoun; in this sentence, the role of "who" is as the subject of the verb "saw."

2. "Whom" is a substitute for objective pronouns, such as "him," "her," or "them."

    ■ Whom did he question for hours?

    The statement, "He questioned her for hours," as a question becomes, "Whom did he question for hours?" "Whom" is substituted for "her" as the object of the verb "questioned." Substitution works the same way in relative clauses. In the sentence, "Marcella was the one whom he questioned for hours," "whom" substitutes for the object "her" in the clause, "He questioned her for hours." Again, it is the role of the pronoun within its subject–verb structure that determines whether it is the subject or the object and therefore "who" or "whom."

That and Which.   Another fine distinction between pronouns is the difference between "that" and "which." Again, the spoken language no longer follows strict rules regarding these subordinate conjunctions, but careful writers need to observe the following guidelines:

1. "That" is a restrictive pronoun, indicating that the information it precedes is essential for correct understanding of the sentence.
   - Dogs prefer bones that improve their dental health.
   - The use of "that" tells us that dogs prefer only this specific kind of bone.
2. "Which" precedes nonessential material; therefore, it typically appears with commas (the ones used to set off nonessential information).
   - Dogs prefer bones, which improve their dental health.

   The use of "which" tells us that all bones improve dogs' teeth.
3. "That" and "which" are not interchangeable. As you can see in the example sentences, the meaning of the sentence is affected when the comma is added in the second sentence and "that" becomes "which." In the first sentence, dogs like only bones that are good for them; in the second, dogs like bones better than other things, and bones just happen to be good for dental health. The second sentence is far more logical.

Slammer for Who/Whom and That/Which

Select the appropriate pronoun in the following sentences:

1. Alvin, (who/whom) everyone adored, absconded with the family fortune.
2. Betty, (who/whom) was the apple of his eye, followed him to Mexico.
3. The FBI agents (who/whom) Alvin had avoided for several months finally arrested him.
4. Veronica, Alvin's sister, (who/whom) needed the money desperately, refused to post bond.
5. Alvin, (who's/whose) health was delicate, wasted away in prison.

Select the appropriate pronoun, then note the proper punctuation as needed in the following sentences:

1. Betty bought a gun (that/which) was on sale and set out to free Alvin.
2. She headed north from Mexico in a stolen car (that/which) had more than 130,000 miles showing on its odometer.

3. The car (that/which) had New Jersey license plates was quickly spotted by police in Texas.

4. The Texans (that/which/who/whom) spoke in a slow drawl told her she was wanted in New Jersey for conspiring with Alvin.

5. She pulled out the gun (that/which) she had in her glove compartment and started shooting.

6. The police officer (that/which/who/whom) was standing closest to her car died after he was struck by a bullet.

7. Other officers took Betty's gun (that/which) now was empty of bullets.

8. They also arrested Betty and placed her in a local jail (that/which) overlooked the Rio Grande.

Check your answers against those in Appendix A and move on to the next grammar problem.

Problem 4: Sentence Structure

Aside from fragments and run-on sentences, two other categories cause most adults problems with sentence structure: faulty parallelism and modifier placement.

Journalists often struggle with giving sentences parallel structure—that is, making sure that series or lists of phrases are parallel in form. Rather than, "He enjoys reading and to go skiing," use the parallel form, saying, "He enjoys reading and skiing." Writers must always remember to check lists within sentences as well as bulleted lists to see that phrases are stated in parallel form, as shown in these examples:

- Marvelene listed steps in planning a successful party: sending invitations early, greeting guests personally, and supplying abundant food and drink. (parallel gerunds: sending, greeting, supplying)
- A successful host always is sure
  —to send invitations early,
  —to greet guests personally, and
  —to supply abundant food and drink. (infinitives are parallel)

Other sentence errors might occur when modifiers are placed incorrectly and give readers an inaccurate, sometimes humorous, picture as, for example, in these sentences:

Wrong: Swinging from an overhead wire, we saw a kite.
Better: We saw a kite swinging from an overhead wire.

Wrong: When wheeled into the operating room, the nurse placed a mask over my face.
Better: The nurse placed a mask over my face after I was wheeled into the operating room.

Wrong: The jury found him guilty of killing his wife after deliberating for three days.
Better: After deliberating for three days, the jury found him guilty of killing his wife.

To solve modifier placement problems, place modifying clauses and phrases closest to what they modify.

Slammer for Modifiers

Rewrite these sentences to correct misplaced modifiers. Some sentences are correct as written.

1. The waiter served ice cream in glass bowls which started melting immediately.
2. The Simpsons gave a toy robot with flashing eyes to one of their sons.
3. We saw a herd of sheep on the way to our hotel.
4. Most people have strawberry shortcake topped with mounds of whipped cream.
5. The house is one of the oldest in Rockville, where Mrs. Rooks taught ballet.
6. Flying at an altitude of several thousand feet, the paratroopers could see for miles.

7. I could not convince the child to stop running into the street without yelling.

8. After the first act of the play, Brooke's performance improves, the critic said.

9. While watching the ball game, Sue's horse ran away.

10. The museum director showed me a spider with the orange diamond on its belly.

11. The bank approves loans to reliable individuals of any size.

12. After being wheeled into the operating room, the nurse placed a mask over my face.

13. Riding in a glass-bottom boat, we saw thousands of colorful fish.

14. Aunt Helen asked us before we left to call on her.

15. Do it yourself: Make up a sentence suffering from modifier malady. Then correct it.

Check your work against the answers in Appendix A, and prepare for the final grammar problem: word usage.

Problem 5: Word Usage

English is a language enriched by words borrowed from other languages, resulting in a rich vocabulary—but also, in many cases, in unorthodox spelling and idiosyncratic usage. It makes little sense to have both "affect" and "effect" in the same language, functioning so similarly but not identically. And why do we distinguish between "pore" and "pour," or "flair" and "flare"? Who cares?

Careful writers have to care because subtle usage errors can cause big misunderstandings. Correct usage leads to credibility; readers have confidence in error-free reading.

Slammer for Troublesome Words

Use a dictionary to help identify correct usage for each of the following troublesome words.

Hopefully
Affect versus effect
Less versus fewer

Lie versus lay
Sit versus set
Comprise versus compose

Math for Journalists

All professional communicators must be able to handle routine computations such as adding, subtracting, multiplying, dividing, figuring ratios and percentages, and rounding off numbers. Such simple calculations routinely are used in daily journalism, and any error would make a story inaccurate.

Professor Emeritus Phil Meyer at the University of North Carolina at Chapel Hill advised mass communication students that if they chose the field because they thought they could escape math, they were wrong. Basic math is necessary.

Here's a typical example of statistical writing that misses the mark: An advertisement tells audiences that computer prices have dropped 200 percent. This news would appeal to someone shopping for a new computer. But what's wrong here? When the price drops 100 percent, the item is free. Below 100 percent means stores are paying customers to take away computers. The writer needs a few quick lessons on math.

Here's another example of a writer in need of math skills: A news story reports that police chased a suspect for 90 minutes from Town X to Town Y, a distance of 300 miles. Possible? Hardly. The cars would be traveling 200 miles per hour to cover that distance in 90 minutes. Something is wrong with the information—unless the cars were literally flying.

Basic Math

Basic math errors show up continually in writing, usually because writers are careless. But a reader somewhere is going to see the error and doubt the writer's and the medium's credibility. Mass communicators need to know some simple math, or at the very least, they need to recognize when data are misrepresented and find someone who can do correct calculations.

Percent.   A lead reports that the president's popularity dropped from 85 to 75 percent, a decrease of 10 percent. Correct? No. The decrease is 10 percentage points, but not 10 percent. That's the first lesson to learn in writing about percent. If you subtract 75 percent from 85 percent, you get a 10 percentage point difference. To calculate the percent difference, you need to find the difference and divide that by the base or original figure: % = d/b (i.e., percent = difference/base). Here, that would be 10/85, a change of 12 percent. It works the same way with increases. If the popularity goes up from 70 percent to 80 percent, the difference is 10 percentage points, which yields 10/70, or a 14 percent increase.

For another example, let's look at a financial story on company revenues. Suppose Midland Trucking Company had revenues last fiscal year of $535,000 and revenues this year of $635,000. The difference is $100,000. If you follow the formula d/b = percent difference, you would divide $100,000 by $535,000. The percent change is 18.6 percent, or rounded off, 19 percent.

If you made an error and divided the difference by the new amount of $635,000, you would get an increase of 16 percent, a significant difference from 19 percent—and one that could affect stockholders' perception of company management. The writer for the company's annual report must be careful in calculating numbers that could influence investments or stockholder confidence.

Rates.   Often, writers will state numbers as a rate—1 in 10 or 3 in 100—so that complicated figures are easier to understand. For example, a writer finds a health department report saying that 0.0021 percent of teens aged 13 to 19 in the county became pregnant last year. The writer decides to translate the percentage into a figure that people can visualize.

One way to calculate the rate is to multiply the percent figure by 100 or 1,000 so that decimals no longer appear. In this case, multiplying 0.0021 × 1,000 gives a rate of 2.1 per 1,000. Rates can be stated by hundreds, thousands, tens of thousands, and on up. More clearly stated, the rate of teen pregnancy is 2.1 per 1,000, or about two teens out of every 1,000 teens aged 13 to 19 living in the county got pregnant last year.

Probability.   Writers need to have an appreciation for probability theory and an understanding of the likelihood that a predicted event will actually occur. If there is a 40 percent chance of rain, how likely is it that we will get wet? Should we write or broadcast the news that rain is on the way? We hear probability each time we listen to a weather report. But if the probability of rain is 40 percent, it's important to remember there's also a 60 percent probability that the weather will be clear.

Writers often make errors when they combine one probability with another, such as "The football coach predicts a 50 percent chance of thunderstorms and a 50 percent chance the game could be delayed." Does that mean a 100 percent chance the game will be delayed? No. To calculate the probability in this case, you must multiply one probability with another. The probability of thunderstorms and a game postponement is .5 × .5 = .25, or a 25 percent chance both will occur.

Reporting Poll Data

Many numbers are reported in poll stories every day in the media. An article notes that the president has a 63 percent approval rating. What does 63 percent mean to the average reader or listener? Translated, the 63 percent means more than six out of 10 people (remember your percentage calculations from earlier in this section) approve of his performance—and four of every 10 do not. You can break that down even further to say simply that three out of five (divide 6 and 10 by 2 to bring to their lowest common denominator) people approve of the president.

When reporting poll data, it is important to make the statistics as clear and understandable as possible. Readers need to grasp what the numbers mean. To report poll numbers correctly, writers must be able to read the charts to determine what the poll figures mean. The following table presents poll results, divided into categories by income. These responses came from people queried at a local mall about whether they support Proposition Y, a proposal for a new city entertainment tax:

	Yes	No	Total
Earn $50,000 or less a year			
Count	148	152	300
Percent	49.3%	50.7%	100%
Percent of total	26%	27%	
Earn $50,001 or more a year			
Count	159	109	268
Percent	59.2%	40.8%	100%
Percent of total	28%	19%	

A writer notes that almost 50 percent of respondents who earn under $50,000 a year support Proposition Y on the ballot. He or she can even translate that 49.3 number to one out of two people interviewed in that income bracket and still be fairly accurate.

But then the writer notes that 59 percent of respondents earn more than $50,000 and support Proposition Y. Is the writer correct? No. The 59 percent figure represents what percentage of those people who earn that amount of money favor the proposition. The total number of people who earn $50,001 a year or more is 159 plus 109 (268). Of the 268 people in that income bracket, 59 percent favor the proposition.

To find out the percentage who actually earn more than $50,000 a year, go back to the actual counts and recalculate from there. If you add all the counts in each box, you will find 568 respondents to the survey. To find out how many earn more than $50,000 a year, divide difference by base, or 268 divided by 568, or 47 percent of those surveyed earn more money—much less than 59 percent.

It is extremely important when reading poll results to read the information correctly and calculate differences correctly. Also, be sure to translate your information to tangible language.

Margin of Error

A necessary part of poll reporting is reporting margin of error. In a poll on the safety of the nation, 87 percent report feeling safe, "plus or minus 3 percent." That "plus or minus" figure is the margin of error.

In simple terms, the error figure, usually from 1 to 5 percent, represents the accuracy of the poll results. Researchers know that in any survey they must allow room for error. Common sense and statistics tell us that the more respondents polled, the more accurately the poll results reflect the opinions of the public at large. Statistically, once the number of people polled reaches a certain level, the margin of error doesn't change or improve much. With several hundred respondents, the margin of error stays around plus or minus 4 to 5 percent. If careful sampling methods are used, poll results will allow researchers to interview 1,200 U.S. residents and then estimate what 280 million people believe. Most pollsters strive for a margin of error around 3 percent. Let's see how that works.

A poll says 45 percent of Americans believe the tax burden is too great on middle-income people. Another 42 percent believe it is just about right, and 13 percent have no opinion. The pollster reports a plus or minus 3 percent margin of error. Here's how the results look in chart form:

Reported results (with error = ± 3%)	
Too great	45%
Just about right	42%
No opinion	13%

The margin of error indicates the 45 percent who believe the tax burden is too great may, in reality, be 42 percent (minus 3 percent). Or it may be as high as 48 percent (plus 3 percent). Likewise, for those who think the tax burden is just about right, the range in reality could be as much as 45 percent to as little as 39 percent. So it's likely neither group can claim a clear majority. With such close percentages, a writer cannot say, "Most Americans said they think the tax burden on the middle class is too great." It would be more accurate to report that many Americans believe the tax burden is fairly distributed.

The Associated Press Stylebook has a separate entry for polls and surveys and lists items that should be included in any poll story. This entry discusses margin of error and urges writers to take care, especially when reporting that one candidate is leading another. According to the stylebook, only when the difference between the candidates is more than twice the margin of error can you say one candidate is leading. The same rule applies to the tax burden survey results presented here: The difference between the two groups is 3 percentage points, not the 6 required to be twice the margin of error of plus or minus 3 percent. So it's clear that in the case of individual opinions about tax burdens—and in many political poll results—a writer would have to say that opinion is just about even.

Tips

Many schools and departments of journalism and mass communication require their students to have basic competencies in math. At the University of North Carolina at Chapel Hill, faculty members in the School of Journalism and Mass Communication have considered adding a math competency requirement for journalism and mass communication majors.

Students who want to test their skills can take a math test online at www.unc.edu/~pmeyer/carstat/. Professor Emeritus Phil Meyer and Associate Professor Bill Cloud at UNC-Chapel Hill produced the test, along with partner *USA Today*.

The Associated Press Stylebook recommends rounding numbers because readers have little use for numbers such as $1,463,729. In this case, the writer needs to round the number to two decimal places, which would convert the number to $1.46 million. Rounding numbers makes it easier for readers to digest numbers and helps avoid inaccuracies.

The Associated Press Stylebook has other entries that relate to numbers, such as those on decimals, fractions, percentages, median, average, norm, and the metric system. Another section explains business terms. All these entries help writers when math is an issue—often the case in communications professions.

Slammer for Math

The following exercises will test your basic math skills. Please use a calculator. Answers are found in Appendix B.

1. The jury has 13 members. There are four members who are women. There are two African American jurors, and only one of them is a man. There also is one Hispanic American man on the jury. (Round percentages to the nearest tenth.)

   a. What is the ratio of men to women on the jury?
   b. What percentage of the jury is female?
   c. What percentage of Hispanic American men makes up the jury?
   d. What percentage of African American men makes up the jury?

2. The town manager tells the town council that he is proposing that the town build a new recreation center. The center would be 15,000 square feet. He has an estimate that the cost to build would be $85 per square foot plus an additional $25 per square foot for furnishings.

   a. What is the cost to build the center?
   b. What is the cost to furnish the center?
   c. What is the total cost for building and furnishing the center?
   d. Round the total cost to the nearest $100,000.

3. A local advertising company is sponsoring a community-wide yard sale in a local middle school parking lot. Each booth space is equivalent to two parking spaces. Each parking space measures 12 feet by 8 feet. The parking lot has 240 spaces.

   a. What is the square footage of one booth?
   b. How many booths can the advertising company rent?
   c. At $30 a booth, how much revenue will the company earn?
   d. You decide to rent two booths to get rid of your old furniture. How much space do you get?

4. Sarah Lamb owns a condominium valued for tax purposes at $175,000. The town's tax rate is 85 cents per $100 valuation, but the City Council is proposing to raise the tax rate by 3 cents for next year.

   a. How much in taxes did Sarah pay this year?
   b. How much will she pay under the proposed tax rate?
   c. What percentage increase will that be in her tax bill?
   d. If her property increases in value 5 percent by next year, how much will her tax bill be under the proposed tax rate?

5. Look at the following chart about support for three candidates for mayor.

	Smith	Small	Tucker
Female			
Count	107	137	31
Percentage	38.9%	49.7%	11.4%
Male			
Count	192	137	23
Percentage	54.4%	39.0%	6.5%

   a. How many respondents were women?
   b. What percentage of the total respondents were women?
   c. What percentage of the total respondents favored Tucker?
   d. What percentage of the total respondents favored Small?

6. Christine wants to go to the state fair Friday night. Her mother said there is a 50 percent probability that she will be able to take Christine to the fair. But Christine's band director said there is a 75 percent chance that he will schedule band practice on Friday night. What is the probability that Christine will actually get to the fair?

7. Jonathan works 40 hours a week at a local hardware store. He earns $7.50 an hour. The manager said he will give Jonathan a 25-cent per hour pay raise. How much will Jonathan earn a week with the raise?

   a. $340
   b. $10
   c. $310
   d. $260

8. Mr. Tennyson is teaching his class how to convert to the metric system. If the average weight for the class members is 135 pounds, what is that in kilograms? (Note: 0.454 kilograms is equal to one pound.)

   a. 61.29

   b. 50.3

   c. 792

   d. 297

   e. 74.2

References

Katherine C. McAdams, *The Grammar Slammer*. College of Journalism, University of Maryland, 1991.

Mary Penny, Class handouts, Needham Broughton High School, Raleigh, NC, 1974.

Web site of Professor Phil Meyer, University of North Carolina at Chapel Hill, at www.unc.edu/~pmeyer/carstat/.

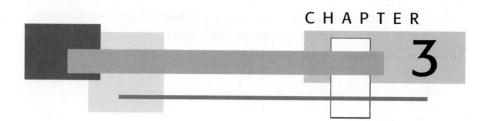

CHAPTER 3

Editing for Audiences

Good writing depends on good editing. Many student or beginning writers assume a writing job is finished once they get a message written. But that's exactly when editing must begin, even in a short text message. With your final reading of any draft, ideas for improving the message begin to flow: How can the message be more focused? Streamlined? Intriguing? What kinds of fine-tuning can send the message on its way, with clarity and accuracy, to target audiences?

While some people choose editing as their job, every writer must be an editor. Self-editing has become even more critical as more and more content is posted online without being edited first. While three or four editors might read a story before it is printed in a newspaper or magazine, a story posted online might not be read by any editor before it is posted. So the burden for editing falls more squarely on the writer.

You already have learned some ways to improve your writing through strategic planning and correct use of language and numbers. These same techniques are applied in the editing process, along with many other guidelines. Hundreds of books have been written about editing (Amazon.com lists more than 1,500), all filled with advice and rules on style and correctness. No writer can remember all the rules while writing a first or even a second or third draft.

Between the first draft and the finished product come polishing and editing. The first draft should be as good as possible; then, self-editing and the editing of others will refine and improve it. Novelist and teacher Doris Betts tells her students: "Handing in your first draft is like passing around your spittle." In other words, an unedited message is unprofessional and offensive.

Editing is more than just a courtesy to readers. It is a necessity because a single set of facts may be edited to produce several messages. For example, a newspaper article on car maintenance may also be edited to appear in the

8139 -

Julianne

****

1137 E. Alosta AvOrder 323918
Azusa CA 91702
626-914-1424

09/14/14 2:32 PM
****

*** TO GO ***
TAB #51

1 Tropical Bowl	0.00
Tropical - Reg	6.25

Total Due: 6.25

Credit Card: 6.25

Item Count:0

Thank you for your business and
please come back again to
Thirsteas!

"Living" section of a Web site, on the "Hot Tips" page of a weekly magazine, or in another writer's automotive blog. Editing is more than just checking for correctness: Today's editor sculpts and reformats information for many presentations to many different audiences.

But first things first: When all is said and done, editors must be sure that messages conform to correct style. In this chapter, you will learn

- basic style and editing rules,
- how different media sometimes require different kinds of editing, and
- steps to guide the editing process.

Watching Style

Part of good editing is ensuring consistency throughout writing. Using a consistent style guarantees a certain pattern persists in word usage, titles, punctuation, abbreviations, grammar, and spelling. If "Dr." means doctor in the first paragraph of an online story, it will not mean "Drive" as part of someone's address later in the piece. Consistent usage builds credibility and reduces chances of audience confusion.

Media organizations follow a style that guarantees consistency. Most newspapers and public relations firms follow the style in *The Associated Press Stylebook and Briefing on Media Law*, updated annually as usage evolves. Others, including *The Washington Post* and *The New York Times*, have their own style manuals. Many universities and publishing houses use *The Chicago Manual of Style* or the style manual of the Modern Language Association.

Online news sites don't yet have an industry standard for style on things such as verb tenses, link text, and site navigation. Media professionals also have to learn the "folk styles" that exist more as tradition than anything else and that change from newsroom to newsroom. But even in a world in which the rules are not yet written, editors will be well served if they remember the reason that style rules exist in the first place—to help the audience more easily understand the message.

The text in this book uses a style that differs from the Associated Press style, so you will notice discrepancies between usage in the text and in examples and exercises.

No one is ever expected to memorize stylebooks, but writers and editors must be familiar with their content. When a question arises, they need to know where to find the answer. Writers will find that certain rules are used so often that they become second nature. For example, most writers become familiar with the capitalization rule for titles: Professional titles are capitalized before a person's name but never after a name. Here's an example, "University President Bill Sandler said classes would end early Tuesday because of the threat of a blizzard." After his name, the title would read, "Bill Sandler, university president, said . . . ."

Basic Style Rules

The most broadly accepted style rules for professional communicators are those set out by *The Associated Press Stylebook*, which covers subjects as diverse as correct abbreviations for military titles, to spellings for Hanukkah and Santa Claus, to capitalization of Kleenex. But several categories in the stylebook are indispensable to media writers. Summaries of those entries that apply to news and online writing are included here. Because the general style rules differ for broadcast writing, they are included in Chapter 13.

Titles.   Long titles should go after an individual's name. William McCorkle's name is not lost if a short title is used before it, such as "University President William McCorkle." But his name would be hard to find if his title were "University Associate Vice Chancellor for Student Affairs and Services." When an individual has a long title, put the title after the name: "William McCorkle, university associate vice chancellor for student affairs and services."

When titles precede names, they generally are capitalized. After names, they are not.

Most titles are written out. The only time some are abbreviated is when they precede a name. *The Associated Press Stylebook* indicates which titles can be abbreviated. For example, "governor" may be shortened to "Gov. Sheila Aycock" and "lieutenant governor" as "Lt. Gov. James Ramsey." Titles that are never abbreviated include "president," "attorney general," "professor," and "superintendent." Most military titles can be abbreviated, and those abbreviations are listed in *The Associated Press Stylebook*.

Stand-alone titles are always written out, and they are never abbreviated or capitalized. Examples are "The vice president said he would turn over the files to the Justice Department" and "The pope will visit the United States in May." Note that "vice president" is not hyphenated.

Capitalization.   The general rule is to capitalize proper nouns that refer to a person, place, or thing. Examples include "Sacramento is the capital of California" and "Mayor Harmon Bowles agreed to lead the town's Independence Day parade."

Abbreviations.   Abbreviate only what your style manual permits. Abbreviate states' names when they are used with the name of a town or city; otherwise, write them out. Note that the Associated Press does not use postal abbreviations in text, except when the complete address is used with a zip code, as in "124 E. Main St., Lakeland, FL 33801." In other instances the Associated Press uses the following abbreviations: Ala., Ariz., Ark., Calif., Colo., Conn., Del., Fla., Ga., Ill., Ind., Kan., Ky., La., Md., Mass., Mich., Minn., Miss., Mo., Mont., Neb., Nev., N.H., N.J., N.M., N.Y., N.C., N.D., Okla., Ore., Pa., R.I., S.C., S.D., Tenn., Vt., Va., Wash., W.Va., Wis., and Wyo. Eight states' names are never abbreviated: Alaska, Hawaii, Idaho, Iowa, Maine, Ohio, Texas, and Utah. You can abbreviate months when they are used with a specific date: "Nov. 12, 1948." Write out "November 1948," however. Never abbreviate March, April, May, June, or July.

Don't abbreviate the days of the week or the words "assistant" and "association."

The Associated Press allows some abbreviations on first reference because people are familiar with them, such as FBI, CIA, UFO, and IBM. But that does not mean to use only the abbreviation. The context of the story may require that the full title be used somewhere in the text. On second reference, use the abbreviation or substitute words such as "the bureau," "the agency," "the object," or "the company."

Acronyms.   Acronyms are abbreviations that can be pronounced as words, such as "AIDS" for "acquired immune deficiency syndrome" or "UNESCO" for "United Nations Educational, Scientific and Cultural Organization." See style manuals for the correct first and second references for acronyms, just as with other abbreviations.

Numbers.   The general rule according to AP style is to write out numbers zero through nine and use numerals for numbers 10 and higher. Always spell out numbers at the beginning of a sentence, however. In writing numbers above 999,999, write out the words "million" and "billion" rather than using all those zeroes. For example: "To clear the site, the construction crew moved 1.2 million cubic yards of dirt" and "Congressional aides discovered the budget would require an additional $1.4 billion in revenues."

AP style lists two dozen or so exceptions to the rule, but the main ones are these:

Age.   Always use a numeral for age: "She has a 3-year-old daughter and an 85-year-old mother."

Percent.   Always use a numeral: "He estimated 9 percent of employees are truly satisfied with their jobs."

Time.   Always use a numeral: "The guests will arrive at 9 p.m."

Dates.   Again, use numerals: "He was born Jan. 3, 1926."

Temperatures.   Use numerals for all temperatures except zero: "The weather service predicted the coldest weather in 15 years for the weekend, noting that temperatures would drop to 2 to 3 degrees below zero."

Dimensions.   Always write height and weight as numerals: "The average height of the team's basketball players is 6 feet 4 inches." "The record-breaking carrot weighed 5 pounds."

Money.   Write dollars and cents as numerals: "The price of an egg is about 18 cents." "Hemming the dress will cost $9."

Editing Responsibilities

As a writer, you are responsible for editing and revising your own work, even if you work in a newsroom with a separate copy desk or in a large corporate communications office where others ultimately will edit your work. You are the originator, the one who must shape and streamline the initial draft of the message. Your copy must be clear, fair, accurate, complete, and in correct style when it leaves your hands.

Many resources are available to help develop your editing skills, such as those listed in Box 2.1 in Chapter 2. One easily accessible guide is EditTeach.org (www.editteach.org), launched under a grant from the John S. and James L. Knight Foundation. Its Web site is geared "for editing professors, students and working professionals to help strengthen the craft of editing and support the work of editors."

As you gain experience as a writer, you also will be asked to revise the work of others. You might be promoted to an editing position or asked for help by others who know less than you do about good writing skills. When you edit others' work, you must apply both editorial and personal skills, coaching and negotiating respectfully with writers. Editing is hard work, and it is time consuming. It can be creative and satisfying. But in any case, it has to be done. Editing is a crucial part of all writing. And like other writing, it proceeds in steps.

The Steps of Editing

Writers should consider editing as a process. Specific tasks allow writers-turned-editors to be focused and thorough in the editing process. Of course, writer-editors approach a news brief differently from a long feature. Sometimes, on first reading, an editor will decide the story needs substantial revisions; other times, only minor changes will be needed. That decision is made in the first step of the editing process and will determine how much time needs to be devoted to editing.

Today's writers learn to edit at the computer. They may not have time to print out a draft and edit on paper. Editing on screen saves time and allows the writer to use computer tools, such as the grammar-checker and Web resources for fact-checking, to help in the editing process.

Editing follows basic steps focusing on these elements in this order: content, completeness, accuracy, language, and final read-through.

Reading the Copy for Content.   The first step is to check for content. Read the written piece from start to finish to get a sense of what has been written. You may fix any minor errors, but at this point, determine whether substantial changes are needed. Underline sections that need attention.

In this step, the ideal scenario is to put away a piece of writing for a few days and come back to it. Then you can look at it with a fresh eye—with the eye of an editor rather than the eye of the writer. But you might not have that luxury. If you are pressed for time, get up, walk around, have a snack, and get some fresh air. Then return to your writing. You will see it from a new perspective.

Read aloud to slow down and "hear" what you have actually written—not what you think is there. The most common errors detected by reading aloud are awkward language, inadequate explanations that confuse the meaning, and too much prose on a particular topic.

As you read and detect weaknesses, you can make simple notes in the margin, such as "fix," "delete," or "explain." If your piece needs substantial revisions, you might need to consider the audience again and ask yourself: "Does the message attract audience attention and meet audience needs? Does the introduction adequately set up the article? Are all the questions raised answered in subsequent paragraphs? Are opening sentences interesting and written to attract an audience to the message?"

To hold the audience to the message, a writer must look at the overall organization and ask the following questions:

- Is the message developed logically? Do facts follow in a clear sequence?
- Is the transition from one point to another effective? Each paragraph should be tied to the previous one.
- Are paragraphs organized so each contains one thought or idea? Readers will be confused if too many thoughts are packaged into one paragraph. Start a new paragraph—basically a unit of organization— with a new quote or a new idea.
- Are there statements or sentences that stop you because they are out of context?
- Do all the quotes add to the message? Would it be better to paraphrase or omit some?

The answers to these questions might require rewriting.

Checking for Completeness.   To determine if you need more information, ask the following questions:

- Is the message current? Are the latest statistics used? For example, a television news story on accidental deaths attributed to alcohol must have this year's figures on reported cases, not figures from two years ago, or even last year. Your audience wants to know how serious the situation is today. If those numbers aren't available, you need to say so, and why.

- Are any questions raised left unanswered? Are all essential elements of the message present, including meaningful context? Each message must be complete. A news release that says a company is privately held must define what privately held means.

Answering these questions as you check your content will show how much reporting and rewriting must be done so that copy is complete and flows smoothly and logically.

Checking for Accuracy.   Once the content is okay, writers and editors must check for accuracy—an intense, time-consuming job. No aspect of writing is more important than accuracy. Employees might ridicule an executive who includes inaccurate information in memos. Readers turn away from publications and advertisements where they repeatedly find errors. Students lose faith in textbooks when they uncover wrong data.

The bottom line is trust: If your audience doesn't trust the validity of any part of your message, it will question the accuracy of the entire message. Once it loses trust, the audience will be less willing to believe in future communications from you and might move to other media, never to return.

Research has shown that even one error in a newspaper can cause readers to doubt the rest of the paper and to have less faith in the reporter's abilities. Accuracy, therefore, can build or break your reputation, not just the reputation of the medium that carries the message. Use the following steps to check for accuracy:

- Check name spellings. Review your notes. Double-check with the researcher or another writer. Use a telephone book, city directory, or other printed reference. Correct names are essential to avoid confusion—and even legal trouble—when people have the same or similar names. For example, in writing about a nightclub singer named Delsie Harper, a reporter inadvertently left off the D, and the newspaper immediately got a call from a church deacon named Elsie Harper.
- Use reputable sources to confirm information. For example, the city budget director will have more knowledge on changes in the next fiscal year budget than will an anonymous city employee who calls a newspaper to complain.

- Make sure quotes that contain opinion or outrageous claims are attributed, such as this one: "Abused women get what they deserve," a self-proclaimed antifeminist said today. The quote has some credibility with the attribution but would have more if the antifeminist were named.

- If quotes are libelous—that is, damaging to a person's reputation—either make sure they can be defended or cut them. A person's barroom allegation about his next-door neighbor's drug use is not protected by law and should never be published. You could quote a witness's remark in a trial, however, because what occurs in court proceedings is protected. See more about libel in Chapter 12.

- Question statistics. For example, a story reports the president received positive approval from "more than half" of the nation. The actual statistic was 53 percent. The margin of error, or accuracy of the poll, was plus or minus 3 percent. Adding 3 percent to 53 percent means as many as 56 percent of the country support the president. But subtracting 3 percent from 53 percent also means that as little as 50 percent of the nation approve of him. And 50 percent is not more than half. More about math is discussed in Chapter 2.

- Recalculate percentages. Your boss may tell you the company CEO will get only a 7.6 percent pay increase. Check it. A raise from $150,000 to $172,500 is a 15 percent pay increase, not 7.6 percent. The inaccuracy would hardly make other employees confident in the public relations department and its message.

- On technical subjects, when there is doubt about an explanation, call an expert source, and read your material to that person for comment.

Getting information right is also important because inaccuracies are audience-stoppers. When radio listeners hear statistics that they question, they puzzle over the error and no longer hear what you have to say. The best-constructed message framed in the finest form means nothing if your information is wrong or even confusing.

What if you cannot check a fact? Enlist someone else, such as a reference librarian, to verify what is in question. If you cannot verify information and you are working on a deadline, leave it out. If the information is vital to the message and it can't be checked, the message will have to wait. Never publish information if you have doubts about its accuracy. In a professional office, writers have help from editors or fact-checkers. But regardless of who helps, writers ultimately are responsible for the accuracy of their work.

Using Clear Language. In this step, you are looking at word usage that will improve your writing. Consider these questions:

- Is the copy clear and easy to read?
- Are words simple, direct, and easy to understand?
- Are jargon and institutional language eliminated?
- Is redundancy gone?
- Are sentences short and to the point?

This step includes spelling, grammar, and punctuation. In the technological age, many writers use computers with spelling and grammar checking systems. Few spell-checkers adequately check troublesome homonyms, such as "affect" and "effect," "red" and "read," "naval" and "navel," "stationary" and "stationery," "trustee" and "trusty," "lead" and "led," and so on. Chapter 2 contains a guide to spelling in the computer age.

Just as you have to check spelling, you have to review grammar. Chapter 2 discusses common grammar problems; consult the reference books listed in that chapter for additional help.

Writers must be on the lookout for jargon. Such language should be replaced immediately with clearer terms, so that, for example, "organizational inputs" becomes "suggestions from parent groups" and "facilitation of new methodologies" becomes "trying a new survey."

In this step of editing, you also should pay careful attention to word choice. Do you want to refer to a hit man as "specializing in conflict resolution"? Remember: The right word enhances audience understanding and willingness to pay attention, whether the message is read or heard. "Let your conscious be your guide" might not affect listeners. And some readers might not even notice the confused choice of "conscious" for "conscience." Those who do notice will not be impressed. If necessary, review the discussion of word usage in Chapter 4.

If you need to shorten your article, do so by looking at phrases, groups of words, titles, and word usage for shorter ways to state the same idea. For example, the statement "He decided to take part in the debate" could be rewritten "He joined in the debate." Or "The banners that were blue and white fluttered in the breeze" could be changed to "The blue and white banners fluttered in the breeze." More on word usage is found in Chapter 4.

Giving the Piece the Last Once-Over.   After revisions are complete, read the entire piece again. At this point, no major reworking should be needed. Check, however, for any editing errors that might have crept in during earlier steps. Check carefully any sections that have been changed. Often, writers make new errors when they revise. The last stage is a final read-through for overall quality and reader appeal. This stage is what some people equate with the term editing. It is the final cosmetic once-over where the writer-editor is pleased with the story. If the writer-editor is not satisfied, then the editing steps should be repeated.

If you have been editing on the computer, you should do one final step: Consult the computer's spelling and grammar checker. It will catch spelling errors and flag repeated words, possible grammar problems, and missing spaces. Such errors often are overlooked.

Some writers may question the sequence in editing. But the reasoning is quite simple: It is efficient. If reviewing for language came first, sentences that had been fine-tuned could be deleted during later content editing. It's far better that the sentences go first. More important, the most critical tasks are done first in case the writer-editor runs out of time. For example, it is more important to write a compelling lead than to smooth out a transition. And it is more important for the piece to be complete and accurate than free of style errors.

Note: Editors should be flexible as they edit. If they see a problem that needs to be fixed, regardless of the step, they should address it then. Editors who wait may forget to make the repair.

Now you might send your copy to your editor or to a corporate executive for review, if you are in an organization or business. If you are an advertising copywriter, the message will go to the account executive and then to the client. In print media, the story will go to an editor and in broadcast, to a news director. If you are a high school principal, your memo might be reviewed by the school system's superintendent before it is sent to parents. If you are a student, you turn the article in to a professor or instructor.

Even if your copy is posted online without ever being edited, your readers will see it, and they won't be shy about letting you know about the errors in your story. Or, even if the grammar is perfect and the facts are correct, the story might change and require you to keep revising the piece with new information.

But do not think that turning in your piece ends the editing process. The copy could come back for another round of editing and changes before publication.

Editing for Online and Other Formats

Online news sites have presented new opportunities for professional communicators. Online news can be published quickly to alert your audience to a breaking news story. But online news—unlimited by the physical space of a print publication or time constraints of a broadcast—can be more in-depth. And, once published, online news often stays online forever and remains findable by anyone with a search engine.

Editors who work online, often called "producers," are often required to work quickly to post stories. But they are also required to be more comprehensive as they enhance the story with photos, audio, and video, and insert links to archive stories or to connect to material on other sites.

Online editors sometimes need to tailor the language of the news for the online audience. People who read news online often are more interested in what is happening now, rather than what is delayed or expected. Online readers often spend no more than a few seconds scanning a story before moving on. This perusal places emphasis on brevity and action.

When working online, editors must remember that their headlines, short descriptions, and key phrases will also function as live links. A click takes the reader to the full story or to a photo essay. So in addition to bearing information, these words must move the reader easily to the related story.

Online news also means more than just Web sites. More and more news is distributed via e-mail or RSS feeds—and is shared by readers on social network sites such as Facebook. Editors should be aware of all the places their words will appear. In some cases—most search engines, for example—only a small portion of the words will appear to the audience. Editors need to stay abreast of continuous changes in tools the audience uses to find your copy.

Regardless of the medium, the same basic editing process is important to a writer's ability to craft a relevant and memorable message.

Well-edited Web sites exploit all the benefits of online communication: brighter pictures, links to original documents or sound, and the potential for instant feedback from an active audience. Readers expect to move quickly among media when they are online—from photos to text to sound to e-mail and back again, many times over in a single seating. Audiences appreciate the extras that come with online stories: more choices, more control, interaction, and variety. Writers and editors must deliver these benefits and remember that one story on a given topic could end up being the only story a reader might see. Editors must check to be sure each story is self-sufficient and fully connected to related materials and sites.

When it comes to feeding content to any Web site, editors function as part of a team that includes artists, writers, photographers, videographers, and others. Even archivists and museum curators get involved when original documents become part of online news. The entire team is important because audiences gravitate toward sites that have strong design and are easily navigated. Content is important, but so is the packaging.

Putting the Editing Rules into Practice

With your knowledge of guidelines for good editing in mind, read the following story:

> A Grove City–area woman has been accused of rigging her ex-husband's washing machine in hopes of torching him and his trailer for the insurance money.
>
> State police at Mercer last week arrested Valerie Norine Lagun, claiming the 43-year-old had hoped to kill semidisabled Thomas Lagun in May when he turned on his washer. She was charged with attempted murder, attempted arson and recklessly endangering another person.
>
> Free on $10,000 bond, Mrs. Lagun is again living with her 57-year-old ex-husband at her home at 458 Blacktown Road, Pine Township, detective Robert Lewis said Tuesday.
>
> "They're still using the washing machine," Lewis said.
>
> According to court papers at District Justice Larry Silvis' Worth Township office, Mrs. Lagun told police she conspired with another man in the plot. She agreed to pay him half of the $5,000 from Lagun's life insurance policy and $10,000 from their renter's insurance.
>
> Police didn't name the man—described as an acquaintance of Mrs. Lagun—because he hasn't been charged, Lewis said. Police know of his whereabouts but are still gathering evidence in hopes of charging him, Lewis said.

According to court papers:

Mrs. Lagun told police she took the man to Lagun's trailer at 169 Jamison Road, Worth Township, after dark.

Once inside, the man wired three bottles containing gasoline to the washing machine. A flip of the washer's switch should have ignited the fire.

"It could've exploded and probably killed him if it blew up. The potential was there," Lewis said.

Lagun discovered the gasoline after an electrical breaker tripped when he attempted to use the machine, according to court papers. He reported the incident to police, and Mrs. Lagun confessed July 24.

She told police she was surprised the explosive didn't work, but happy that her ex-husband wasn't killed, according to court papers.

Mrs. Lagun has a preliminary hearing at 1 p.m. Jan. 8 before Silvis.[*]

*Reprinted with permission of The Sharon Herald Co.

The story has compelling interest: potential death, oddity in an alleged method of killing someone, human interest because the ex-husband and wife are still living together despite the charges, and the twist about the washing machine.

Consider this edited version of the story that includes most of the original information. But it is rewritten to apply good writing rules and reorganized in a format to pull readers through the story and reward them at the end:

A Grove City–area woman has been accused of rigging her ex-husband's washing machine to explode, killing him and destroying his trailer so she could collect the insurance money. But that's not where the story ends.

Valerie Norine Lagun, 43, was arrested last week by police who claim she had hoped to kill semidisabled Thomas Lagun in May when he turned on his washer. She was charged with attempted murder, attempted arson and recklessly endangering another person.

Mrs. Lagun is free on $10,000 bond and has a preliminary hearing at 1 p.m. Jan. 8 before District Justice Larry Silvis.

According to court papers, Mrs. Lagun told police she conspired with another man and agreed to pay him half of the $5,000 from Lagun's life insurance policy and $10,000 from their renter's insurance.

The man—described as an acquaintance of Mrs. Lagun—hasn't been charged, detective Robert Lewis said Tuesday. Police know of his whereabouts but are still gathering evidence and hope to charge him.

Mrs. Lagun told police she took the man to Lagun's trailer at 169 Jamison Road, Worth Township, after dark. The man wired three bottles containing gasoline to the washing machine. A flip of the washer's switch should have ignited the fire, according to court papers.

Lagun discovered the gasoline after an electrical breaker tripped when he attempted to use the machine, according to court papers. He reported the incident to police, and Mrs. Lagun confessed July 24.

"It could've exploded and probably killed him if it blew up. The potential was there," Lewis said.

Mrs. Lagun told police she was surprised the explosive didn't work, but happy that her ex-husband wasn't killed, according to court papers.

Despite the charges, Mrs. Lagun is again living with her 57-year-old ex-husband at her home at 458 Blacktown Road, Pine Township.

And, noted detective Lewis, "They're still using the washing machine."

The following exercises will require you to apply the guidelines in this chapter. When you have completed them, take a message you constructed during the last week and rewrite it to be clearer and simpler.

Exercises

1. Check your ability to apply the rules you have learned so far. On a separate sheet of paper, copyedit the following sentences according to Associated Press style. Also check for any grammar, spelling, or punctuation errors. Use proper copyediting symbols to save time.

   1. Lieutenant Governor Stanley Greene was stripped of his powers by the N.C. Senate.
   2. William Williams, Dean of the Graduate School of Journalism, will speak to students about graduation requirements on Wed. afternoon.

3. The students are expected to begin the test at 9:00 a.m. Tuesday.

4. The President lives at 1600 Pennsylvania Avenue, but his mail is delivered to the U.S. Post Office on Twenty-second Street.

5. The state Senate is expected to enact a bill to require polio vaccinations for children under the age of two.

6. The airport in Medford, Oregon was closed yesterday after an Alaskan airlines jet made an emergency landing on the runway.

7. The Atty. Gen. has a B.A. in history from American University.

8. The then-Soviet block countries sponsored the Friendship Games rather than attend the 1984 olympics in Los Angeles.

9. The city and county used thirteen busses to transport the children to the July Fourth picnic.

10. Water freezes at 0 degrees Centigrade.

11. Three houses on Sims street were destroyed by the fire, which began at 112 Sims Street.

12. Following the Federal Reserve action, three banks announced a one percent increase in the prime rate, putting it at six percent.

13. The late Senator Jesse A. Helms (R-North Carolina) used to be city editor of The Raleigh Times.

14. John L. Harris, 48 years old, of 1632 Winding Way Road was charged Tuesday with cocaine possession.

15. The champion wrestler measured six feet six inches tall and won 4/5 of his fights.

16. Army Sergeant Willie York was charged with misappropriating $1,000,000 dollars in construction equipment.

17. Hurricane Diana, blowing from the East, caused millions of dollars in damages to the east coast of the United States.

18. Colonel Max Shaw, who has served as a national guardsman for more than 20 years, is Ed's commanding officer.

19. Ability with a frisbee is not a valid measure of IQ.

20. We heard the kickoff announced over the radio at the Laundromat.

21. The stockings were hanged by the chimney with care, in hopes that Kirs Kringle soon would be there.

22. Travelling the 48 miles, or 60 kilometers, to Kansas City, we got 32 miles per gallon in our new minivan.

23. The five-year-old boy got on the wrong bus and was missing for two hours.

24. Sarah sold two hundred and two boxes of Girl Scout cookies to her neighbors on Sweetbriar Pkwy. and Pantego Ave.

2. Read the following message. Assume the audience for this information is readers of the campus newspaper. Using only the available information, edit this message according to Associated Press style, and use proper spelling and grammar. Watch out for usage errors and redundancies.

> All of the faculty members from the School of Journalism and Mass Communication will be attending on Thursday of this week a regional meeting of the Association for Education in Journalism and Mass Communication at the Holiday Inn in the state capitol.
>
> The meeting will commence at 10 a.m. in the morning and conclude at 2 p.m. in the afternoon following a noon luncheon.
>
> In the morning, sessions will offer journalism educators the opportunity to have discussions on current issues addressing journalism and mass communication.
>
> At a luncheon program, professor Walter Blayless will be speaking on the topic of cigarette advertising and the effect on the nation's young people of today.
>
> The meeting sponsored by AEJMC is exemplary of the several regional meetings the organization holds across the country each year. The National meeting is always held in August each year at different locations around the country.

As you edit, make a list of questions you would like to ask about information that would improve the message. Also make a list of the steps you followed in editing. Take these two lists and your edited story to your next class where you can meet with a group of other students to discuss the strengths and weaknesses of various approaches to this editing task.

3. Look at the story you edited in Exercise 2. Now edit it as an online story that will be posted to the campus news Web site on Thursday morning, the day of the meeting. Which elements of the story are now most important to your audience? Is your lead the same? Or did it change? Also, add three links to related content on the Web and determine which words in the story should be linked.

References

Clair Kehrwald Cook, *Line by Line: How to Improve Your Own Writing*. Boston: Houghton Mifflin, 1985.

Norm Goldstein, ed. *The Associated Press Stylebook and Briefing on Media Law*. New York: The Associated Press, 2005.

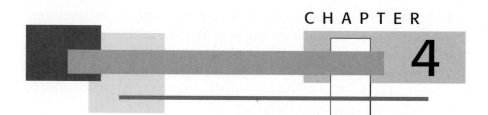

Guidelines for Good Writing

For years, writing coaches have worked to distill a set of qualities in writing that will catch and hold readers. Many people, such as Roy Peter Clark at the Poynter Institute in St. Petersburg, Florida, have spent a great deal of their professional careers analyzing the qualities of good writing. Authors such as William Zinsser, best known for his book *On Writing Well*, offer advice on how to strengthen and improve prose. Even communication researchers, charged with finding out what makes publications sell, have considered which qualities are valued in messages. The research shows the most effective writing is simple and forceful; that is, it says it straight without flourishes and pomp.

In this chapter, you will learn

- four essential qualities in writing: accuracy, clarity, completeness, and fairness,
- five broad rules for good writing, and
- specific tips to improve writing.

Watchwords of Writing

No message will succeed if it does not have four essential qualities: accuracy, clarity, completeness, and fairness. We know from the discussion in Chapter 1 that audiences can be fickle; once lost, they may not return. Writing that is accurate, clear, complete, and fair has a better chance of holding audiences, particularly those who might be clicking through a Web site or leafing through a magazine.

Accuracy ensures the credibility of all writing. When the audience catches a misspelled name or an erroneous date, it doubts the accuracy of the information that follows. An audience will abandon a communicator it cannot trust.

Clarity means the writer uses language an audience understands. Simple language is preferred over complicated words. Jargon and technical language are avoided. The message comes through.

Completeness anticipates and answers an audience's questions. A complete message satisfies the audience and does so quickly.

Fairness occurs when the writer uses a variety of sources to keep an article balanced, excises any editorial opinion, and is as objective as possible.

Let's look at each element more closely.

Accuracy

Good communication of any kind always contains accurate information. Accuracy is comforting to audiences, who depend on information. Errors can occur at any stage in writing: gathering information through research and interviewing, transcribing notes, calculating figures, and creating the copy (when typos can occur). To ensure accuracy, writers must use good information-gathering techniques. They must obtain information only from reliable sources, then check and recheck it against other sources. If they find a discrepancy or an error but don't have time to check it, they should follow the adage, "When in doubt, leave it out."

We are all prone to committing errors on occasion. Just because a well-known person recites a fact or the fact is found in a computer database does not mean it is correct. The potentate might be wrong, and humans type information into databases. Name spellings, middle initials, street numbers, birth dates—seemingly trivial details—become monumentally important once they become part of a message. Such details might be accurate in notes but then could be transcribed erroneously into copy.

Today's information environment constantly tests accuracy. Deadlines, competition, and 24/7 news cycles push reporters and editors to publish and air the news quickly—sometimes, too quickly. In their hurry to produce copy, writers run a greater risk of getting information wrong.

Errors have always been a danger to a communicator's credibility, but the Internet has made it even more treacherous for writers who don't take the time to get it right. Once incorrect information is cached on the Web, it often remains there for others to pick up and reuse. Always available from search engines, this incorrect information can then be found and repeated by other writers who may also fail to double-check for accuracy.

The ease of publishing information online has made it easier for malicious or lazy writers to spread inaccurate information, but at the same time it has also increased accountability for professional communicators. Some bloggers closely monitor professional news sites, standing ready to criticize inaccuracies. Two of the most prominent sites dedicated to correcting inaccurate information are Snopes.com, a semi-professional site run by a California couple, and Factcheck.org, funded by the Annenberg Public Policy Center of the University of Pennsylvania.

If messages are wrong, people are misled. Writers and audiences rarely forget the mishap when a name is misspelled or an address is wrong. Inaccuracies in messages lead to distrust among audiences—and they can lead to libel suits. Once audience members are misled by a source, they have difficulty trusting it again. Even the venerable *New York Times* has struggled with lost credibility because of inaccuracies. Recently, bloggers have recalled information they posted too quickly, such as reporting that political candidates were dropping out of races or that certain individuals were vice presidential nominees—and none of the information was true.

Clarity

A message will have impact if it is clear and straightforward and everyone in its audience can understand it. "Send a check for $75 by February 1 if you want to ski with the Seniors Club in February" makes the requirement clear. The writing is direct and uses simple, to-the-point language.

A message needs to be so clear that no misunderstanding or confusion can possibly result. People rely on media for information on where to vote, get flu shots, take vacations, enroll their children in school, and find cheap gasoline. If the directions to a polling site are unclear, such as "the church on Capitol Square," people will be unhappy when they arrive and discover a church on each corner of Capitol Square.

Completeness

Useful messages also are complete, giving sufficient information for real understanding and guidance. A news story that omits an important fact can be misleading and even harmful.

When an important highway intersection outside Washington, D.C., was under construction, traffic was rerouted for a 12-hour period. News reports warned drivers about the detour, but some neglected to mention the additional 45 minutes of drive time required to navigate the detour. This problem with completeness caused headaches for the many travelers who missed important appointments.

Fairness

Messages will be more believable if audiences sense the stories are fair. Readers or viewers will turn away from reports they feel are skewed or one-sided.

For a story to be fair or balanced, it must have a variety of sources. That doesn't mean that every story must present each side of an issue in the same detail and the same number of words. Such balance is not possible in most writing. A reporter might not be able to get in touch with sources on one side of an issue, but in the story, the reporter should let readers know that he or she tried.

Writers must be careful about the language they use so audiences don't ascribe any specific leaning or viewpoint to the story. Language should be neutral. Quotes can be inflammatory or weighty—but such language should be reserved to quotes attributed to specific sources, not to the writer.

Keys to Good Writing

Researchers, language professionals, and experienced writers agree on five basic tenets of good writing: (1) use short sentences, (2) use short words, (3) eliminate wordiness, (4) avoid jargon, and (5) come to the point quickly. Anyone can apply the rules while writing and editing.

Good Writing Uses Short Sentences

Most readability experts argue that regardless of age, education, or economic status, people prefer and understand writing that uses short sentences. Humans have little patience with long, complicated sentences that tax their brain power. Of course, not all sentences should be short; sentence length should vary. A short sentence can have impact. A long, complex sentence can set up an idea for the audience or create a mood, and a short sentence can follow immediately—almost as a punch line. Get the point?

A study at the American Press Institute showed that reader understanding drops off dramatically if sentences exceed 20 words, and comprehension continues to drop as sentences grow longer. Only about one of 20 people studied could clearly comprehend 50-word sentences, a common length in newspapers and in academic writing. Short sentences are critical in broadcast writing or descriptive links on Web sites. People tend to skim online news stories more quickly than print stories, and search engines have difficulty classifying Web pages containing more than about 1,000 words.

Short-term memory rarely exceeds 15 seconds, which might not be enough time to read one of the many 50-word sentences in traditional magazines and newspapers. Consider this lead:

> LAS CRUCES—James McDonough has withdrawn his acceptance of New Mexico State University's interim presidency, and the president of the board of regents said he plans to nominate Waded Cruzado, the university's executive vice president and provost, in McDonough's place.

By the time many readers reach the end of this 38-word sentence, they have forgotten whom the Board of Regents named as interim president.

The English language is based on a pattern of simple, subject–verb–object constructions. Most are short. Because people learn and use English this way in everyday life, they prefer this pattern in messages.

Readers would be more likely to warm up to a straightforward approach to the news, such as:

> LAS CRUCES—James McDonough has decided to turn down the offer as interim president of New Mexico State University, citing personal reasons.
>
> A successor has already been identified. Waded Cruzado, the university's executive vice president and provost, will be nominated for the position, said the president of the board of regents.

Retired journalism Professor Fred Fedler of the University of Central Florida said that simplicity makes stories more interesting and forceful. He cites as an example a prize-winning story by World War II journalist Ernie Pyle; the average sentence length was 10.6 words.

Good Writing Uses Short Words

Perhaps your high school English teacher praised you for using "penurious" rather than "stingy," or "inebriated" rather than "drunk." Then you were expanding your vocabulary, but now your audience will thank you for choosing the simpler word.

Just as with long sentences, readers and listeners become tired and discouraged when faced with too many complex words—usually those exceeding three syllables. To be sure, you can use commonly known, longer words, such as "responsibility," "establishment," "participate," and "governmental." Be sure, however, that the longer words are a better choice than a shorter version, such as "duty," "founding," "join in," or "federal" or "state."

When writing, select the simplest word possible to convey the meaning. For example, in a police story, a writer said, "The contents of the suspicious package were innocuous." Some readers might wonder if the contents were dangerous or not. Use "fight" instead of altercation. Replace "finalize" with a word such as "conclude" or "finish." Rather than "exasperate," use "annoy" or "bother." Instead of "terminating" this paragraph, we will "end" it.

Good Writing Eliminates Wordiness

"You can almost detect a wordy sentence by looking at it—at least if you can recognize weak verbs, ponderous nouns, and strings of prepositional phrases," Claire Kehrwald Cook writes in her book, *Line by Line: How to Improve Your Own Writing*. Her advice gives writers clues about where to find wordiness and where to improve sentence structure.

Author William Zinsser notes that the secret to good writing is to strip every sentence to its cleanest components. Writers must detach themselves from the information and chisel it to the bare essentials. Writers must throw out extra words and phrases—even extra sentences and paragraphs. Remember this adage: "Two words are never as good as one." Consider the simple word "new." When used in the following sentence, it is unnecessary: "Crews expect the new building to be completed within two months." All buildings under construction are new. Leave the word out.

Audiences can find the facts only when excess is trimmed. Sparse writing is more professional, more informative, more objective, and more likely to be read. In Saltzman's *If You Can Talk, You Can Write*, writer Stanley Elkin describes the process of eliminating excess in writing: "[It's] a kind of whittling, a honing to the bone, until you finally get whatever the hell you're looking for. It's an exercise in sculpture, chipping away at the rock until you find the nose."

Wordy writing is likely redundant. No writer needs to say a fire "completely destroyed" a downtown block; if it was destroyed, the destruction was complete. This classic often appears: "Jones is currently the manager of consumer services." "Is" means "now," and "now" means "currently." Kill the word "currently." Think about other phrases such as "past history," "acres of land," "4 p.m. in the afternoon," "at 12 midnight," "dead body," and "totally incomprehensible."

In seeking wordiness, look specifically for unnecessary adjectives and qualifiers. For example, a project cannot be the "most" unique. "Unique" means one of a kind. Qualifiers such as "very," "truly," and "really" can generally be cut without damage to copy.

Sometimes a statement or entire paragraph that repeats a speaker's direct quotes can be deleted:

> Jones said he was delighted the school would receive $40,000 to use for purchasing audiovisual equipment materials for the library.
>
> "I am just delighted that we will have the $40,000 to buy audiovisual equipment for the library," Jones said.

Delete the first paragraph. It does more than serve as a transition to the direct quote—it steals it.

As in art, too much embellishment in writing only detracts and distracts. Consider the effectiveness of the following message before and after its extra words are deleted:

> More than 100 years ago, the Tung Wah Dispensary attempted to cure the ailments and afflictions of the San Francisco Chinatown community from its humble outpost at 828 Sacramento Street. When the institution realized that its cramped quarters were counterproductive to the logistics of health care, it expanded its services and relocated to 845 Jackson Street, eventually being renamed the Chinese Hospital.

Simplified, the history looks like this:

> A century ago, the Tung Wah Dispensary treated sickness in San Francisco's Chinatown from its humble outpost at 828 Sacramento Street. Cramped quarters and expanded services led to a new location at 845 Jackson Street, the building that eventually was named the Chinese Hospital.

Without its embellishments—"ailments and afflictions," "institution," and "counterproductive"—this message is much more readable and just as informative.

Good Writing Avoids Jargon or Technical Language

In our high-tech society, so much jargon exists that it is difficult to tell what is jargon and what is plain English. Few people recall that "input" and "output" originated in computer jargon. The same is true of the terms "bottom line," "24/7," and "in the red." The Internet has introduced "google" to mean "look for" and "blog" for weblog as part of common language.

Jargon abounds in everyday life. For example, in listing its objectives for the year, an annual report from an elementary school stated:

> Objective Three: The mean score for the kindergarten program will increase from 5.1 to 5.4 as measured by the FPG Assessment Report. The lead teacher for developmentally appropriate practice coordinated the efforts of our kindergarten teachers to enable our program to meet this objective.

For parents, what does this say? Not much. What is a mean score? What is the FPG Assessment Report? What is developmentally appropriate practice? When people see or hear such words, they stop. Confusion sets in. Parents just want to know how their children are doing in school.

Why Is Jargon Such a No-No? Jargon should be avoided for several reasons. First, it makes too many assumptions about audiences. Technical language reserves a message for insiders: those who are familiar with the lingo. "Outsiders" who could benefit from the information might be put off. For example, an art exhibit notice that contains artistic jargon might scare away potential visitors to the gallery. Technical terms might create a feeling that the gallery is reserved for an elite group. As a result, town residents might feel excluded or perceive the message as exclusive. For the same reason, it is also wise to avoid foreign words and phrases in published writing—unless those words are commonly used, such as *voila*!

Second, jargon is precise only to the insiders who use it. Once again, consider the word "input," which may be anything from telephone conversations to cash contributions. A more specific term is better.

Third, jargon usually is ambiguous. The "bottom line" mentioned in a school newsletter could mean many things: expenditures, income, or both; parent satisfaction; student learning outcomes—or almost anything. Skilled writers avoid vagueness by avoiding jargon.

Of course, whether writers use jargon or technical language depends on the audience. If they are writing for a medical publication whose audience is nurses and doctors, the language can be more specific to that profession.

Too often, though, messages for general audiences or laypeople are filled with educational, legal, economic, or medical jargon. Some technical language has become more understood by the general public, such as "SAT" scores for "Scholastic Assessment Tests" and "AIDS" for "acquired immune deficiency syndrome." But language too often goes unexplained.

Institutional Language.   Another problem related to jargon is the use of institutional language: abstract terms and phrases that might communicate well in a specific workplace or institution but that lose meaning for a general audience. For example, medical professionals use the term "treatment modalities." That terminology is nonspecific and lacks meaning and interest, even to a well-educated general audience. Treatment modalities should be named in terms an audience can understand: a series of shots, an antibiotic for 10 days, physical therapy for several months, and so on. It is easy to find words to substitute for institutional terms, and the simpler words are always more specific.

A professor wrote, "Shrinking and unstable sources of funding lead to short-term dislocations." What he meant was a lack of funding interrupts research. Some terms cannot be avoided such as the nation's "gross domestic product (GDP)." Writers must explain such words adequately when they use them. As *The Associated Press Stylebook* explains it, "The gross domestic product is the sum of all the goods and services produced within U.S. borders."

Although institutional language may be the conversational standard at work, it rarely works in writing. When you are talking, you can be sure how much your audience knows about your topic; you can supplement messages with hand gestures, facial expressions, and other visual aids; and you can clarify or define confusing terms if your audience looks puzzled or asks questions.

But when you are writing, your text stands alone and must be absolutely clear. Your goal as a writer is to eliminate misunderstanding, and omitting jargon and technical language is a giant step toward that goal.

Good Writing Comes to the Point Quickly

Chapter 5 will focus on the need for writers to come to the point quickly, perhaps the most problematic of writing challenges. A writer might not want to come to the point because the point is unpleasant: A company has lost money or laid off employees, or a popular program has been discontinued. But audiences see through attempts to delay bad news and interpret them as sneaky ways to hide information. However unwelcome the message, direct communication conveys a feeling of openness and honesty.

Some writers fail to come to the point because they are in "writer's mode," self-indulgently crafting a long introduction to the main points rather than getting to those points. Readers of nonfiction want information rather than art, and they consider the most direct messages to be the greatest masterpieces.

Still other writers have trouble coming to the point because they do not know what the point is. Critical thinking—deciding on the main goal in communicating—precedes every writing task. To come to the point, writers must know their audiences and analyze information carefully enough to know the point audiences will want to know.

Writer and filmmaker Nora Ephron tells a story about her high school journalism teacher. In one lesson, he taught his class to recognize main points by telling them their faculty members would be attending a major conference the next day. He asked them to write a news story about it. In the students' articles, the introductory paragraphs summarized the facts: All teachers would travel to a nearby city and hear famous speakers. After collecting the papers, the teacher threw them away and told the students, "The point is that there will be no school tomorrow." Ephron says she never forgot the point:

> It was an electrifying moment. So that's it, I realized. It's about the point. The classic newspaper lead of who-what-when-where-how and why is utterly meaningless if you haven't figured out the significance of the facts. What is the point? What does it mean? He planted those questions in my head. And for the first year he taught me journalism, every day was like the first; every set of facts had a point buried in it if we looked hard enough. He turned the class into a gorgeous intellectual exercise, and he gave me enthusiasm for the profession I never lost. Also, of course, he taught me something that works just as well in life as it does in journalism.

Words

Three of the five keys to good writing just given—using short words, avoiding wordiness, and eliminating jargon—focus on words, the basic unit of any oral or written message. A good writer also needs knowledge of language, a good vocabulary, and the sense to know when a word is inappropriate or unnecessary.

The Power of Little Words

Most of the little words in our language come from the original language spoken in England before Roman and French invaders added their vocabulary to the mix. The English common folk retained their own words for everyday things, and they borrowed from Latin and French only when they had to.

As a result, the things nearest and dearest to us still are called by their original English names—home, fire, food, and mother, for example. And it is these words to which English-speaking people still respond emotionally. The word "home" has much stronger emotional appeal than the cooler, more technical word "domicile," which is borrowed from Latin. Likewise, "food" sounds good; "nutrients," a Latin-based word, is another matter.

How Little Words Are Successful

Professor and writing coach Carl Sessions Stepp says people respond to small words because they usually are "first-degree" words, or words that are immediately understood. Everyone has a single, readily available mental picture of "home," along with a host of meanings and feelings associated with that mental picture. But few people can respond so completely to "domicile." The writer who uses "mother" taps the audience's rich reserves of emotion and information.

Stepp points out that larger, multisyllabic words, many of which have origins in other languages, are "second-degree" words. Such words are abstract rather than concrete. They produce no immediate images in the minds of readers or listeners and are often ambiguous when other information is given. Take, for example, the word "nutrition." Does it mean food substances, or measures of vitamins and minerals? It is a second-degree word because the audience needs more information for full understanding.

Consider other second-degree words, such as "facility" and "output." Compare them with these first-degree words: "school" and "grades."

Stepp argues that writers are more likely to appeal to audiences if they choose first-degree words and avoid second-degree words. In writing, we deal with many second-degree words that are part of science, technology, education, and almost every other field. Writers need to remember to define such words in first-degree terms whenever possible, as in this sentence:

Nutrition—the kinds of foods patients eat every day—is the topic of a workshop for nurses at Sibley Hospital on Saturday.

Little words are more heart-warming and more easily understood. They also save space, time, and the reader's energy. They are more readable. In an Associated Press article about a Dallas drug bust, the language could not be much simpler (see Box 4.1). Most fifth graders could read the story with very little trouble.

BOX 4.1   Crime, Fear, Poverty—All Part of Life in America

Young Woman's Eyes Reflect Despair of Violent Nation

BY JULIA PRODIS
Associated Press

DALLAS—Her eyes are the color of earth, and as vacant as the lot next door.

She's sitting on a concrete step holding a baby that's not hers. Her 16-year-old friend is lying face down on the sizzling sidewalk beside her, his arms arched awkwardly behind him, his hands cuffed in plastic police ties. A girlfriend is similarly contorted at her feet.

"What's your name?" a policewoman asks this hot August day in Dallas.

In a low, slow whisper, she answers, "Latasha."

"La-what?"

"La-Tasha," the thin, moonfaced 19-year-old says with slightly more effort, her blank gaze never looking higher than the holster holding the officer's 9 mm semiautomatic.

Minutes ago, eight muscular members of the Dallas drug enforcement squad, wearing black boots and bulletproof vests, had stormed the faded yellow bungalow behind her. It took two heaves of "the slammer" to break down the door, blocked only by an empty bookcase.

Shrieks from inside, then blurs of motion as the young man bolted out the rear and the woman ran toward the back fence. Latasha

Smith never said a word, and the baby didn't cry.

She has the dull look of someone who had seen this rerun too many times. Her look of despair, so deep it turns everything gray, is the same look that flattens the faces of the young and hopeless in poor, violent American neighborhoods everywhere.

Neighborhoods where crack heads fear friends and neighbors more than the cops. Where homes are so filthy detectives can't pickup evidence without something crawling on it. Where neighbors scatter when someone screams for help.

For Americans who say crime is their gravest concern, these calloused Latashas and their criminal friends stir angry fear. But for Latasha, it's just another day.

The baby with cocoa skin and wavy brown hair spits up on Latasha's chest as she rocks negligibly back and forth. Indifferently, she wipes his face with her droopy white tank top.

"Who's payin' for that baby?" the policewoman asks.

"It ain't MY baby," she retorts.

"It's my baby," says the 16-year-old boy, squirming awkwardly on the sidewalk. As he strains to lift his head to speak, the pebbles clinging to his cheek dribble to the ground.

Latasha tells the officer she has three children of her own and she's on welfare. She quit the last job she had washing dishes because she didn't like it. Her children are scattered with relatives and friends today.

"Did you grow up like this baby is growing up?" the reporter asks.

"My daddy shot my momma dead when I was 2." She speaks flatly, like a kid bored with homework. She was raised by her grandfather.

She doesn't explain why she is at this house that isn't hers holding somebody else's baby.

An undercover officer recently bought drugs at this house. The police had come back to clean it up and close it down—one of nearly 400 Dallas dope houses stormed this year.

After running background checks on the three, the sergeant in charge decides to arrest the handcuffed youths on drug charges and ticket Latasha for failing to appear in court after being cited for driving without insurance.

"Do you ever dream of a better life?" the reporter asks.

She shrugs.

She doesn't watch the van carry her two friends away. She just sits in front of the house with the For Rent sign and the broken door, holding someone else's baby, and stares blankly at the vacant lot next door.

The Right Word

Wordsmiths such as the late Theodore Bernstein and the late John Bremner have long decried the lack of precision in language. Bremner lamented what he called "the surge of literary barbarism" in English usage. Both stressed the importance of knowing language and definitions. To language lovers like

Bremner, writing is a love affair with language. In his book, *Words on Words*, Bremner wrote,

> *To love words, you must first know what they are. Yes, words are symbols of ideas. But many words have lives of their own. They have their own historical and etymological associations, their own romantic and environmental dalliances, their own sonic and visual delights.*

A careless writer describes a basketball player as "an intricate part of the team." Perhaps his footwork is intricate, but what the writer really meant to say was "an integral part of the team."

A letter from a university provost to a newspaper columnist thanked her for "the prospective" she gave to a local issue. The provost meant "perspective."

In a news story, a student quoted a speaker as saying the decision "reaped haddock" on the school's admissions procedures—a fishy end to "wreaked havoc." Language needs to be specific and correct. When writers misuse or misspell words, such as "brew ha-ha" for "brouhaha," we laugh. As writers, we do not want our audiences laughing at us—unless we mean for them to chuckle.

Similar Words

Words that sound alike are troublesome for writers. Among the most common homonyms are "principal" and "principle," "affect" and "effect," and "its" and "it's." Such words are particularly troublesome today when writers depend heavily on computer spell-checkers. Few programs will know the difference between "naval" and "navel" or "stationary" and "stationery," as we discussed in Chapter 2. The resulting confusion can be misleading and embarrassing. Writers must be comfortable in reaching for a good dictionary or other reference books to check correct spelling and usage. Other references, such as those listed at the end of this chapter, are valuable for writers who are choosy about words. Refer to Chapter 2 for help with spelling in the computer age.

Writers should pay heed to synonyms. Many writers haul out the thesaurus when they are weary of using a word too often. But a synonym might not be specific. One editing teacher advises against using a thesaurus and prefers a dictionary. Remember that repetition of a word or words throughout a message is acceptable. Repetition can unify a message. For instance, use the phrase "online news site" throughout a story about the launch of a television station's Web site. It unifies the story and is more specific than "media product."

Word Choice

While taking care with word usage, writers should strive to choose words that are universally accepted and understood. If they are unsure about a word or its use, they should consult a stylebook or a dictionary. *The Associated Press Stylebook*, for example, adds cautionary notes about how specific words in its entries should be used. The note might warn that the word is offensive or derogatory. Dictionaries will include in the definition whether the word is below the normal standard for literate writing. Dictionaries also will indicate spellings of words and correct usage, as in the case of homonyms.

If a dictionary or a stylebook warns against usage of a word, as profanity perhaps, writers should use it only if they have a compelling reason. They might also have to explain in a note at the beginning of the article or the broadcast that the message contains offensive language. Using profanities and vulgarities is discussed more fully in Chapter 10 on quotes and attribution.

Sentences

Sentences should be complete. Each must have a subject and a verb and must state one complete idea, thought, or meaning. Granted, some writers use short but incomplete sentences for emphasis, such as "The day he left was cold and in the dead of winter. January 22, to be exact." Sentence fragments or stray phrases generally have little place in straight writing, and beginning writers should avoid using them.

This is a fragment:	"January 22, to be exact."
This is a sentence:	"The day he left was cold and in the dead of winter."
This is a sentence:	"That day was January 22, to be exact."

Sentence Types

Grammarians define different types of sentences on the basis of structure.

- A simple sentence is one independent or main clause. It can have more than one subject and verb, object, and modifying phrase.

  The tanker ran aground, spilling 11 million gallons of crude oil into the bay.

  Six seniors and two juniors are on the University's debate team.

- A compound sentence has two or more simple sentences that may be joined by a conjunction such as "and" or "but" or by punctuation such as a semicolon.

  Homer used his share of the settlement to buy a fishing boat, but within two years his business was bankrupt.

  Many people have changed their diets to cut out high-fat foods; others have ignored warnings that a high-fat diet might cause heart disease.

- A complex sentence has at least one independent or main clause and other clauses dependent on the main clause.

  Downloading applications on a social networking site might open your private information to third parties, despite your belief those details are locked away from public view.

- A compound-complex sentence is a compound sentence with at least two independent clauses and one or more dependent clauses.

  When the album was released in May, investors expected it to do well, but it zoomed to No. 2 on the charts, exceeding all their hopes.

Vary Sentence Types

Good writers use a variety of sentence types, but they prefer the simple sentence. A good guideline is to use many simple sentences and to use compound sentences formed from short simple sentences.

Writers use complex sentences because of the need for attribution, amplification, and identification. But they work hard to avoid compound-complex sentences, saving them to express ideas difficult to state any other way.

Studies show that people of all ages and levels of education prefer simple sentences, in which subjects come before verbs and verbs before the remainder of the sentence. A series of simple sentences relaxes your readers or listeners and prepares them to encounter something more complex when it occurs in your text, as it inevitably will.

Look at the sentence variety in the story by Alison Delsite of *The Patriot-News* in Harrisburg, Pa., in Box 4.2. She uses a mix of complex sentences and simple sentences. Paragraph 5 is one complex sentence. But in the next paragraph a series of short, simple sentences carries the action.

BOX 4.2   Life-Saving Tickets Win Fame, but No Fortune

BY ALISON DELSITE
The Patriot-News

Patrick Gayle's lottery tickets weren't losers after all.

Not only did they help deflect a bullet and possibly save the Harrisburg man's life, they brought him a few days of fame and, maybe, a little extra cash.

Gayle was interviewed on CNN. Crews from TV's "Hard Copy" taped a segment outside the Allison Hill convenience store where he was shot.

He was interviewed for publications nationwide, including The National Enquirer and a lottery magazine in Florida. He did radio shows. "I told them, 'I feel blessed,'" Gayle says.

On April 23, Gayle was walking into a Regina Street store to play the Daily Number when he was struck by a bullet during a shooting that police say was a continuation of the long-standing Allison Hill-Uptown rivalry.

The bullet was deflected by a cigarette lighter and a wad of tickets in his shirt pocket. The lighter shattered. The tickets were tattered. The shirt had a hole in it. He wasn't injured.

The Patriot-News story about the shooting made the Associated Press' wire. Since then Gayle's phone has been ringing.

Edward Meyer, vice president for exhibits at Ripley's Believe It or Not, said Ripley's intends to do a cartoon on Gayle and hopes to purchase his tickets. For now, they are evidence, in the custody of Harrisburg police.

Meyer wouldn't say how much Ripley's would pay. "Probably a couple hundred dollars. Stories like this are right up our alley," he said. "We'll make it worth his while, but not make him rich." Gayle, a forklift driver, said he spends $40 a day on the lottery.

Meanwhile, the phone in Patrick Gaylor's home in Swatara Twp. also has been ringing.

It seems callers—including ones from TV's Montel Williams and Maury Povich shows—unable to find Gayle's number, have called Gaylor's instead.

"They ask, 'Are you the person who was shot and saved by a pack of lottery tickets?'" said Gaylor. "No," he laughs. "But I hope he makes a lot money off it anyway."

Reprinted with permission of *The Patriot-News*.

Common Sentence Errors

In constructing sentences, some writers forget the rule of parallel structure, noted as a grammar problem in Chapter 2. In writing, all parts of any list or series must be parallel—that is, if the first element in the list starts with a noun, all others must be nouns as well. For example, the structure of this sentence is not parallel:

> Plaintiffs reacted to the court's decision with sorrow, rage, surprise, and vowing to appeal the ruling.

Nouns in the list, "sorrow, "rage" and "surprise," are not parallel with the verb form "vowing." The sentence should be rewritten to read:

> Plaintiffs reacted to the court's decision with sorrow, rage, surprise, and vows to appeal the ruling.

When writers start with a specific verb form, such as an infinitive with "to," they must keep the same format. The structure of the following sentence is not parallel:

> In the new budget, the county will have funds to expand social services, to hire five police officers, and for adding bike lanes to Main Street.

It should be rewritten to read:

> In the new budget, the county will have funds to expand social services, to hire five police officers, and to add bike lanes to Main Street.

Another common sentence error is the incorrect placement of modifying phrases or clauses. Such misplaced elements can lead to humorous and misleading sentences, such as the following:

> After wheeling me into the operating room, a mask was placed over my face.

> The bank makes low-interest loans to individuals of any size.

> Mrs. Rogers was arrested shortly after 3 p.m. at the home where the couple lived without incident.

Once spotted, modifier problems are easy to repair. Good writers train themselves to check modifier placement: Did the mask really wheel me into the operating room? Does the bank make loans based on height and weight? Did the couple really live in the house without incident? The questions can be cleared up by quick rewriting:

After I was wheeled into the operating room, a mask was placed over my face.

The bank makes low-interest loans of any size to individuals.

Mrs. Rogers was arrested without incident shortly after 3 p.m. at the home where the couple lived.

A good sentence can never be interpreted to mean more than one thing. Linguists say it has a "single reading"—meaning the reader never needs to go back and read it again to understand it. If the reader goes back, it should be to savor the quality of the writing. Good writing aims for a single reading, so readers move unobstructed through messages to meaning. Once they understand the message, then readers can act or react—and communication is complete.

Paragraphs—Short Paragraphs

Words become sentences, and sentences become paragraphs. English composition books devote entire chapters to the topic of writing good paragraphs. When writers are concerned with transmitting information quickly, their ideas about paragraphing change. A paragraph is a whole presentation or argument on a topic in an essay for an English composition or literature class, whereas in mass communication, a paragraph is a single fact, thought, or "sound byte." That single thought or idea might take several sentences to explain. In newswriting, paragraphs often are short to break up blocks of gray copy. Journalists talk about "graphs," a shortened version of "paragraphs." One thought or idea is in a graph, and graphs are one sentence on occasion.

Effective use of three graphs of varying lengths is shown in the opening of this story written by *St. Pete Times* reporter Michael Kruse to describe damage from Hurricane Katrina:

> WAVELAND, Miss.—City Hall is gone.
>
> The post office is gone.
>
> The restaurants, the condos, the houses. Gone, gone, gone.
>
> In this coastal town of about 7,000 people, on a wide swath of land that stretches about a mile up from the Gulf of Mexico, almost everything south of the railroad tracks is gone.

Newspaper and magazine writers start a new graph to signal a new fact or a change of speaker—and sometimes just to give the reader a break. Readers appreciate white space in a publication, and frequent "graffing," as it is called, gives such visual relief by making space—literal and figurative—between ideas.

New Speaker Equals New Paragraph

One of the most useful functions of frequent graffing is that it effectively signals a change of speakers. Notice how Associated Press writer Timberly Ross moves smoothly from one quote to another, just by starting new graphs and giving background in between. The story focused on a tornado that hit a Boy Scout camp:

> Taylor Willoughby, 13, said several scouts were getting ready to watch a movie when someone screamed that there was a tornado. Everyone hunkered down, he said, and windows shattered.
>
> "It sounded like a jet that was flying by really close," Taylor told NBC's "Today" on Thursday. "I was hoping that we all made it out OK. I was afraid for my life."
>
> Ethan Hession, also 13, said he crawled under a table with his friend.
>
> "I just remember looking over at my friend, and all of a sudden he just says to me, 'Dear God, save us,'" he told "Today."
>
> "Then I just closed my eyes and all of a sudden it's (the tornado) gone."

With quotations, the short graph adds a lively, conversational air to newswriting and holds the audience's attention. "New speaker, new graph" is a writer's rule that can add clarity to all writing.

Most writing can benefit from shorter paragraphs. Bite-sized paragraphs may not be appropriate in all settings, but leaner paragraphs tend to streamline messages of all kinds, saving time and space—the most precious resources in any medium.

The Way to Clearer Writing

Writing often moves from the general to the specific, and this chapter is following such a path. At the outset, we discussed broad principles of accuracy, clarity, completeness, and fairness. We then looked at the basic tenets of good writing and the components of any piece of writing—words, sentences, and paragraphs—as summarized in Box 4.3. When listed, the rules seem more manageable.

Now for the specifics. Additional guidelines can help you say it straight. Keep the guidelines in mind as you write, but do not be so tied to them that you stop after every sentence to analyze whether it meets the standards of good writing. Go ahead and write, then go back and apply the guidelines.

Memorize!

BOX 4.3   Good Writing Rules

1. Good writing uses short sentences.
2. Good writing uses short words.
3. Good writing eliminates wordiness.
4. Good writing clears away redundancy, jargon, and institutional language.
5. Good writing comes to the point quickly.
6. Good writing has a mix of sentence types.
7. Good writing has short paragraphs.

Write the First Draft as You Would Say It

Writing coach Robert Gunning said writers should write the way they talk. He argued that all writing would improve if people simply talked and wrote down what they said. Gunning was onto a great idea: First drafts are most effective when a writer puts down on paper what he or she would tell someone about a topic. Most people talk in subject–verb–object order that is easy to understand. The result is text that is conversational, uses simple language, and is easy to revise into a well-organized written message.

Colorful Description

Author Tom Wolfe made his mark among fiction writers by writing the way he talks—frankly, and with rich description. In his bestseller, *The Bonfire of the Vanities*, Wolfe describes Maria, the girlfriend of his anti-hero, Sherman McCoy:

> *Now Maria pushed the door all the way open, but instead of ushering him inside, she leaned up against the doorjamb and crossed her legs and folded her arms underneath her breasts and kept staring at him and chuckling. She was wearing high-heeled pumps with a black-and-white checkerboard pattern worked into the leather. Sherman knew little about shoe designs, but it registered on him that this one was of the moment. She wore a tailored white gabardine skirt, very short, a good four inches above the knees, revealing her legs, which to Sherman's eyes were like a dancer's, and emphasizing her tiny waist. She wore a white silk blouse, open down to the top of her breasts. The light in the tiny entryway was such that it threw her entire ensemble into high relief: her dark hair, those cheekbones, the fine features of her face, the swollen curve of her lips, her creamy blouse, those creamy flan breasts, her shimmering shanks, so insouciantly crossed.*

In this passage, all parts of speech become part of the description. The verbs are active: pushed, leaned, folded, worked, and threw. The nouns—doorjamb, pumps, flan, shanks—are concrete and tangible, and the adjectives appeal to the senses: high-heeled, black-and-white, checkerboard, tailored, fine, swollen, creamy, and shimmering. All writers can learn from Wolfe's gift for conversational, dense description that leaves readers with strong sensory images.

Don't Begin at the Beginning

After seeing a four-car collision, the typical observer arrives home and blurts out: "I saw an incredible wreck on Highway 501. Four cars collided; all the drivers were injured, and one car burned." Only then will the observer back up and give background: "I was in the left lane, coming home from the mall," and so on.

Like urgent conversation, writing needs to jump straight to the point, then fill the reader in—just as we will discuss in Chapter 5 on writing leads. This technique gives writing a conversational tone and at the same time gets to the ever-so-important point of the message.

Starting with salient facts is a natural way to tell about important information. Unfortunately, it is a form that most people forget after years of reading stories and writing essays, both of which usually start with formal introductions. If your goal is to say it straight, say it—your main point—soon in your message. Suspenseful beginnings work best in drama.

Writing and Editing: Two Compatible Tasks

When you spill out your conversational first draft, write it without stopping to edit. Mixing writing and editing wastes time and effort. If you edit as you go (and most amateurs do), you might fuss over a sentence you eventually cut. At the very least, you will interrupt your own thought processes and conversational flow. So write first. If you pause to ponder sentence structure or information, that's okay. But do not wander or stray from the effort.

Some beginning writers lack the confidence to sit down and write. But author Joel Saltzman points out that we all are more competent wordsmiths than we think:

> *When you're talking, odds are that 98 percent of the time you don't even think about grammar. You're doing fine and it's just not an issue....I am suggesting that you don't worry about it right now; because the more you worry about grammar, the less you're going to write.*

Stick with Subject–Verb Order

Most human languages prefer to place subjects before verbs, and English is no exception. Curious people want to know who did something, then what they did (and to whom or what). Keep these audience interests and preferences in mind when you write. Subject–verb–object order generally gives the sentence action.

> Soldiers of the People's Liberation Army cleared rocks the size of houses from blocked roads.

> A massive earthquake registering 6.8 on the Richter scale rocked Japan early Tuesday morning.

Readers get confused if subjects and verbs are scrambled, regardless of how artistic the result may be:

> Came he swiftly to her bower?

Not in the information age.

Choose Active Verbs

Verbs are action words, but not all verbs are active. Some show no action at all, such as the verb "to be" in all its forms (is, am, are, was, were, be, being). Such verbs are less interesting and harder to picture than active verbs.

Writers prefer active verbs because they contain more information and sensory detail. "He was president" is vague compared with "He dominated the country as president." "Lightner whacked the ball with such force that it sailed over the right outfield wall" evokes the sound of the bat striking the ball. Good writing is filled with active verbs that evoke images in the mind of the reader or listener. In the following lead, the writer uses active verbs in a weather story:

> MOSCOW, Ind. (AP)—Tornadoes ripped through this central Indiana community and skipped over National Guard barracks full of sleeping soldiers as thunderstorms battered the Ohio Valley, authorities said Wednesday.

Choose the Active Voice

When writers use active verbs, they write in active voice.

"Lightner whacked the ball." The subject, Lightner, performs the action. The object, the ball, receives action. This sentence format is called *active voice*, and it is the natural order of English. "A man wearing a stocking mask robbed the university dining hall" carries more action than "the university dining hall was robbed by a man."

Every now and then, a sentence has no obvious subject and must be written in another format, called the *passive voice*. Take, for example, this sentence: "The law was changed several years ago." It is in passive voice. The recipient of the action, the law, has been moved into the subject position—probably because a long legislative process kept the writer from isolating a single person or session responsible for changing the law.

Research shows that people prefer active sentences over passive ones. The sentence "Congress passed the bill" is easier to read and comprehend than its passive equivalent, "The bill was passed by Congress." Skilled writers prefer the active voice and use passive sentences only when necessary. In our example about Lightner, a passive structure would hardly have the same effect: "The ball was whacked by Lightner."

Sometimes writers use passive sentences for emphasis: "The anticrime bill that will give police departments more powers was passed by Congress." Here the writer wants to focus on the provisions of the bill rather than on congressional action and writes the lead accordingly.

Generally Put Time Elements after the Verb

Because verbs are stimulating to readers, they should come before less interesting elements. Audiences need to know when something happened, but they can wait to find out. The time element, a necessary but often dull part of a message, can be relegated to a place after the verb. Some writers prefer to put it immediately after the verb. Here are a few examples:

> The second annual Wiener Festival, featuring dachshunds of all sizes and breeds, will be held Saturday in Laurel.

> Grant applications requesting up to $100,000 for research on learning disabilities may be submitted through June 15 to the National Institutes of Health.

Sometimes, however, the time element carries importance and needs to go elsewhere—even first in the sentence:

> On Wednesday, a 14-year-old youth collected $125,000 he found in a paper bag a year ago. No one claimed the money.

In the above example, the beginning and end of the sentence set up the time span: On Wednesday, the youth cashed in after waiting a year.

> Beginning July 1, North Carolina residents will need to show their Social Security cards or verify their numbers when getting new or replacement driver's licenses.

Right away, people know the laws will change.

Be Specific

Always give the most specific information you can. Significant details enlighten and delight readers and pack information into a few words. Instead of saying singer Mariah Carey went shopping, tell what she bought: cosmetics. What kind? Inquiring minds want to know! Instead of saying a reporter had a messy desk, try:

> On his desk, Howard had a can of unsharpened pencils and two potted ferns, both of them dead.

Watch out for words that have almost a generic quality, such as "facility." Be specific: bank, gymnasium, recreation center, high school. Use the specific noun.

Author Tom Wolfe has a marvelous talent for combining simple words into colorful, entertaining description. In *The Bonfire of the Vanities* excerpt we discussed earlier, Wolfe creates pictures with his prose. Like other excellent writers, he uses language to appeal to the senses. Wolfe gives specific details, such as the skirt riding "a good four inches above the knees" and the "checkerboard pattern worked into the leather." His technique is one that all good writers use, regardless of the medium.

Appeal to the Senses

Whether reading or listening, an audience still can use the full range of senses as it absorbs information. That means writers must pay attention to their senses when gathering information. Writers can report the facts or describe the scene without being subjective—a fear that keeps many beginning writers from using descriptive writing.

Through writing that appeals to the senses, *New York Times* reporter Mark Landler takes readers inside an Austrian monastery:

> HEILIGENKREUZ, Austria—As noon draws near, the monks glide into the church, their white cowls billowing behind them. They line up in silence, facing each other in long choir stalls. Wood carvings of saints peer down on them from the austere Romanesque nave.
>
> Bells peal and the chant begins—low at first, then swelling as all the monks join in. Their soft voices wash over the ancient stones, replacing the empty clatter of the day with something like the sound of eternity.
>
> Except, that is, for the clicks of a camera held by a photographer lurking behind a stone pillar.
>
> It has been like this since last spring, when word got out that the Cistercian monks of the Stift Heiligenkreuz, deep in the Vienna woods, had been signed by Universal Music to record an album of Gregorian chants.

The reader sees the monks and senses the stillness that precedes the bells and chanting. Writing that creates mental pictures, aromas, and sensations is more memorable and more appealing because it transports the audience to the scene of the message. Once captured, the audience is likely to remain in the writer's world long enough to get the message.

You don't need to be a feature writer to use sensory appeal. It works well in everyday forms of communication, such as directions to the company picnic. Instead of "turn right two blocks after the fork in the road and proceed to 1511," how about:

> Look for a grove of tall pines two blocks after the fork in the road; turn right and go to the red mailbox marked 1511. You'll smell pungent smoke from Marvin's famous barbequed ribs.

With such sensory appeal, it is doubtful anyone will get lost.

Use Statistics Sparingly and Powerfully

We live in an era where numbers make powerful messages: A basketball arena will cost $121 million. A pharmaceutical company will lay off 1,600 workers.

Audiences become desensitized if bombarded by alarming numbers, regardless of how striking those numbers may be. Statistics of any kind should be delivered one at a time. Never let two numbers touch in written copy; avoid putting numbers close to one another except in direct comparisons:

> The report assumes oil prices ranging from a low of $113 a barrel to as high as $186 a barrel by 2030; a barrel was trading above $133 on Wednesday.

Another good rule of thumb is to limit yourself to no more than three numbers in any paragraph to avoid overwhelming your reader or listener. In a business story, for example, numbers can be confusing, so spread them out and keep them simple. Consider the following lead packed with numbers:

> Dr. Marcy LePique, a Flagstaff obstetrician and gynecologist since 2003, has delivered more than 10,000 babies and about 20 litters of puppies in her 25-year career as a physician and 30-year career as a breeder of golden retrievers.

Professor Emeritus Philip Meyer, a former consultant at *USA Today*, suggests that in any statistical report one or two numbers stand out as crucial. The important numbers should appear early in your message, and others may be summarized in lists or tables outside the written text.

Translate Statistics into Everyday, Tangible Terms

People have little intuitive understanding of large numbers. The citizen who learns that a sports arena will cost $121 million is left with many questions: Is that a good price for an arena? How many new schools would that buy? How much will my county taxes increase?

Good writers provide an understanding of big numbers in several ways. One way is to compare one number with another:

> The $121 million price tag compares with the $58.2 million cost of an arena built in 1989 in Springfield.

Another way to present numbers is to give them in terms the average person deals with each day. Few of us can visualize $121 million, but many people can understand a 3.5 percent tax increase to fund the stadium.

The clearest way to present costs is to use an individual citizen as an example:

> A person owning a home with a tax value of $154,000 will pay about $200 more each year in taxes to finance the arena.

Such writing allows the audience to understand personal gains or losses that may be obscured in reports of large numbers.

Double-Check Your Math

Many writers jokingly say they went into communications because they could not do math. But any writer needs to use numbers and must be sure they are correct. Errors can be embarrassing.

In a news story about salary increases at city hall, a reporter looked at the current year's salary for the city attorney: $130,000. The proposed salary for the next fiscal year was $138,000. The city attorney would get a 5 percent pay increase, she wrote. The actual increase was 6 percent. The reporter erroneously divided the difference of $8,000 by the new salary rather than the current salary. Other city employees were upset that the city attorney was getting 5 percent compared with their 2 percent. When the real difference eventually was published, the unhappiness grew. (And the city attorney expressed his anger that the figures were published at all, forgetting that the salaries of public officials are public record.)

When in Doubt, Leave It Out

Unless you check the accuracy of a number, spelling, or surprising fact, leave it out or hold publication until you can verify it. Accuracy is linked, in the minds of audience members, with quality—with media quality and writer quality. Your reputation is riding on what you write.

Some errors are painful to people in the community. A university magazine noted offhandedly that a famous scientist had discovered a new kind of plant. His research assistant, who in fact had made the discovery and received credit for it in scientific journals, called the reporter to correct the error. Few people will ever see a small correction notice, but people such as the offended research assistant will remember the slight for years.

Mistakes, no matter where they appear, also may lead to legal problems. Chapter 12 discusses libel.

Rewrite Long Introductory Phrases

Audiences are eager to get to the point, and long introductory phrases slow them down. Long phrases also interrupt the subject–verb–object pattern that readers and listeners prefer.

Avoid:

Because the Cardinals had been waiting all season for a victory and had received what they considered to be negative media attention, several players refused to be interviewed.

Prefer:

Several Cardinals players refused to be interviewed after a winless season amid negative media coverage.

Eliminate Long Strings of Prepositional Phrases

Any group of two or more prepositional phrases makes a sentence meander rather than flow. Too many prepositional phrases strung together within a sentence are undesirable but easy to fix. Prepositional phrases are among the movable parts of any sentence; they also can be placed in new (short) sentences.

Avoid:

The school's marching band will appear in a series of performances on three consecutive Tuesday afternoons on the athletic field near the gymnasium on the school campus beginning this Tuesday.

Prefer:

The school's marching band will present a series of Tuesday afternoon performances beginning this week. The band will play on the athletic field near the gymnasium.

Look for unnecessary prepositional phrases everywhere in writing. Take

> Marilyn Jacobs, one of the writers of the letter, said the group wants action immediately.

and edit it to read

> Marilyn Jacobs, who helped write the letter, said the group wants action immediately.

Avoid Making Everything Look IMPORTANT

Some writers like to add emphasis by underlining text or using capital letters, exclamation marks, bold type, and even quotation marks. Frequent use of such elements detracts from professional polish. Once in a while, everyone needs to add emphasis. Save it for when it really counts. In some messages, such emphasis can be interpreted as anger, exasperation, and even sarcasm.

Avoid a message that looks like this sentence:

> If you don't get your information sheet in today, you WON'T be in the new directory AT ALL.

Try:

> If you don't get your information sheet in today, you won't be in the new directory.

Clear Out Euphemisms

Most of us were taught to use euphemisms in polite conversation—to say "expecting" rather than "pregnant," "plump" rather than "fat," and "passed away" rather than "died." Most euphemisms are designed to be imprecise—to mislead or give false comfort. In fact, we like euphemisms because they are handy substitutes for embarrassing words. In media, straight talk is preferred.

Avoid:

The guard said two residents of the correctional facility had gone to "their just reward."

Prefer:

The guard said that two prisoners had died.

Using the straightforward "prisoners" and "died" instead of the longer euphemisms keeps the sentence short and the reading easy. Once euphemisms are removed, the meaning is clear and timeless.

Watch Out for Language Trends

Writers should avoid popular trends in writing that substitute a myriad of words and phrases for ones that had been part of common language. In many cases, the new language is wordy and less precise.

The use of such "pop" language excludes segments of the audience that might not be cued to the lingo. Certainly language evolves. Each time a new edition of *Webster's Dictionary* comes out, new words are included. Many of us can remember when "ain't" was not in the dictionary. Dictionaries list and define words common in the English language, but a dictionary is just one of many sources writers use.

One trend that has caused extreme pain to language experts is the conversion of nouns to verbs. Host has become "to host," and conference has become "to conference." An advertising director notified clients: "We will deadline ad copy for Friday's paper on Wednesday." Many computer terms already are accepted usage, but some writers still cringe when they hear nouns such as "text" used as a verb for the act of contacting someone via the short messaging service on a mobile phone or "fiend" as a verb for the act of connecting with another user's profile on a social networking site.

Another trend that offends many writers is the addition of "-ize" to create new words: "prioritize," "finalize," "maximize," "accessorize." Again, although the words have found their way into everyday usage, language professionals try to find better and more accurate verbs.

Keep Writing Readable

Readability is defined most simply as the level of difficulty of a given message. Readable, or high-readability, writing is easy to understand. Several ways to measure readability have been found, most of which are based on (1) sentence length and (2) concentration or number of multisyllable words.

One common readability measure is the Fog Index, developed in the 1940s by Robert Gunning for United Press International wire service. Despite its age, the Fog Index is still used as a measure of readability. To compute a Fog Index, (1) calculate the average number of words per sentence in a given message and (2) count the number of difficult words, or those with three syllables or more, in a 100-word sample from the message. Add these two figures together and multiply by 0.4.

The resulting number—the Fog Index—corresponds to the number of years of education a reader would need to read and understand the copy. For example, a publication with an average of 22 words per sentence and 15 difficult words in the 100-word sample would have a Fog Index of 14.8. That means its readers would require some college education to read the piece comfortably.

Most readability experts agree that clear writing is geared to the 11th- and 12th-grade levels. Even people with a great deal more education seem most comfortable reading at this level. Many grammar-check software packages have readability measures that automatically tell writers the readability of any piece. *The Wall Street Journal's* Fog Index routinely falls into the 11th- to 12th-grade range, despite the complicated nature of financial reporting. A clever marketing strategy is operating here: Dow Jones knows that to make business reports palatable, they must be readable.

Exercises

1. Change the words used incorrectly in the following sentences:

   ▪ The perspective budget for the coming year will include raises for the city's fire fighters.
   ▪ An incoming ice storm will effect whether we can drive to work tomorrow.
   ▪ The state historical society will reenact signing the state constitution in the Capital.
   ▪ The country's navel force has been reduced.
   ▪ His desire for money is his principle guiding force in business.
   ▪ The coach said the team ignored his advise to make it a passing game.

- Jiminy Cricket said Pinocchio should let his conscious be his guide.
- The engineer eliminated the High Road sight because it sloped to much.
- Returning the stolen car to it's owner is the best decision.
- The most affective writing follows good writing principals.

2. Edit the following sentences to make them shorter and to the point:

- In order to expedite the delivery, the company will add a third delivery truck for its routes on Monday.
- We will have pizza for dinner whether or not you choose to come.
- She is presently employed as the assistant to the president, but she expects to make a decision whether or not to change jobs by the end of the year.
- If they are willing to pay the difference between the economy pack and the family pack, customers will learn that the family pack will save them more money in the long run.
- Students voted Thursday to conduct a poll to determine the status of living conditions in dormitories.
- Clarendon Park residents will march Saturday to protest the city council's decision to annex the neighborhood over residents' objections.
- If the school maintains lines of communication and makes the alumni feel as if they are still a part of the school even though they have already graduated, the school should have no problem reaching its fund-raising goal.
- The residents of the neighborhood said they would petition the city council to reconsider again the decision to allow beer sales before 11 a.m. on Sunday morning, which would be against the wishes of many church-going citizens.
- Fifteen scholarship winners, who were chosen because of their high academic achievement, will be given $15,000 in scholarship money to use at the college of their choice after they graduate from high school.
- Child-care experts disagree over whether or not children should be spanked as part of a parent's disciplinary techniques or whether or not putting children in a time-out away from activities is punishment enough.

3. Edit the following to eliminate redundancy:

- Susan is currently director of marketing sales.
- He served as past president of the Rotary club.

- The elementary school will need twenty-five acres of land for a multipurpose building, playground, and ball fields.
- Fire completely destroyed the town hall in the month of June.
- The future outlook for the economy indicates interest rates may rise slightly.
- The circus will be at 3 p.m. Sunday afternoon and 7 p.m. Sunday night.
- Due to the fact that more than two-thirds of the people did not respond, the picnic will be canceled.
- She climbed up the tree in order to get a better look at the defendant.
- John went on to say that any student's effort should be recognized.
- The Broadway show will close down six months after it first began.

4. Look through newspapers, magazines, and Web sites and select an article or blog that shows five or more of the characteristics of good writing mentioned in this chapter. Clip or print out the piece you selected and write a short paper, listing the guidelines for good writing that are followed. For each guideline you mention, quote a passage or paragraph that shows how the writer used the good writing rules or techniques.

References

Henry Beard and Christopher Cerf, *The Official Politically Correct Dictionary and Handbook.* New York: Villard Books, 1992.

Theodore M. Bernstein, *Dos, Don'ts and Maybes of the English Language.* New York: The Times Book Co., 1977.

John Bremner, *Words on Words.* New York: Columbia University Press, 1980.

Nora Ephron, "Writers' Workshop," video series produced by South Carolina Educational Television, 1980.

Robert Gunning, *The Technique of Clear Writing.* New York: McGraw-Hill, 1954.

Ernie Pyle, *Here Is Your War.* New York: Pocket Books, 1945.

Joel Saltzman, *If You Can Talk, You Can Write.* New York: Ballantine Books, 1993.

Carl Sessions Stepp, excerpt from videotape, "Taking Charge of Your Local Paper," National Rural Electric Cooperatives Association, Washington, D.C., March 1993.

William Strunk, Jr., and E. B. White, *The Elements of Style,* 3rd ed. New York: Macmillan, 1979.

Tom Wolfe, excerpt from *The Bonfire of the Vanities.* New York: Farrar, Straus & Giroux, 1987.

William Zinsser, *On Writing Well.* New York: Harper & Row, 1976.

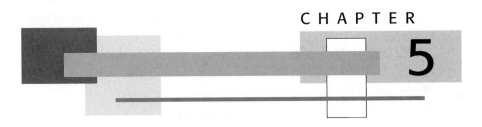

CHAPTER

5

Getting to the Point

When the president of a university spoke at her installation ceremony, she discussed the broad issue of improving undergraduate education and specific points to achieve that goal. Media began their respective stories from different angles. The student newspaper focused on greater rigor in classroom teaching. A television station with a broad viewing audience began its 6 p.m. report with her call for accountability to state legislators, then posted video and the text of her speech on its Web site. A business publication examined her challenge for a more aggressive investment policy to increase the school's endowment. The university's alumni publication looked at the outcome: the continued strength of the university's reputation and the value of its degree. A donor newsletter picked up her request for additional funds for scholarships and teaching excellence awards.

Because audiences are information-seeking, writers have to let them know right away what is in the message. Writers familiar with their audiences know which information will be relevant and appealing. Writers must alert audiences to important messages. They know what will attract the attention of the individual who juggles time for job, home, spouse, children, hobbies, and friends.

Messages must therefore hook the audience. The hook must be set in the first few sentences or paragraphs, the *lead* of the message. That is where writers must show the relevance of the message and attract, entertain, and inform. Readers or listeners then will decide whether the message is compelling, entertaining, or informative enough to warrant their attention.

Leads must fit the medium's style and format. While a longer descriptive lead might work in the print edition of a newspaper, a shorter version with important elements that can also help index the story's content would appear on the online site. Writers today need to know how to write all types of leads.

This chapter will discuss lead writing, specifically

- the role of leads in capturing audiences,
- elements in lead writing,
- news values, and
- types of leads.

What's the Point?

To hook a particular audience, writers must know why they are writing. It sounds simple enough. But many people regard writing as an artistic endeavor, not as a craft. They avoid thinking about the substance of what they are going to say. Instead, these writers sit down to write with a broad purpose or goal in mind, such as informing an audience about government waste. Their copy might ramble because they have not figured out the main point of the specific message, an essential element in hooking the active audience.

Determining the point requires critical thinking. Writers must look at the components of the message and weigh each as it pertains to audiences. They must lay out the facts and evaluate their importance and relevance. The steps are part of the stages of writing discussed in Chapter 1.

What does a rural community need to know about issues in a state legislative session? How about a professional association of school board members? These two audiences will need different hooks when a bill is introduced in the state House. As writers consider information and audiences, they get closer to the point of the message, establishing where they want to start.

Getting to the point is like opening a package: As you open the carton, you get closer to the real heart of your search. You might toss out styrofoam popcorn, then layers of tissue paper. Finally, you uncover the gift—the point of your search.

Finding the point of your story is essential to writing. Along the way, writers will discover facts and pieces that relate to the main point, surrounding and supporting it like the tissue paper. Other pieces could be discarded. But the examining process must be completed first.

Consider the advertising copywriter who says, "I want to write an ad that will get more business for my client." He or she is still handling the whole package—a big and unworkable problem. Thinking and planning—a stage of writing—will help in moving from the broad idea of producing an ad to the task of communicating the benefit of the service or product. The writer will get to the point.

If the client makes hand lotion, the advertiser's point might be beautiful hands or healthier skin or convenient packaging. If the client owns a tax service, the point might be customer peace of mind and the accountant's knowledge of tax laws. Once that benefit—the point—has been identified, the writer's job is to select precise words that will emphasize that point and grab a consumer's attention. And once writers have established where to start, they will know the direction to go.

In crafting messages, writers focus on the point, the hook, the lead, and the copy.

- The *point* is crucial information that justifies creating a message in the first place: A bill is passed. New funds are available. A road is closed.
- The *hook* is an enticing opening phrase or sentence that draws audiences into a message.
- The *lead* is the opening few sentences of a media message. Typically, it contains the hook and the point.
- The *copy* is the entire body of a media message, including a lead and all supporting information, such as new facts, background, quotes, and statistics.

In the Beginning Comes the Lead

In journalism, the first sentences or paragraphs of a story are called a *lead*. The lead has a heavy responsibility: It is the bait to hook the reader. By educating, entertaining, or enlightening, it stimulates the reader to pay attention. The lead shows relevance and is relevant to the audience. It also entraps. A publisher once wrote that a lead must be provocative, vigorous, and even at times startling to the reader.

Every piece of writing has a beginning or opening statement; every piece of writing has a lead. Long-time syndicated columnist James J. Kilpatrick once wrote:

The lead is vital to any writing, whether one is writing a novel, a short story, a book review, a term paper, a newspaper editorial, or a homily to be read in church on Sunday morning.

A lead needs to establish relevance for readers:

If you plan to have a summer internship next year, be aware that editors often begin their searches in October and November and make offers in December.

The lead contains the stimulus for reading, sets out the message's relevance, and gives readers the most important information first. As the stimulus, the lead entertains, enlightens, and educates. As it sets out the relevance, it whets the reader's appetite to stay with the message. In giving the most important information first, the lead ensures that readers get the point quickly. They can stick with the story or even move to other messages.

The lead must also set up the story. After reading or hearing the lead, audiences should know the main points of the message that follows. If not, the lead has misled them, and the writer's credibility is damaged. How does a writer know whether the lead sets up the story? When the story is complete, a writer must consider the main points in the body of the message and ensure they are noted in the lead. The lead sets up the story; the story backs up the lead. For example, a story reports a robbery at the campus dining hall and includes details about the robber locking the dining hall manager in a closet. That fact should be noted in the lead, along with the information about how the robbery occurred and how much money was taken. The chronological details of the robbery appear in the body of the story.

Journalists, primarily print journalists, have recognized for decades that getting to the point is essential to attract and retain readers. Media writers have found they immediately must set out the critical aspects of the message for their readers, listeners, consumers, or other audience members. Writing a lead is a crucial assignment for any writer.

Leads and Audience

Different audiences will react differently to leads. That makes sense. The audience of a local newspaper expects writing and prose that differ from what readers of a campus newspaper want. In a campus newspaper, leads will be focused for a university audience and its interests. The local newspaper has to attract an audience that includes students and university staff as well as people with no connection to the campus. The local newspaper might consider the language in a campus newspaper inappropriate for its audience.

Writers, whether for newspapers, Web sites, television stations, or magazines, have to structure their leads and stories to suit their audiences. When Republican presidential nominee John McCain announced Alaska Gov. Sarah Palin as his running mate, the media covered the story with an angle that would relate to readers. Many noted her relative obscurity on the national political scene. Consider these leads from *The New York Times* and the *Anchorage Daily News*, respectively:

> DAYTON, Ohio—Senator John McCain astonished the political world on Friday by naming Sarah Palin, a little-known governor of Alaska and self-described "hockey mom" with almost no foreign policy experience to be his running mate on the Republican presidential ticket.

> Alaskans woke to a new kind of earthquake Friday.
> So did the other 49 states.
> Instead of making a scheduled appearance at the Alaska State Fair, Gov. Sarah Palin stepped onto a stage in Ohio as Sen. John McCain's running mate on the Republican presidential ticket.

In each lead, the writer focused on Palin's selection. The Anchorage paper, however, brought the story closer to home with references to earthquakes and the state fair.

How to Get Started

Before constructing a lead, writers must know their information thoroughly. They must look at information collected via research or interviewing, then evaluate it, using judgment and experience, to determine what is most relevant to their audiences. As a prewriting activity, some writers go through their notes and add priority numbers next to information.

For example, before writing the lead that tells readers they should plan in the fall for the next summer's internship, a writer should list information to be included: students want internships; editors plan eight to ten months ahead; offers are made in December; don't wait. Next to each fact, the writer should put a number corresponding to its importance to the audience.

In writing the lead, the writer determines that the audience does not need to know the specific date that editors begin to interview or how many editors interview in the fall. Priority No. 1 is that editors will start looking soon and readers can avoid missing out on an internship if they plan ahead. The writer sets out the main part of the story—getting ready for internships—and then the relevance—students can miss the opportunity to apply if they wait until spring.

Writers can try another prewriting approach to evaluating information. They can simply ask, "What must my audience know?" and then list three to five things in order of importance. In the case of internships, the list would look something like this:

1. It is almost time to start planning for next summer's internship.
2. If students want to have an internship, they need to be prepared now.
3. Editors make hires in December for next year's interns.

The main point would become the lead. Other main points would be fashioned into the rest of the copy. Writers then have followed the format many journalists use—the inverted pyramid, which ranks information in descending order of importance. That format is discussed in Chapter 6.

Writers who struggle with ranking information and its relevance should remember that most people want to know the personal angle first. It all comes down to the audience's automatic question, "How does this message affect me?" The audience immediately looks for the explanation.

Sometimes stories or messages don't have that simple, personal component. Then writers must look beyond the "what about me?" question or relevance rule to other factors that make some pieces of information more important than others. Such factors are also guides to the selection of information for the lead. Those elements are called *news elements* and *news values* and are discussed next in this chapter.

News Elements

Certain elements are of interest in all writing. Journalists over the years have spelled out the elements that must appear in news stories: who, what, when, where, how, and why. This list is a basic starting point for any writer in determining what will go first.

These news components can form a question: "Who did what to whom, how, when, where, and why?" Every letter, news story, news release, or advertisement will answer this question.

Why are these elements important? Because people are most interested in other people, who they are, what they say and do, where they live and work, what happens to them, why they make certain choices, and how they deal with those choices. They are interested in conflict, competition, and achievements. People want to know about other people who overcome adversity, who are defeated, and who do the unusual. Look at this example:

> A Hollywood, Fla., man and woman exchanged wedding vows at 1,300 feet as they plummeted to earth hand-in-hand under silver parachutes five miles west of here Wednesday afternoon.
>
> Grace Mason and John Kempner met while skydiving at a local club and decided it would be the most significant way to start their married life together.

The elements are there:

Who:	Grace and John
What:	Got married
When:	Wednesday
Where:	Near Hollywood, Fla.
How:	By parachutes
Why:	Because they wanted to start married life in a manner meaningful to their courtship and to them

The two-paragraph lead summarizes what happened. Readers can decide whether they want to read further to learn more about Grace and John. The author has also set it up so that after two paragraphs, the reader knows the most important information and can turn to another message.

Where to Put *Who* and *What*

Putting all the elements in the first sentence can result in a long, convoluted sentence. Consider the following lead and its clearer rewrite:

> Sam Atwood, an associate professor of political science at the University, told students in a speech Thursday in MacPherson Hall that they should be more concerned about world events that more and more directly affect their lives and their future.

Rewritten:

> Students should be concerned about world events that more and more directly affect their lives and their future, an associate professor of political science at the University said Thursday.

In the rewrite, students get the content first. Rather than the professor's complete name, a descriptive phrase or identifying label describes him. The location of the speech and why he was giving it can be included in a subsequent paragraph.

Writers must decide which elements deserve emphasis and are most relevant before they write a lead. All elements will be included somewhere in the story. As a general rule, *who* and *what* will be included in the first sentence. *Where* and *when* will also appear here because they take up little space. This formula also follows the natural order of the English language: subject, verb, object. *Who, what, when,* and *where* set up an active structure: "A masked man robbed the university dining hall of $3,000 Wednesday night and locked the dining hall manager in a closet." *How* and *why* can be included in the first sentence if they are unusual. A full explanation usually will require several sentences or paragraphs.

Consider this lead from the *Great Falls Tribune* that focuses on *who, what, when,* and *where.*

> A man who witnesses say was driving erratically and clutching his chest drove through a fence and into the fairgrounds Tuesday morning, hitting a woman who was on a riding lawn mower, police said.

Again, the elements are there:

Who: A man driving erratically
What: Drove through a fence and hit a woman
When: Tuesday
Where: The fairgrounds

A Closer Look at the Elements

Let's define the lead elements and what role they play in the copy.

Who defines the person carrying out the action or affected by the story. *Who* may not be a specific name, such as Grace or John, but rather an identification or label. For example, a news release may say in the first sentence that two marketing employees have been promoted and in the second sentence give their names and titles. But if the president is retiring, his name will be given first because it has recognition among company employees and in the community, as in the following:

> Charles Southwick, chief executive officer of Englewood Mills, who began his career sweeping floors, will retire April 1 after 42 years with the company.

The *who* is Charles Southwick, specifically named because of the role he plays in the local business community. *What* represents the action: will retire. Usually, *what* can be simply stated in a verb. Consider this news lead:

> CAPE CANAVERAL, Fla. (AP)—To everybody's relief, astronauts fixed the toilet at the international space station on Wednesday and opened up a grand new science lab.

The phrases "fixed the toilet" and "opened a science lab" tells *what*. Similarly, in a letter to a high school's alumni, the verb "donate" tells *what*:

> Southeast High School's PTA is asking alumni to donate money to put at least two computers in every classroom by the end of the year.

What in the example is asking alumni for money.

When tells the audience the timeliness of the event or the time frame of specific actions. Often it is one word. In most writing, *when* will go after the verb because the time element rarely is the most interesting information. Few leads begin with *when*. In the space station example above, "Wednesday" tells when the events occurred. In the lead on the alumni letter, the time frame is less specific. But an alumnus reading the letter will know the goal for installing the computers is December 31, so contributions should be made between receipt of the letter and well before December 31.

When can also be used to set up a longer time frame, as in this *San Antonio Express News* lead:

> NATCHEZ, Miss.—Fifty years ago today, the civil rights movement began when racist thugs butchered Emmett Till, a Chicago youth visiting relatives in Money, 150 miles from here.
>
> And for 50 years, nobody has been punished for the crime, or for many other racially motivated killings.
>
> It's taken decades, but America is finally bringing justice to the Old South, with an unprecedented campaign to reopen unresolved civil rights murders such as Till's.

The writer sets up the time frame between what happened 50 years ago and today.

Where gives the reader the geographic context of the story. In many cases, this information will pique audience interest because readers want to know about events that affect them. The closer the story is to the reader's backyard, the greater the interest will be.

Wire service and other stories in newspapers often start with *where* by using a dateline—the name of the city in capital letters—to let readers know immediately where the event occurred.

> BLENCOE, Iowa—Frightened Boy Scouts huddled in a shelter as a tornado tore through their western Iowa campground, killing four teens and injuring 48 others who had little warning of the approaching twister.

In stories without a dateline, the exact location would be the first word or words in the lead only when it offers some unusual aspect to the story. Usually, the *where* is tucked elsewhere into the lead.

> A slice of history awaits you at the Tastee Diner in Silver Spring.

How expands on the what aspect. Look at the following lead from the *Wyoming Star-Tribune:*

> Power Resources, Inc., will pay $900,000 in penalties to the state to settle a
> long list of violations at its Smith-Highland Ranch in-situ leach uranium mine in
> Carbon County.

The lead tells *who, what, when,* and *where* but also talks about *how:* how the company will settle the violations.

Why gives the audience the reason a decision or a change was made or is pending or the cause of an event. In the Boy Scout example, the audience knows why the youngsters died: because tornadoes destroyed shelter in their campground. In the alumni letter, alumni are asked to give money. Why? So the school can buy computers. *Why* is often oversimplified or overlooked. Writers should go beyond superficial explanations.

Remember: *How* and *why* should appear in the first sentence or lead if there is some unusual aspect or if they are essential to understanding the message. Consider this lead from the *Reno Gazette-Journal:*

> Unable to cope with soaring fuel costs, Texas-based ExpressJet will cease
> all flights under that brand name, including five daily flights out of Reno,
> on Sept. 2.

Why and *how* ExpressJet is handling higher costs are immediately clear to the reader.

Watch Out for Too Much

Sometimes all elements fit concisely into a lead, as in the ExpressJet example. But because all elements do not have to appear in every first sentence, a writer can set up the point of the story using a few elements in the first sentence and explain the other elements in later paragraphs. Consider this lead:

> A major housing development that preservationists believed had died last year
> has been resurrected by developers who say local planning officials are much
> more receptive to the revised version.

Are *who, what, when, where, how,* and *why* all answered in this first sentence? No.

Who:	Developers
What:	Are resurrecting a housing development plan
When:	Implied now, but not stated
Where:	Implied in the county, but not specifically stated
How:	Not stated
Why:	Because planning officials seem more receptive

The lead would have been complex if the writer had included more elements, such as adding that preservationists will fight the renewed development with a door-to-door campaign before a planning board hearing next month and the exact location of the 300-acre site. With complicated material, the writer should consider a lead that sets out the new information in the first paragraph followed by some context or an explanatory quote in the second graph.

A lead attracts readers to the story because it has other elements—not just *who, what, when, where, how,* and *why*—that must be considered when the writer is structuring the first sentence. These other elements are called *news values.*

News Values

In structuring leads, writers are guided by what journalists traditionally have called *news values,* or aspects of an event that the audience might want to know about. The more writers know about their audience, the easier it is to predict the news values that will interest people or satisfy them in some way. These values or qualities carry over into any type of writing.

The traditional news values taught by journalism professors become second nature to reporters: *prominence, timeliness, proximity, impact, magnitude, conflict, oddity,* and *emotional impact.* News values are important in any media writing because they guide writers in identifying and listing crucial information. Let's look at each of the news values and how they affect lead writing. Several are closely allied to the elements *who, what, when, where, how,* and *why.*

Prominence

When the main characters in your story are well known, that is a signal to put those names in the lead. Readers recognize those names and are drawn into the story.

When well-known figures die, the obituaries become front-page news. When celebrities end up in divorce court or have custody battles, again, their lives make headlines. When prominent people have a medical issue, their names draw attention to treatments, such as actress Christina Applegate who opted to have radical mastectomies when she learned she had the breast cancer gene. Even people who are merely related to famous people are lead-worthy, such as Jamie Lynn Spears, Britney's sister. Prominence extends even to pets, such as Paris Hilton's Chihuahua, Tinkerbell.

Timeliness

One adage in journalism is "old news ain't news." People want to know what is happening as soon as it happens. They want newness in the news. They want to know information they did not know yesterday. They want timely, up-to-date news and depend increasingly on television, radio, and online services as initial sources of information. Therefore, *when* an event happened is almost always included in the first sentence of a story so that people will have a context for that event.

> The official ceremony for east Montgomery's latest new school took place this morning, which is named in honor of an icon of Montgomery's civil rights movement.

> ISTANBUL, Turkey (AP)—Turkish authorities captured a gunman Thursday wanted in the deadly attack on the U.S. consulate after rounding up suspects who had communicated with three other assailants killed by police, local media reports said.

Proximity

People are most interested about news that happens close to them. Audiences easily identify with stories with a geographic proximity—that is, those in their own community, town, county, or state. They like to read stories about their neighbors' successes and even defeats.

Audiences are also interested in what happens to people from their communities in other locations. For example, people in Cleveland would want to know about an airplane crash in Washington state that kills residents from their city. A Cleveland newspaper might run this lead:

> SEATTLE, Wash.—Two Cleveland businessmen were among 19 people killed early this morning when a jet struck a radio tower just outside Seattle.

The lead emphasizes Cleveland's loss while reporting that the plane crash occurred. Writers call this *localizing a message*, or putting a local angle on a story that originated miles away so that audiences can see how the message relates to them and their community.

News reports might also have an emotional or nonspatial proximity, whereby readers identify with a certain group of people. People who have suffered heart attacks are interested in articles about how other heart-attack victims have coped. People who live in a college town may be more inclined to read about stories originating from other cities with campuses, even if the cities are far away. Parents anywhere could relate to the following *Ames* (Iowa) *Tribune* lead about the return to school:

> The kids arrived by the busload and carload, on foot and on bikes, toting back-packs and dragging parents behind them.
> The first day of school was upon Ames.

Impact

Audiences always want to know how they will be affected, whether by a road closing while a sewer line is being laid or by a sale at the local supermarket. Reporters often hear people ask, "But how does this affect me? What does this have to do with me?" High in any message should be an explanation of how an event affects individuals' daily lives or why they should be concerned.

When possible, the impact should be translated into tangible terms. For example, a water and sewer rate increase approved by the Cityville Town Council Tuesday night will mean that the average resident will pay $3.52 a month more for service, bringing the average monthly bill to $31.96.

Sometimes impact is harder to detect. In such cases, it may be even more important for the writer to point out effects on ordinary individuals. Many stories will begin with anecdotal leads that give an example of how an event, decision, or medical breakthrough will affect specific individuals. Readers often can identify their own family and friends who would fit in the scenario. Using the example brings impact close to home.

In natural disasters, the impact might be stated in terms of how people are affected. When a hurricane, earthquake, wildfire, or tornado occurs, thousands of residents will probably be without electricity and potentially hundreds of houses damaged.

Consider the impact clearly outlined in this lead from *The Associated Press:*

NEW YORK (AP)—Floods that have inundated the Midwest could reduce world corn supplies and drive food prices higher at a time when Americans are already stretching their grocery budgets and people in poor countries have rioted over rising food costs.

Impact can be positive, such as free bus service:

Residents can ride the town's buses for free, beginning Monday, the first time the transit service has been offered at no charge to riders.

University students, staff, and faculty will also benefit from the free bus service, made possible by a $200,000 grant from the university to the town.

Magnitude

Some folks like to distinguish between impact and magnitude in defining news values. *Magnitude* is defined as the size of the event. Death, injury, or loss of property are all elements of magnitude that attract audience attention. Large amounts of money, such as lottery winnings, as well as disasters, such as earthquakes, carry magnitude and are always big news. When wildfires ravage the California hills, the acreage burned as well as the speed and intensity of the flames are part of the magnitude.

Consider this lead, which has magnitude and an understood impact:

Tuesday morning 54 school buses will drive more than 1,000 miles as they pick up 2,500 school children for the first day of classes this year.

The magnitude is represented in part by the 2,500 students, the 1,000 miles traveled, and the 54 school buses. The understood impact of the first day of school is much broader, affecting any household in the county that has school-age children, an employee of the school system, or an early morning commuter.

Conflict

Most news reports contain some kind of conflict: contract disputes with striking workers, continuing struggles in African countries and in the Middle East, the battles between neighbors in rezoning issues, or a grievance filed by an employee against a supervisor. People like to read about conflict. The extent of the conflict, either its size or its duration, will determine whether conflict is included in the lead of the message.

Conflict permeates the news. For example, when a devastating cyclone hit Myanmar, the country's leaders prevented the entry of much-needed aid, as noted in this lead:

> YANGON, Myanmar (AP)—U.S. Navy ships laden with relief supplies will steam away from Myanmar's coast Thursday, their helicopters barred by the ruling junta even though millions of cyclone survivors need food, shelter or medical care.

Or as shown in this lead by Susana Hayward of the *Miami Herald*:

> FORT SAM HOUSTON, Texas—Clutching their children, siblings, spouses and parents amid tears and applause, three former American hostages held captive for more than five years by Colombian guerrillas denounced their captors Monday as terrorists who kept them chained by their necks.

Oddity

Editors often encourage writers to look for oddity or some unusual twist to a story, such as a police officer who responds to the accident call and discovers that one of the injured people is his son. When a doctor used a claw hammer to pull a nail out of a 60-year-old man's skull, the man survived—except for some lingering headaches—and kept the nail as a souvenir. This *Miami Herald* lead sets up an unusual story:

> A shopper looking for a deal in the garden department of a South Florida Wal-Mart found more than he bargained for when he startled a poisonous pygmy rattlesnake hiding in some plants.

The article tells readers that emergency medical services crew gave the man an antidote and explains the risks of a pygmy rattler bite.

Consider this lead from the *Detroit Free Press:*

> Nothing wrong with teaching your kid your trade. But when your line of work is shoplifting, well....

Or this lead from the *Bismarck Tribune:*

> Riding a bike while intoxicated is still considered driving drunk, police say.

Whenever a writer is working on a message that has an element of oddity, care must be taken to ensure that people are not portrayed as freakish or unnatural. For example, a story on the largest baby born in the county in 30 years might not need to be written at all.

Emotional Impact

Writers are recognizing more and more that people like stories that affect them emotionally and that have emotional impact. This news value is also called *human interest* and *universal appeal*. It is the quality that draws audiences to children, young people, and pets, as well as stories tied to love and romance. Emotional events are important elements in stories and generally should be included in the first paragraph, as in this example:

> MADDOCK (AP)—Most 3-year-olds don't have much of a story to tell. Barkley is an exception, though he's not much of a talker.
>
> Barkley is a handsome, 98-pound golden retriever who has just found a new home at the Maddock Memorial Home, nestled next to a rolling prairie in the small central North Dakota community of Maddock.

The story continues, revealing that Barkley is a refugee of Hurricane Katrina who eventually finds a new home at a retirement community.

Think about your own interests. In looking at a page of a company newsletter, the photo of children and balloons at the company picnic will probably have more appeal than the picture of the president presenting a $5,000 check to the local PTA president. Death and injury convey emotional impact. A spousal murder also captures audience attention, from the arrests through the trial.

Remember the Audience

In applying news values, writers must think about what is important to their audience. Knowing the audience determines what's in the lead and affects how the writer will rank information. For example, a college community audience hears the mayor speak in a lecture series. What he says looks like this in the college newspaper's lead:

> Students play a vital role in boosting the town's economy when they shop at downtown businesses, Mayor Leo Ryan said Wednesday.

The primary audience for the college newspaper is students. What the mayor said has a different focus for the lead in the town's general-circulation newspaper:

> Town and college administrators need to develop a joint long-range plan that will address growth, particularly along the campus perimeter, during the next 20 years, Mayor Leo Ryan said Wednesday night.

A general-interest audience, primarily made up of town residents, would be more interested in what the mayor said that affected them directly.

News with a local angle will have more appeal to audiences. Think of interest in concentric circles: People are interested first in what happens in their neighborhoods, then their towns, their counties, their states, their countries, and the world. Leads should be written to focus on the local angle, such as this one for readers in Annapolis, Maryland:

> If you are planning to drive to Ocean City for the weekend, avoid Maryland Highway 113 near Dagsboro where highway crews are working and traffic is slowed to one lane.

Television satirist Jon Stewart often makes fun of reporters who introduce news that they say is "the story everyone is talking about." The humor of this phrase, as Stewart points out, is that the audience isn't talking about the story—it's only the reporters and TV anchors. Apparently, "everyone" doesn't include the audience. The serious point that Stewart makes is that writers, if they aren't careful, can easily mistake their own interests with the interests of the audience.

And just because everyone is talking about a story doesn't necessarily mean it is true. One day in late June 2008, people using the online messaging service Twitter helped spread a false rumor that Subway spokesman Jared Fogel had died. The rumor spread so quickly that his name became one of the hottest search terms on Google that day. People who had heard the rumor were apparently hunting for news of Fogel's demise. Even though traditional news sources like CNN or the Associated Press didn't report on it, this item was "the story everyone is talking about."

Sorting It Out

At this point, you are educated about the elements of a lead, but you still may be unclear about the sorting process. Let's walk through it.

Suppose you are a business writer for a local newspaper. In three months, a major employer in town will open a fitness center for employees. The center will be in the old YMCA building next door to the bank's corporate headquarters. You have collected the needed information. Your list of elements looks like this:

Who:	Amana Savings and Loan
What:	Will open a fitness center
Where:	Next door to corporate headquarters in the old YMCA
When:	In three months
Why:	To improve employee health and to provide a benefit to employees
How:	By renovating the old YMCA

Now make a list of news values as they relate to the story. Ask whether each applies and if so, how:

Prominence:	No
Timeliness:	Yes, within three months

Proximity:	Yes, in downtown
Impact:	Yes, the renovation will mean local jobs and other economic benefits to the town. It will affect the lives of the company's 275 employees and the townspeople who have been wondering what will happen to the old YMCA.
Magnitude:	Yes, the acquisition and renovation will cost the company almost $1 million.
Conflict:	None internally—shareholders approved the expenditure at the annual meeting. None externally—town residents want the building saved.
Emotional impact:	Possibly, for people who remember using the old YMCA

In writing the lead, you as the writer must consider the newspaper's audience—the townspeople, including employees of the bank—and ask, "What will they want to know first?" The answer is the timeliness of the renovation. The renovation is new news. A first draft of the lead might read like this:

Amana Savings and Loan will spend $1 million to renovate the vacant YMCA downtown on Sycamore Street to create an employee fitness center that will open within three months.

Here, you have answered *who, what, when,* and *where*. You also have addressed the *magnitude* of the project. The second paragraph will answer *why* and *how*, and the third paragraph will explain *impact*:

The bank will renovate the old YMCA building to provide a convenient way for employees to remain physically fit, said employee manager Kay Barnes. The bank will use the existing layout and install new equipment and furnishings.

The project will mean additional jobs during the renovation and later when the center opens, Barnes noted.

The story can continue with information on the actual renovation, such as the construction company that will do the job, types of equipment and furnishings, how many jobs created, among other facts.

General Rules for Leads

No matter what type of lead you choose to write, all leads have common features.

Leads should be short.   As a guide, some writers use no more than 30 words. Many wire service stories have leads no longer than 20 words in the first sentence or paragraph. This *Bismarck Tribune* lead sets up the story in nine words:

> He lost his home, but saved a wedding dress.

Readers know what happened, but will continue to find out exactly how he lost his home.

Leads should be concise and to the point.   Writers must eliminate unnecessary words. Look at the following lead and see what has been eliminated in the rewrite and how the focus has changed:

> A local daycare center was broken into Wednesday night and property vandalized, toys overturned and a pet rabbit, named Ray, killed with a broom.

Rewritten:

> Vandals broke into a local daycare center Wednesday night, killed the center's pet rabbit with a broom, overturned toys, and damaged property.

Words in the lead should be precise and in general vocabulary.   The words in the following Associated Press lead are precise and show the impact:

> LAND O'LAKES, Fla.—When 3-year-old Mikey Spoul took his father's car for a joyride last month and explained "I go zoom," the act grabbed national attention and even became fodder for late-night show monologue jokes.
>
> But nobody's laughing now. Mikey torched his bedroom curtains with a cigarette lighter and burned down his family's home, authorities said.

Leads should use active verbs.   Consider the verbs in the preceding lead example: "grabbed," "torched," and "burned down," or the verbs in this lead:

> A Cityville man smashed the glass door on a Laundromat washing machine and yanked a 3-year-old child from the swirling waters Saturday morning.

Leads should be simple, not rambling, convoluted sentences.   No one wants to work too hard at understanding most communication. The writer has lost if the "huh?" factor enters in. That's when a person has to stop and reread a lead to understand what the writer is saying. Compare the simple lead about the Cityville man in the Laundromat with this more convoluted lead:

> Under a handgun-control plan, announced by state and county grassroots organizations Monday, a person who sells a handgun to an unlicensed customer would be liable to a victim for three times his losses if that handgun is used to commit a crime.

Apply what you have learned about leads so far to untangle this report on controlling handguns. What's the point? Some grassroots organizations have come up with an idea for making handgun salespeople more responsible for crime. What does the audience have to know? How about this lead:

> If a local citizens group gets its way, people who sell guns will help pay for the lives and property lost in handgun crimes.

Writers base the structure of their leads on the type of story and the audience. Some information, such as police reports, lend themselves to summary leads. Other material works better in a descriptive or anecdotal lead. The next section looks at leads and where each works best.

Summary Leads

The most common lead format is a summary lead that tells or summarizes the most important information:

> Four Cityville teens will receive all-expenses-paid trips to the U.S. city of their choice, their prize in a local essay contest.

To reduce attrition, Telstar Corp. will build an on-site day-care center that will enroll 125 children of its employees in May.

World leaders meeting at the G-8 Summit endorsed a plan Tuesday to halve the world emissions of greenhouse gasses by the year 2050.

The summary lead serves the audience members who skim newspaper stories, online articles, company newsletters, or handouts from school; who listen with one ear to radio news reports and one ear to the kids in the backseat of the car; or who casually tune into the morning television news while getting dressed. Because of the crowded field of communication today, summary leads are used often to give people information quickly.

Summary leads are useful. They can be the introduction of a letter, the hook of an online story, the beginning of a news release, the headline of a broadcast story, or the homepage link to the complete story.

Beyond One Paragraph

Although most summary leads consist of one sentence or one paragraph, they may be longer to provide adequate information and context. Leads must be clear and easy to understand. Look at this Associated Press lead:

BELLEVILLE, Ill.—James Dowdy has gone to prison three times, and may go there again, for the same crime: burglarizing homes and stealing women's socks.

Dowdy had been free on bond in one alleged sock caper when police say he was caught with socks that had been taken from someone's laundry room Monday morning in Belleville, a St. Louis suburb. The 36-year-old remained jailed Wednesday on a felony burglary count filed the previous day.

The writer needs the second graph to set up the context and bring readers up-to-date.

A writer in a company's corporate communications department needs to tell employees about payroll changes. She must do so in a way that is informative, pertinent, and clear:

Long Branch Entertainment employees will see in their paychecks next month some changes that represent good news and bad news.

> The good news is the company's across-the-board 3 percent pay raise.
>
> The bad news is each employee with a family plan will pay $52.22 more a month in health insurance premiums and employees with individual plans $26.32 more a month.

The three-paragraph summary lead contains information essential to employees: how the company's health insurance plan will change and how much their raises will be. The writer wanted employees to know right away they were about to be hit in the pocketbook and why. Employees who want to know more about how and why the changes occurred will continue to read the message.

Multiple-Element Leads

The Long Branch lead on health care also illustrates how a writer presents more than one aspect to a message. Often, a lead has multiple elements or more than one point it must convey to readers. A *multiple-element lead* summarizes information for readers and sets up what will be covered in the rest of the copy. It presents a challenge to the writer, who must be wary of complex or convoluted sentences. The best approach is to rank the elements, put the most important in the first sentence, and then create a second or third paragraph to present the other points:

> A group of university students has presented a list of concerns to Chancellor Paula Walls, asking foremost that the university put a moratorium on tuition increases.
>
> The letter, hand-delivered to Walls on Wednesday, also asks the administration to name more students to campus-wide committees, to recruit minority faculty members, and to renovate the Student Union.

From this lead, readers have the most important information first: the list of demands and the high-priority demand. And they know the content and structure of the message. For writers, the lead sets up how to organize the story: in order of the points listed in the lead.

Delayed-Identification Leads

Another type of summary lead is the *delayed-identification lead*. When individuals in a news story carry no prominence, their proper names are not given in the first paragraph. Rather, they are identified by a generic label: "An Orange County woman died when..." or "A Lockwood High School student has been named a National Merit Scholarship winner...." Immediately, in the next paragraph, the individual is named. If more than one person is in the lead or first paragraph, the individuals are renamed in that order in the next paragraph. Consider this:

> WOBURN, Mass. (AP)—A British man convicted of shooting to death his 9-month-old baby and wife as they cuddled together in bed showed no reaction Thursday as he was sentenced to two life prison terms without the opportunity for parole.
>
> Neil Entwistle was found guilty Wednesday of two counts of first-degree murder in the 2006 deaths of his wife Rachel and their baby, Lillian Rose, in their rented home in Hopkinton. He fled to his native England afterward.

Other Lead Formats

Although the summary lead is the most useful, writers sometimes find other lead formats better suited to the kind of message they need to send. Some types of leads, such as anecdotal or descriptive, are popular in media today. They can be risky because they don't hook readers soon enough. They must therefore be well written to entice readers to stay long enough to find out what the message is about.

In general, when using other lead formats, make sure you get to the point by the fourth paragraph. Otherwise, you might lose your reader. If you are writing for a newspaper, the story might have jumped to another page before the reader ever gets to the point. Let's evaluate some types of alternative leads.

Anecdotal or Affective Leads

Many newspapers have developed a lead style that uses an anecdote to illustrate how one person is or has been affected by a social, health, political, or economic problem. The lead makes readers feel the abstract on an interpersonal and even emotional level. The abstract then becomes real. McClatchy reporter Tim

Johnson used the following lead to get into the broader story of China's security sweeps prior to the 2008 Summer Games:

> BEIJING—When Dechen Pemba, a British citizen, walked out of her Beijing apartment at 8:55 one morning this week, she found seven to eight security agents milling about waiting for her.
>
> They allowed her to throw some clothes in a rucksack, then took her in a whizzing convoy to the airport, ordering her deportation on a flight to London.
>
> The expulsion of Pemba, who's of Tibetan descent, is part of a broader campaign to sweep away anyone deemed a potential troublemaker before the Aug. 8–24 Olympic Games.

In the story, Johnson uses sources to explain to audiences how China's fears of any embarrassment have affected people, such as Pemba. Her experience opens and closes the article.

The key to using the anecdotal or affective lead is to keep it short and get to the point right away. Writers must quickly reveal the message's social or economic issue. Writers must use the anecdotal example throughout the story, not solely as a hook dropped after the lead. Consider this *Associated Press* lead:

> WINONA, Minn.—On the morning after the house party on Johnson Street, Jenna Foellmi and several other twentysomethings lay sprawled on the beds and couches. When a friend reached out to wake her, Foellmi was cold to the touch.
>
> The friend's screams woke up the others still asleep in the house.
>
> Foellmi, a 20-year-old biochemistry major at Winona State University, died of alcohol poisoning on Dec. 14, one day after she had finished her last exam of the semester. According to police reports, she had three beers during the day, then played beer pong—a drinking game—in the evening, and downed some vodka, too.
>
> Foellmi's death was tragic but typical in many ways.
>
> An Associated Press analysis of federal records found that 157 college-age people, 18–23, drank themselves to death from 1999 through 2005, the most recent year for which figures are available. The number of alcohol-poisoning deaths per year rose from 18 in 1999 to 35 in 2005.

The writer sets up the subject through an anecdote as a way to get to the point in paragraph 5: The numbers of college-age individuals dying from alcohol poisoning is on the rise. The reporter interviewed Foellmi's mother, who is quoted throughout the story.

Descriptive Leads

Like an anecdotal lead, a descriptive lead puts emotion or a human element into a message. It sets the scene for the reader. Consider *The New York Times* lead in this story:

> HEILIGENKREUZ, Austria—As noon draws near, the monks glide into the church, their white cowls billowing behind them. They line up in silence, facing each other in long choir stalls. Wood carvings of saints peer down on them from the austere Romanesque nave.
>
> Bells peal and the chant begins—low at first, then swelling as all the monks join in. Their soft voices wash over the ancient stones, replacing the empty clatter of the day with something like the sound of eternity.
>
> Except, that is, for the clicks of a camera held by a photographer lurking behind a stone pillar.
>
> It has been like this since last spring, when word got out that the Cistercian monks of the Stift Heiligenkreuz, deep in the Vienna woods, had been signed by Universal Music to record an album of Gregorian chants.

The writer, Mark Landler, uses the description to launch a story about the monks and their profitable music.

Consider this *Associated Press* lead:

> SAN FRANCISCO—Serenaded by a gay men's chorus, showered with rose petals and toasted with champagne, hundreds of tearful same-sex couples got married across the state Tuesday in what some are calling California's new Summer of Love.
>
> Wearing everything from T-shirts to tuxedos and lavish gowns, they rushed down to county clerks' offices to obtain marriage licenses and exchange vows on the first full day that gay marriage became legal in California by order of the state's highest court. They were joined by jubilant crowds that came to witness the event.

In the following descriptive lead from the *Seattle Times*, a human element is ascribed to a machine. Writer Lisa Heyamoto has taken a subject that affects Seattle residents—drilling under Queen Anne Hill—and presented it in a readable, interesting manner.

> She weighs 305 tons, is 27 feet long and creeps forward in four-foot intervals, her teeth gnashing through clay and rocks like corn nuts in a blender.
>
> You can call her Cassandra, and she's been burrowing her way 150 feet beneath Queen Anne Hill all summer.
>
> Cassandra isn't a Tolkien-esque subterranean monster. She's basically a drill—a giant one—carving a tunnel beneath Seattle that will store storm-water runoff until it can be treated and piped into Puget Sound.

Question Leads

Question leads should be avoided. They rarely are successful. In most cases, they are the lazy writer's way out, and they turn off audiences. In almost every case, they give the audience the option to turn elsewhere.

> Who will pay to build the county's new schools?

The reader might say, "Not me, and I don't care who pays." Think of another angle such as:

> The average Cityville resident will end up paying the cost for building new schools, a local watchdog group stated today.

On rare occasions, a question lead can work, as in this one from the *Arkansas Democrat Gazette:*

> What's a prairie dog worth?
> Two to six years, Little Rock police say.

The reader at first mentally guesses a dollar figure, but then is surprised immediately that the correct answer is a prison term. The reader is hooked into the story on prairie dog-napping.

Quote Leads

Quote leads should be used sparingly because rarely does someone sum an entire speech or premise for a decision in one simple quote. A quote can be used if it is short, is relevant to the rest of the message, and does not need any explanation. It must be clear within itself. Look at this newsletter lead:

> "Taking advantage of the different opportunities available in the Scholars program is what made a difference in my academic career," said a University of Maryland senior who will attend Georgetown Law School next year.

The lead here is empty and nonspecific. It fails to point out that the senior is a semifinalist for a Rhodes scholarship, is the Student Government Association vice president, and was an intern at the FBI. A stronger lead would have focused on his accomplishments and linked them to his involvement in the Scholars program:

> Randy Cates, a senior at the University of Maryland, is a semifinalist for a Rhodes scholarship, one of the most prestigious international academic awards; an FBI intern; and vice president of the student government association.
>
> He is also a College Park Scholar, and he says that award "is what made a difference in my academic career."

A partial quote is used effectively in this example from the Associated Press:

> Smoking and drug use among U.S. teenagers are increasing after a decade of decline, a study showed Monday, and its author warned that "the stage is set for a potential resurgence of cocaine and crack use."

Direct Address Leads

The direct address lead talks straight to the reader or consumer. It usually gives advice or has a "hey, you" aspect to it. Consider Shauna Stephenson's lead in the *Wyoming News:*

> If you've been to the national parks during the height of tourist season, you know how grandeur can suddenly become a grand headache.
>
> So if you're looking for a bit of solitude, go to a place so quiet that the National Park Service won't speak above a whisper about it: the Laurance S. Rockefeller Preserve.

Writing Leads for Online Media

Sometimes the medium can dictate the type of lead. The more time you anticipate a reader will spend with a story, the longer you can make your lead. Anecdotal leads, for example, are particularly well-suited for longer stories often found in magazines or in the Sunday editions of newspapers. However, online readers often quickly skim stories, or they may only see the headline and first paragraph before deciding whether to click and read the whole piece.

Writers who work for online publications must balance two influences that sometimes compete with each other. On one hand, many readers turn to the Web for breaking news. This usage suggests that online writers should put an emphasis on immediacy by clearly and prominently telling readers *when* something is happening.

On the other hand, online readers use search engines to find old stories relevant to an area of interest. Search engines use the first dozen or so words of a Web page to deliver the pages that are most relevant to a person's search terms. This process suggests that online writers should make an effort to use in their leads keywords that potential readers might search. People tend to search for nouns more than verbs or adjectives, so writers concerned about search engine optimization will emphasize the *who, what,* and *where* in their leads. This lead was written for a story published by WebMD Health News:

> Intense control of blood glucose levels in type 2 diabetes helps reduce the risk of kidney and eye complications, but not cardiovascular risks such as heart attacks and strokes, researchers said at a news briefing during the annual meeting of the American Diabetes Association in San Francisco.

Count the number of nouns that someone with Type 2 diabetes might use to look for information about treating the disease, and the potential side effects of the treatment: "blood glucose," "type 2 diabetes," "kidney," "eye," "complications," "cardiovascular," "heart attacks," "strokes," and "American Diabetes Association." Now, look where those keywords are located in the paragraph. "Blood glucose" and "type 2 diabetes" are the most widely used keywords, and they appear high in the lead. The writer emphasizes the results of the study, saving the attribution information until the end of the paragraph.

You may also have noticed other nouns, such as "San Francisco," that are popular search terms—probably even more popular than "diabetes." But someone looking for this information probably doesn't care where the meeting was held. And someone planning a vacation in San Francisco probably isn't interested in attending a meeting of the American Diabetes Association. Remember: only the relevant keywords are important.

Now, compare this lead from a *New York Times* article on the same topic:

> Two large studies involving more than 21,000 people found that people with Type 2 diabetes had no reduction in their risk of heart attacks and strokes and no reduction in their death rate if they rigorously controlled their blood sugar levels.

This story has some keywords—"type 2 diabetes," "heart attacks," "strokes," and "blood sugar"—but not nearly as many as the Web MD article, and they aren't as high in the lead. This lead puts the attribution of the news—"two large studies"—and even some details about the scope of the studies—"involving more than 21,000 people"—ahead of the findings. While a study's size is important, people with diabetes probably are less interested in "two large studies involving more than 21,000 people" than in information about "intense control of blood glucose levels in type 2 diabetes."

Google has two tools to help online writers learn which search terms people are most likely to use. To find these tools, do a Web search for "Google keywords tool" or "Google trends." For example, using the Google Keyword Tool, a writer would have seen in 2008 that "presidential election" was a far more popular search term than "presidential campaign," even though journalists often use those terms interchangeably. And using Google Trends, we can see that the number of searches for information about the "presidential election" spiked in February 2008 and then declined throughout the summer.

Before writing their lead, online writers should ask themselves a few questions:

- Is this story valuable to readers because of its immediacy or because of its in-depth and relatively timeless account of a subject in which people will be interested for some time to come?
- What are the key search words most likely to be used by people interested in my story?

Choosing a Lead Type

In many cases, the information will dictate the type of lead. A crime story, for example, generally will use a summary lead. A story on a city council meeting will need a multiple-element lead to cover the council's different actions. Lack of prominence will dictate a delayed-identification lead. But sometimes a writer must ponder and decide which lead will set up the story best. Look at this Associated Press lead about a 911 operator:

> NEW YORK—"You want the police to your house because your mother didn't come home?"
>
> It's nearly 7 p.m. on a Wednesday in the weeks before Christmas and somewhere in New York City, two scared young girls watch the clock, more frightened by the minute. They call 911 and reach Ivey Bruce.
>
> Her voice is soothing and steady. "OK, what apartment are you in? And what's the telephone number? And how old are you and your sister?"
>
> As she speaks Bruce types on a battered gray computer. The figures 10 and 11 appear on her screen, then "HOME ALONE." Another tap of a key speeds the girls' telephonic SOS to a police dispatcher in a nearby room.
>
> Bruce, a 45-year-old mother of two sons, nods as if to reassure the unseen child and then tells her police will be there soon.
>
> Like a novel half read, a mystery never solved, this story has no end for Bruce. After 14 years on the job, she knows that's as it must be.
>
> It's only suppertime in New York, and by the end of her 3:30 p.m. to 11:30 p.m. shift, this 911 operator will have heard accounts of panic and terror by the score.

The writer chose a long, anecdotal lead to set up a story about 911 operators. The story specifically follows one operator, Ivey Bruce, before it gives information about 911 services. By focusing on one typical call, the writer lets readers know how a 911 operator reacts to a call and interacts with the caller. The writer could have written this lead:

> NEW YORK—The hectic and gargantuan New York City 911 service will field more than 10 million calls this year.
>
> The system represents a lifeline found in 89 percent of the country. The operation rests largely with the 911 operators, who answer scores of accounts of panic and terror during their shifts.

Which lead works? The one with the human element referring to children and their missing mother will draw more people into the story than one that tosses out numbers. The faces behind the digits set up the story, and readers know by the end of the second paragraph that the key elements are 911, operators, Ivey Bruce, and calls.

Does It Work?

Once you have written a lead, scrutinize it, keeping in mind the guidelines in the leads checklist at the end of the chapter. Consider this lead from a daily newspaper:

> Ten-month-old Betssie Martinez-Oidor's fever soared to 105 degrees Monday. Her mother, Isabel Oidor, called York Hospital. Oidor and her husband, Gabriel Martinez, told a Spanish interpreter they had never seen their baby this ill.
>
> "They both got scared," interpreter Carmen Bones said. She told them to bring the baby to the hospital. They stayed until late Monday so the baby could be observed because of her fever. Betssie also had a runny nose, mild cough, and little appetite for her formula.

As the reader, what do you think the story is about? The lead says that the baby is ill with a high fever. Is the story about the effects of fevers on infants? No. See how far you have to read before you know what the story is really about.

> Periodic doses of Tylenol® helped bring the fever down to 100.6 degrees by the time they returned Tuesday for a follow-up exam by Dr. Mary Barnes in the Mother/Child Clinic.
>
> Applying her stethoscope to the baby's back and chest, Barnes ruled out bronchitis and pneumonia.
>
> "I think the baby has the flu and an ear infection," Barnes said. "It's out there. There's so much of it around."
>
> "Maybe she got it through me," the baby's father said to Barnes in Spanish.
>
> Betssie's parents have been ill with flu-like symptoms. They're far from alone. Pennsylvania is one of about 20 states experiencing an earlier-than-usual start to the flu season. The state's physician general, Dr. Wanda Filer, issued a statement that some flu cases of a Type A strain known as A/Nanchang have been confirmed in residents of several counties.

By paragraph 7, the story is clear: Pennsylvania is having a flu epidemic. All the discussion about the baby's illness makes readers wonder about fevers, immunizations, colds, or perhaps care for children. The example of the sick baby could be used, but readers need to know sooner what the actual topic is. Consider the rewrite:

> Ten-month-old Betssie Martinez-Oidor's fever soared to 105 degrees Monday, scaring her parents who took her to the hospital. Betssie has the flu. She is among the latest and youngest victims of this year's flu season. Pennsylvania is one of about 20 states experiencing an earlier-than-usual start to the flu season.

Then the writer can proceed with quotes from the parents and other details of the flu, its symptoms, and treatment.

Leads Should Do the Job

Remember to read through your stories carefully and ensure your leads are honest and set up for the reader what the story covers. Review the checklist in Box 5.1. In addition, remember that deaths, injuries, or substantial loss of property are other items that should be included in leads. All relate to news values that capture audience attention.

Readers will be disappointed if they believe that a story is about one topic only to discover that it is about another. Writers will lose credibility if they make false promises in their leads.

You can become a good lead writer, whatever the copy, by focusing on what is important to your audience, learning the guidelines of good writing, and reading good leads that are specific and present information accurately, clearly, and concisely. Look for such leads in everything you read.

BOX 5.1   Leads Checklist

Essential Lead Elements

1. I have looked at the facts and decided which are the most important.

2. My initial sentence is simple and complete.

3. My lead is accurate.

4. My lead is relevant to my audience, and includes keywords they might use to find the story online.

5. My lead comes to the point, is well edited, and makes sense.

6. I have used understandable, fresh words and strong, active verbs.

7. My lead sets up the story.

Desirable Elements

1. I have emphasized the latest information.

2. I have included unusual aspects of the message.

3. If possible, I have used a local angle to show how the information relates to readers.

4. I have kept my lead short and readable—no longer than 30 words.

5. My lead attracts the audience's attention.

6. My lead summarizes the message.

Exercises

1. Read the following lead. Identify the elements and the news values present:

> A third elementary school in Johnston County will be delayed for a year because school officials have asked architects to revise the plans to include more space for computer labs, the school board chairman announced Monday.
>
> The school will be a model for schools across the state and will take about 14 months to build.

Elements

Who:

What:

When:

Where:

Why:

How:

News Values (identify only those present; not all will be)
Conflict:
Timeliness:
Proximity:
Prominence:
Magnitude:
Impact:
Oddity:
Emotion:

2. Read the following lead. Identify the elements and the news values present:

> Two fishermen whose boat capsized in the Atlantic Ocean were rescued Sunday after spending 24 hours floating in life preservers.
>
> George Blackburn and Brian Livengood, both of Wilmington, Del., went fishing off the coast early Saturday. Their boat capsized about 2 p.m. that day after a fire burned a hole in their boat. The Coast Guard rescued them about noon.

Elements
Who:
What:
When:
Where:
Why:
How:

News Values (identify only those present; not all will be)
Conflict:
Timeliness:
Proximity:
Prominence:
Magnitude:
Impact:
Oddity:
Emotion:

3. Read the following lead. Identify the elements and the news values present:

WASHINGTON—Hospital leaders told members of Congress Tuesday that reductions in Medicare and Medicaid could have great impact on the people they care for.

The federal budget calls for $115 billion less for Medicare and $21.6 billion less for Medicaid. More than 1,000 hospitals across the country depend heavily on the two federal programs for about two-thirds of their annual revenues.

Elements

Who:

What:

When:

Where:

Why:

How:

News Values (identify only those present; not all will be)

Conflict:

Timeliness:

Proximity:

Prominence:

Magnitude:

Impact:

Oddity:

Emotion:

4. Read the following lead. Identify the elements and the news values present:

The Cityville Town Council approved a 3-cent property tax rate increase for the coming fiscal year budget and more programs to assist in low-income housing.

The tax rate increase means a person who owns a home valued at $100,000 will pay $30 more a year.

Elements

Who:

What:

When:

Where:

Why:

How:

News Values (identify only those present; not all will be)

Conflict:

Timeliness:

Proximity:

Prominence:

Magnitude:

Impact:

Oddity:

Emotion:

5. You are a reporter for the Cityville Chronicle. Write leads for the following information. List for each exercise *who, what, when, where, how,* and *why.* You may want to list the news values to help you determine what information should go into the lead. Think about the local audience. Write just the lead, not the entire story, for each.

   ▪ A Johnston Community College student died yesterday. He was working at a construction site at Town Hall. The construction company he worked for was building an addition to the Town Hall. He was dead on arrival at Cityville Hospital. He died when scaffolding he was standing on collapsed and he fell three stories to the ground. One of the cables holding the scaffolding broke and he slipped off the scaffolding. A board from the scaffolding, which came apart, fell on his head as he lay on the ground. He worked part time for the construction company while he was in school.

   ▪ The Natural Resources Defense Council had a news conference today in Washington. The NRDC is a national environmental lobbying group. It said that smog is getting worse in metropolitan areas across the country and is reaching the stage of "a public health emergency." The group also said the government is seriously understating the problem. Smog is the polluted air that irritates eyes and lungs and causes long-term health problems. The Council said unsafe levels of smog occur in many large cities twice as often as the federal Environmental Protection Agency says it does.

- The Cityville Planetarium has regularly scheduled programs at 7 p.m. and 8 p.m. on weekdays and 10 a.m. Saturdays. This weekend, the planetarium will expand its offerings to the afternoon. "Sam, Space Cat" will be at 1 p.m. and 3 p.m. on Saturday and Sunday. The film "Beyond the Earth" will be shown at 2 p.m. each day. The planetarium director said the additional showings will allow more people, particularly those who work during the week, to see the special offerings.

- Workforce.com, a local company in the Cityville Research Park, employs 85 people. Company officials have announced a restructuring that will layoff 60 employees and that they hope will allow them to save the company. Profits have dropped 40 percent in the last six months. Workforce.com was founded five years ago. It is an online employment company that had targeted a national clientele, but company officials said the number of clients did not reach expectations.

CHAPTER 6

Beyond the Lead
Writing the Message

Once writers have fashioned the lead, they face the task of organizing the rest of the message. They must decide what will come after the first sentences or paragraphs that hook the audience. The ranking decisions discussed in Chapter 5 that help them write the lead are invaluable in helping them develop the body of the message. Again, with audience needs and interests in mind, the writer outlines how the message will evolve.

As mentioned in Chapter 5, journalists have traditionally used the inverted pyramid form of writing to get to the point quickly and to set priorities for basic news stories. The principle behind the inverted pyramid style—to order information according to its value to the audience—is valuable in much writing today and is becoming more valuable as audiences read more news online and spend less time with each story they read there. The process of ordering information for the inverted pyramid involves critical thinking, an important skill for all writers.

Different styles of writing might be more suitable for other audiences or for a particular medium. Students will find various organizational styles in print and online publications: newspapers, magazines, company newsletters, and so on. If you find yourself reading a story from start to end, study it to identify the elements that pulled you into and through the message. Save it. Some day you may want to adopt the style for a piece of your own.

This chapter discusses

- the inverted pyramid form of writing,
- news peg and nut graph,
- other organizational formats, and
- how to unify writing.

The Inverted Pyramid

Leads must get to the point quickly, and messages must provide important information right behind the lead. Newspaper editors have recognized that need for decades. Henry A. Stokes, as an assistant managing editor for projects at the *Commercial Appeal* in Memphis, Tennessee, once wrote in a staff memo that reporters had to ensure stories attracted reader attention.

Stokes told staff writers they were to "tell the news in an identifiable, functional format that guarantees the reader will receive the best information we can provide, written in a way that the reader can quickly and easily understand."

As a result, the newspaper adopted the four-paragraph rule: Tell the essential message in the first four paragraphs of the story. Details that could be cut would follow.

The format Stokes advocated was the inverted pyramid style of writing, long a standard in journalism. With the inverted pyramid, information in a message is organized in descending order of importance. The most important and compelling information comes first and is followed by information of lesser value. His advice years ago still applies in today's electronic and online media world where important information must be stated immediately.

To be successful at using the inverted pyramid, writers must be able to evaluate and rank information, and they must know what is most important to their audiences. This simple model shows how the inverted pyramid works:

Lead summarizes information. Next few paragraphs back up the lead.

Next section provides background and additional important information.

Next section has information of lesser importance about the topics introduced in the lead.

Final section contains least important information, which could be cut.

In the inverted pyramid, the lead paragraph or paragraphs summarize the most important news values and elements and hook the audience.

The next paragraphs usually give additional crucial information that would not fit into the lead. Background information to provide context comes next. From there, subsequent paragraphs develop the topics presented in the lead, introduce other important information, expand the significance of the information, and give details.

Each section will vary in length, depending on what the writer has introduced in the lead and whether he or she is building the message with quotes. A local government reporter might devote four or five paragraphs to dialogue from a meeting before moving on to other city council actions set forth in the lead paragraph.

The inverted pyramid format helps a writer organize information logically, whether the topic is a single subject or has multiple subjects or elements. If the writer plans to develop several issues in the message, the summary multiple-element lead would set up the organization in the following way:

> The Cityville City Council voted unanimously Tuesday night to renew the city manager's contract for three years with a raise each year and to annex 325 acres south of town and just west of the Newtar River.

Through the inverted pyramid, the writer sets up the order of importance in the lead and how the message will be organized. The most important item is the city manager's contract, which includes a pay raise. Because no one objected to the annexation of acreage, it carries less importance because it is not controversial. It can be discussed second. The important point, the action of annexation, is contained in the lead. The rest of the story follows the lead like this:

> In discussing City Manager Larry Morgan's new contract, council members agreed that Morgan had done an exemplary job in his six years as manager.
>
> "We couldn't find anyone better," said Council Member Dick Haynes, who made the motion to give Morgan a 10 percent pay raise in the first year of the contract and 5 percent in the second and third years.
>
> "We have maintained quality town services with only modest tax increases while Larry has been here," added Council Member Loretta Manson.
>
> The council voted to annex the Heather Hills subdivision following a public hearing in which no one objected to the annexation plan. Residents who spoke said they wanted to come under the town's water and sewer services and to gain improved fire and police protection.

The inverted pyramid is more than just an organizational tool. It has been identified traditionally as a writing style that uses simple words, short sentences, and one idea to a paragraph. It also represents critical thinking: It forces writers to evaluate information and rank it in order of importance. Some critics have said the inverted pyramid puts pressure on reporters to craft an attention-getting, information-packed lead, leaving them little time to follow through with a well-organized message. To be successful, writers must do both: write a compelling lead and organize a story logically. In reality, time constraints or deadline pressure may interfere with both functions.

Why Use the Inverted Pyramid for Media Writing?

Newspapers traditionally have used the inverted pyramid format for two primary reasons: to give readers the most critical material quickly so they can move to other stories if they wish and to allow a story to be cut easily from the bottom, leaving important information intact at the top of the story.

Newspapers have a limited news hole, or space, to fit editorial content, so story lengths can change at the last minute, depending on where a story is placed on a page. For online sites, the story length is potentially limitless, but online writers and editors know audiences have limited time and their work must capture and retain readers.

Many beginning writers question why they should follow the inverted pyramid style of writing when they plan careers in public relations, advertising, or marketing. They object to what they see as a rigid way of writing or formula writing—a basic format devoid of creativity.

At first glance, the objections seem valid. But as students use the inverted pyramid, they will discover plenty of opportunities for description and for their own style to develop. They will also learn that their audiences expect upfront delivery of essential information and that critical thinking goes along with the inverted pyramid style. For the inverted pyramid, writers must gather information, list or rank information, write a draft, and rewrite, as outlined in Chapter 1.

John Sweeney, professor in the School of Journalism and Mass Communication at the University of North Carolina at Chapel Hill, teaches advertising courses. He advises all students, no matter their major, on the value of learning the inverted pyramid structure.

"Before you can develop your own style, you have to master the basics," he tells introductory writing students. "You have to be taught to be meticulous. To say it succinctly, concisely, precisely. You have to be able to distill information, whether it's a 30-second TV spot, or a piece of newswriting, or an ad distilled from a 100-page document on product data.

"Writing also has to have access: Anyone can read it and understand it," Sweeney advises. "You have to focus on what's key, get to the heart of the matter, and put the issue in perspective."

Communicators first must be able to master the traditional before they can be avant-garde. Mastering the inverted pyramid style of writing gives any student journalist or communicator the basic plan for writing messages that focus on what is important and emotionally compelling for the audience. Whether writing for print or online, the inverted pyramid style organizes information so that it is accessible, appealing, simply stated, and easy to understand.

The Inverted Pyramid for Other Media

Research supports the belief that the inverted pyramid retains value today, when the majority of messages are becoming shorter and more direct. Consider broadcast messages, which usually begin with a short, catchy headline to grab the viewer's attention and then summarize the main points. Because broadcast news stories are short, it is imperative for TV and radio reporters to fit in as many compelling facts as possible in the few seconds allotted. The inverted pyramid allows for the speedy, information-rich writing that broadcast demands.

Corporate communication offices and nonprofit agencies, whether staffed by professionals or volunteers, more and more follow the traditional inverted pyramid style. It puts their agenda where readers and editors can see it. Even advertising depends on the inverted pyramid style, communicating to consumers in an abbreviated way a product's qualities and the reasons for buying it.

Although it works best in shorter pieces, the inverted pyramid style can be adapted for longer, more complex pieces, many of which use the inverted pyramid format early and then other organizational patterns later. For example, nondeadline pieces, such as feature stories and documentaries, attract readers best by getting to the point and summarizing first. Simple pyramiding in nondeadline writing can attract readers by creating a mood, setting the stage for more detailed information, or providing a memorable image.

The growth in online news consumption has made the inverted pyramid more important than ever. Many online news readers are quickly skimming the Web or their mobile phones for the latest headlines. Bombarded with an increasing array of news sources, online readers want to know quickly what is the point of a story.

In one sense, news Web sites themselves are one giant inverted pyramid. News sites put the most important information on their homepage, often in the form of brief one-paragraph story summaries called "blurbs." If the blurb entices a reader, he or she may click deeper in the site to get the full news story. And from that news story, the reader may have the option of reading original source documents, archival material, or other news stories related to the original article. Because the online reader with each click can exercise the choice to go deeper in to the material, online writers don't have to cram tangential information in to every story, but they do need to think about ways they can construct an inverted pyramid of links that will make it easer for the reader to read more information if he or she desires.

Organizing a Story

The basic work of organizing a message in inverted pyramid style is done when you use the steps outlined in Chapter 5 for writing leads. The writer first identifies news values and the elements needed to structure a lead. News values and elements introduced in the lead will be developed in greater detail within the message. The writer will use the remaining news values and elements in subsequent paragraphs based on ranking information important to audiences.

In summer 2008, a sailboat operated by a student crew from Texas A&M University capsized in the Gulf of Mexico. The initial stories reported the boat missing after the crew failed to check in by radio at a specific time. Updated stories followed the 26-hour search, then the rescue efforts.

Broadcast media and online sites continually updated the leads and information at the top of their stories as the ordeal unfolded. Reporters had basic information to consider:

Who:	Four student crew members and two coaches
What:	Capsized, then were found after drifting
When:	26 hours Friday to Sunday
Where:	Gulf of Mexico
How:	Boat rolled on its side
Why:	Boat lost its keel

Look at the news values we discussed in Chapter 5 and determine which ones apply here. The human interest angle is crucial as is the timeliness as the news is updated. Conflict and oddity could be relevant in man versus the sea and the rarity of a student crew floating in the Gulf of Mexico for more than a day. Other news values such as impact, prominence, or magnitude may not exist.

Consider the lead from MSNBC after the crew was found:

> Four student crew members and the captain of a capsized Texas A&M University sailboat are alive after 26 hours in the Gulf of Mexico without a life raft—thanks to a heroic coach who gave his life to save two students, as well as their own survival training.

The lead identifies the elements *who*, *what*, and *how* with the elements *when* and *where* understood. A second paragraph—a direct quote—expands on how they survived.

> "The students are here today because they did a great job. They were positive, they didn't panic. They kept working as a team and taking care of each other," Steve Conway, skipper of the "Cynthia Woods," told TODAY's Matt Lauer Monday from Galveston, Texas. "We pretty much did a textbook drill. We held onto each other very tightly, and we used our belts and our rigging to lash ourselves together."

Later graphs answer why the accident happened.

For any natural disaster or breaking news event, reporters will update information continuously. Story angles will focus on what readers and viewers need to know to prepare for storms and protect themselves and their property, or the details as police search for suspects.

Applying News Elements and News Values

A news value, such as oddity, may be referred to in a lead but then be developed fully later in the message. Remember the lead in Chapter 5 about the wedding dress? Although readers have the basics from the lead that something was lost, they may want more information about how the house was lost. The body of the message answers that question.

FARGO (AP)—He lost his home, but saved a wedding dress.

Joe Westbrock dashed back into his burning apartment building Saturday afternoon in south Fargo after alerting others to the blaze.

Westbrock, who lives on the third floor with his girlfriend, said there was little smoke or fire on the floor when he rescued his girlfriend's wedding dress. He said he also grabbed a laptop computer.

"She said her wedding dress was up there, and without even thinking, I just ran back in," Westbrock told Fargo's KFGO radio.

No one was injured in the fire.

Westbrock said he saw the fire after hearing a loud banging noise. When he realized the danger, he pulled the fire alarm and knocked on doors to alert others.

"My dad was a volunteer firefighter, so I've seen all the videos growing up," he said. "I've gone through all the drills with him. I used to be a lifeguard in high school…everything just kicks in to be calm, collected and try to be levelheaded. Some type of instinct told me to run and grab the fire alarm and knock on people's doors."

He has not been able to get back into the building to see if anything else is left.

The wedding is set for early next year.

Damage to the apartment building has been estimated at more than $750,000. Dozens of people were displaced by the blaze.

Fire officials say they cannot determine the cause of the fire, but Fire Department Capt. Dan Freeman said officials do not consider it suspicious.

In this story, the writer uses a short lead that focuses on *who* and *what*. Graph 2 gives readers information about *where* and *when* and answers how he lost his home and saved the dress. Readers reach paragraph 5 before they learn no one was injured.

Beyond the news value of oddity, the story has impact because of the dozens of people displaced, human interest because of the dress and Westbrock potentially saving lives by pulling the alarm, and magnitude in the damage estimate. Conflict and prominence are not relevant.

Instead of writing a straight news story about a fire that caused $750,000 in damage and displaced dozen of residents, the reporter chose to emphasize one aspect to attract readers and make them pay attention.

You also might have noticed in the organization of the story that the information came in paragraphs of varying lengths. Paragraphs in an essay for an English composition or literature class differ from paragraphs in all forms of media writing. In an essay or composition, a paragraph can be a whole presentation or argument on a topic. But in mass communication, a paragraph is identified as a single unit of timely information and usually is one to three sentences long. It conveys a solitary fact, thought, or "sound bite" from the larger message. When a writer is concerned with transmitting information quickly, his or her ideas about paragraphing change.

As mentioned in Chapter 4, journalists rarely use the word "paragraph." In the newsroom, a paragraph is a "graph." This abbreviated word symbolizes the abbreviated form that paragraphs take in news stories. A graph generally will have several sentences, but on occasion it may be one sentence long and transmit a single news element or news value.

News Peg and Nut Graph

Newspaper reporters talk about the *news peg* when developing stories. The peg, just like a peg on the wall where you hang a coat, is what a writer hangs the story on. It is the reason for writing the message. In the sailboat story, the news peg comes in the lead: The crew has been rescued.

Every piece of writing—whether it appears in print or is aired or shared—has a news peg. Writers, no matter their skill or medium, have a reason for composing a message. That reason is spelled out in the *nut graph:* the paragraph that defines the point the writer is making. The rest of the message expands and clarifies the singular idea in the nut graph.

In some cases, the lead serves as the nut graph, particularly if it is a summary lead, and sometimes the nut graph is more than a paragraph long. The nut graph should be in the first four to five paragraphs or writers risk losing audiences who want the point quickly. In today's writing of shorter paragraphs, the nut graph might be lower because audiences don't have to wade through long copy. When writers use anecdotal or descriptive leads, as described in Chapter 5, they must summarize and focus the message for audiences after drawing them in.

Look for the nut graph in this *Washington Post* story by Dan Morse:

> We could all use one from time to time: a dog that can find the darn cellphone.
>
> Maryland has three. Their job is to sniff out phones smuggled into prisons.

"Seek," Sgt. David Brosky told his dog Alba yesterday, offering a public demonstration at the former Maryland House of Correction in Jessup.

Alba made her way through an unoccupied prison cell until she came upon a rolled-up pair of jeans on a bed. She sat, a signal she had found something.

"Good girrrrrrrrrrl," said Brosky, a corrections officer, handing the dog a ball, a reward for finding the black cellphone tucked in the pants.

The state's trained dogs—Tazz and Rudd, along with Alba—could be the solution to a problem facing prison administrators nationwide, a solution taking hold in the Washington region.

Smuggled cellphones allow inmates to run criminal enterprises, threaten witnesses and warn fellow inmates about the movements of correctional officers, state officials said.

By the second paragraph, readers have a clue to the story: dogs sniffing phones in prison. In graph 7, the actual nut graph, readers learn the point: Smuggled cellphones allow inmates to continue criminal activities from within prison walls.

Remember *The New York Times'* descriptive lead about the Austrian monks from Chapter 5:

HEILIGENKREUZ, Austria—As noon draws near, the monks glide into the church, their white cowls billowing behind them. They line up in silence, facing each other in long choir stalls. Wood carvings of saints peer down on them from the austere Romanesque nave.

Bells peal and the chant begins—low at first, then swelling as all the monks join in. Their soft voices wash over the ancient stones, replacing the empty clatter of the day with something like the sound of eternity.

Except, that is, for the clicks of a camera held by a photographer lurking behind a stone pillar.

It has been like this since last spring, when word got out that the Cistercian monks of the Stift Heiligenkreuz, deep in the Vienna woods, had been signed by Universal Music to record an album of Gregorian chants.

> When the album, "Chat: Music for Paradise," was released in Europe in
> May—and shot to No. 7 in the British pop charts, at one point outselling releases
> from Amy Winehouse and Madonna—the trickle of press attention turned into a
> torrent. (The CD will be released in the United States on Tuesday.)

By graph 5, readers learn the news peg that is included in the nut graph: The CD
will be released within days in the United States, hence coverage by U.S. press.

Other Organizational Styles

Although the inverted pyramid works for much writing, other formats might
seem better for a particular message because of the event reported. Some formats
use the inverted pyramid format to introduce material, then move into another
organizational pattern.

Chronological Format

In some cases, making the decision about how to organize the body of a message is easy. Chronology—telling events in the same order in which they
occurred—often can meet audience needs. A breaking news story about a bank
robbery, for example, would have a summary lead telling that the robbery
occurred, where, and when. Then, after the nut of the news is clear, events
would be revealed chronologically. The writer would organize the rest of the
story by using time elements, as in the following article:

> A masked woman robbed the First Guaranty Savings and Loan on Main Street
> shortly after 9 a.m. today and escaped into a thickly wooded area nearby. Police
> have made no arrests.
>
> The robbery occurred when the woman entered the bank and approached
> a teller. She handed her a note asking for money and saying she had a gun in the
> sleeve of her sweatshirt.
>
> Although the teller did not actually see a gun, she gave the woman an
> undisclosed amount of cash. The woman put the money into a purple sack, ran
> from the Savings and Loan, and disappeared in the woods behind the bank's
> parking lot.

At 6 p.m., police were still looking for the suspect, who was described as a white woman in her mid-20s. She weighs about 150 pounds and stands about 5 feet 6 inches. She has shoulder-length blonde hair. She wore a purple sweatsuit and had pulled a stocking as a mask over her face. Bank employees could not describe her facial features.

Here, the lead, or the first paragraph, states *who* did *what*, *where*, and *when* and the latest information. Graph 2 starts *how* events unfolded. The last time element tells readers the status of the investigation at the newspaper's deadline.

In breaking news stories that are continually updated, such as those online, chronology works well as a format. New information can be added in the lead and first few paragraphs. All the details that have unfolded chronologically can remain. Any additional information that adds to the timeline can be inserted easily.

While some messages can be developed chronologically, organization generally is not that simple. Not all messages involve action that evolves over time. For example, a high school principal writing in the school newsletter cannot use chronology to inform teachers about changes in ordering classroom supplies. Although teachers may be interested in the events that led up to the changes, they want to know the specific changes immediately. That is when another format, such as inverted pyramid, is needed.

Hourglass Format

Some writers have adapted chronological development to longer stories in what they call the *hourglass format* of writing. A summary lead followed by the inverted pyramid style gives readers the most important information in four to six paragraphs, allowing them to stop at the end of the inverted pyramid segment. Then the writer sets up more information with a simple statement by a source, such as "The police chief described the events this way."

Beyond the transition statement, the message unfolds chronologically. Writers can use the style for many kinds of stories, such as telling of the search for a lost child, recounting a day in the life of a popular singer, or bringing out the details of a baseball game. Electronic media writers often use the hourglass format. For example, a local television station aired a story about a crime that police had been unable to solve. After noting the latest information, the reporter said, "Here's how police have recreated the sequence of events." The details that followed were a chronological account of the crime. The story ended with the reporter showing the local telephone number for Crimestoppers.

Mapped Format

Assistant Professor Jacqueline Farnan and newspaper copy editor David Hedley discussed another variation on the inverted pyramid style called the *mapped format*. They noted that the inverted pyramid becomes confusing for longer pieces, but they believed it served as a way to introduce the most important elements of the message.

Mapped format is a technique to indicate points of interest within the message, just as a map includes highlights for its readers. The mapped format benefits topics, such as business and government, that are of interest to readers. It also aids readers in finding information of particular interest to them in longer stories.

A mapped message is organized into sections. The first is the inverted pyramid lead. Following the lead, a series of subheads in a subject–verb–object form define categories of information. Readers can quickly find the segments of information that most benefit or appeal to them.

Subheads for an expanded story on the bank robbery would look like this:

Robber Approaches Teller
Escape into Woods
Police Still Searching

The mapped format can also help the writer organize. Assume you are writing a story on the cost of funerals and the alternatives to traditional burial. Your research finds categories of information: reasons why funerals are expensive, caskets and their costs, funeral home expenses, cost of burial plots, cost of cremation versus burial, memorial services, and how to cut costs. After drafting the lead, you can group categories of information under subheads, which help organize the story and readily identify parts of the story for readers.

Newspapers are not the only medium to use mapped formats. For example, CNN.com uses subheads in its full stories. This style helps readers quickly find information and helps search engines better understand the key topics on each page.

Numerical Format

A writer might organize a message numerically or by points. For example, a city council votes on three issues: water and sewer rates, a rezoning application, and the town manager's contract. The writer would list in the multiple-element lead the actions taken and the votes, thereby setting up the three points to be expanded, in that order, in the body of the story.

Writers covering a speech will often use a numeral or point-by-point format that follows the organizational structure of the speech. For example, a speaker discusses three major risk factors in heart disease. The writer notes the three risk factors in the lead: smoking, lack of exercise, and lack of a well-balanced diet. The points serve as transitions from the lead to the sections of the message. The reporter's story might read:

> Cardiovascular disease is the No. 1 cause of death in the United States, but it can be reduced with lifestyle changes such as no smoking, regular exercise, and a well-balanced diet, the chairman of the American Heart Association's Wayne County chapter said Tuesday.
>
> Gus Rivas said Americans should pay attention to the risk factors at an early age and get children to be aware of healthy lifestyles.
>
> More than 3,000 children smoke their first cigarette every day. This number will translate into more adults who are at risk for cardiovascular disease.
>
> "Children consume more than 947 million packs of cigarettes in this country per year," Rivas said. "More than 25 percent of high school students who smoke tried their first cigarette while in the sixth grade."
>
> Youngsters need to exercise, he noted. Studies show that today's youth do not get enough regular exercise.
>
> "Riding a bike, walking, even doing household chores can establish fitness patterns," Rivas said.
>
> A well-balanced diet low in fat is essential to reduce the risk of heart disease, Rivas said. About one out of four children is obese, and obese children are at a risk for obesity as adults.

The writer followed the lead, using the three points or risk factors as a way to organize and unify the story.

Unifying Writing

Any story, memo, news release, or online message needs unity to be a coherent and complete piece. Each paragraph in a written piece must follow the preceding paragraph logically and build on previous information. Each section of the piece must fit the subject or theme. Unifying writing takes careful thought and planning, and it requires rewriting or reorganizing after a draft is done.

Transitions and repetition of certain words are ways to unify writing and to get readers from the beginning to the end. The first two or three paragraphs set up many of the unifying elements—for example, people, places, things, controversy, or chronology.

Repetition of Words

Some writers are uncomfortable repeating words in their writing. They pore over the thesaurus or dictionary, looking for synonyms that might not be as good as repeating the word itself. Repetition is okay; it offers unity in a message and gives readers familiarity. Repetition is also clearer; readers are not stopping to match synonyms and words.

The topic will determine the words repeated. A memo that covers changes in employee benefits should use the word "employee" throughout rather than switching from "worker" to "staff" to "professional." The same applies in writing about an organization; "organization" or the organization's name can be used throughout rather than "group," "agency," or "company."

Transitions

Transitions are cues for readers. They set up changes in location, time, and mood, and they keep readers from getting lost or confused.

A simple sentence or word might be needed as a logical bridge from one section of the message to the next. Any transition should wrap up the previous thought and introduce the next one.

> "We must continue our efforts to reduce teenage pregnancy, and our programs are aimed to do that," the governor said.
>
> While the governor defended his policies, others in state government cited lack of action on welfare issues for his dwindling popularity.

The second sentence uses "while" and "others" to indicate a shift from the governor's words to those of state government officials.

Most writers are accustomed to simple words or phrases as transitions. Look at some of the following words and phrases that give readers certain information about where a story is going:

A change in opinion:	but, on the other hand, however
Clarification:	in other words, for example, that is, to illustrate, to demonstrate, specifically, to clarify
Comparison:	also, in comparison, like, similarly, on the same note, a related point
Contrast:	but, in contrast, despite, on the contrary, unlike, yet, however, instead of
Expanded information:	in addition, an additional, moreover, in other action, another, further, furthermore, too, as well as, also
A change in place:	above, higher, beneath, nearby, beside, between, across, after, around, below
Time:	while, meanwhile, past, afterward, during, soon, next, subsequently, until then, future, before, at the same time

Look at how a few transitions work. In developing a story chronologically, time serves as a transition. Refer to the First Guaranty bank robbery story earlier in this chapter. The time elements pull the reader from shortly after 9 a.m., when the robbery occurred, until 6 p.m., when the woman still had not been caught. In other stories, time-oriented words and phrases could be "at the same time," "later that day," "Tuesday," and "last week."

A story about voter reaction on election day uses polling sites around town as geographic transitions: "Voters at Precinct 35 (Town Hall) said...," "Those voting at Precinct 15 (Main Street Presbyterian Church) said...," "Precinct 2 voters (Blackwell Elementary School) said...." Other geographical phrases would be "on the other side of town," "at his father's 25-acre farm," "next door," and "at the White House."

Tone to Unify a Message

Familiarity with your audiences will help determine what tone to set in organizing and writing a message. The tone of a story can act as a unifying device. A PTA newsletter editor knows that her audience is busy, fast-moving, and distracted by children, work, day-to-day routine, and a deluge of information. She knows her audience is in need of quick tips about kids and school. She must write lively copy with short, pithy sentences and paragraphs. Active parents need newsletter copy that looks like this:

> Spring cleaning may leave you with trash and treasures. Please donate them to Southview School's Trash and Treasure sale! This year's sale is planned for May 9.
> Jennifer Chen will begin receiving donations April 26 at her home, 322 Dale Drive. For more information, call 499-2342.

In contrast, a lead in *The New York Times* on a story about a Supreme Court ruling has a more formal, serious, thoughtful tone that will carry into the story:

> WASHINGTON—The Supreme Court on Thursday embraced the long-disputed view that the Second Amendment protects an individual right to own a gun for personal use, ruling 5 to 4 that there is a constitutional right to keep a loaded handgun at home for self-defense.

A writer's knowledge of audiences will determine the mood or tone that will best maintain interest and retain it throughout the message.

Quotes to Unify Stories

Quotes can be effective transitions throughout writing. They add liveliness and allow people to speak directly to readers and listeners, helping them feel more connected to personalities and events. They can supplement facts and add detail. News stories and news releases should have a good balance between direct and indirect quotes. Information on direct and indirect quotes, attribution, and punctuation of quotes is given in Chapter 10.

In a profile story about boxer Tony Thompson, writer Zach Berman of *The Washington Post* uses quotes to pace the story and allow Thompson to explain why he fights.

Thompson doesn't love boxing. He derives no joy from training. He fights for the reward, not the act.

"I really don't like getting hit," he said. "I really don't like to train for boxing. I'm just good at it. It's what I do to make a living. If I had my choices of making a living, I'm not one of those people who would say boxing…Boxing was so far down the list for me."

Quotes can refer to the lead and wrap up a piece, they can leave the reader looking to the future, or they can add a touch of humor. But sometimes writers have to be careful in using a quote at the end. If the story is cut from the bottom, readers should miss only a chuckle, not important information.

Unifying Devices in Practice

Let's go back and look at the short article on the wedding dress and the fire. What are the unifying devices? First, see what the lead set up.

He lost his home, but saved a wedding dress.

Throughout the story the writer refers to wedding and dress.

The second paragraph identifies Joe Westbrock and makes it clear that a fire is the cause for Westbrock losing his home and identifies the home as an apartment building.

Joe Westbrock dashed back into his burning apartment building Saturday afternoon in south Fargo after alerting others to the blaze.

Graph 3 uses an indirect quote from Westbrock as reasoning why he went back into the burning building. Repeated are the themes of smoke, fire, and the wedding dress.

Westbrock, who lives on the third floor with his girlfriend, said there was little smoke or fire on the floor when he rescued his girlfriend's wedding dress. He said he also grabbed a laptop computer.

Graph 4 alerts readers that although he went back into the building, no one was injured.

No one was injured in the fire.

Graph 5 gives readers more information about Westbrock and his actions. The word "wedding dress" is repeated.

"She said her wedding dress was up there, and without even thinking, I just ran back in," Westbrock told Fargo's KFGO radio.

Graph 6 continues explanation about Westbrock's actions to save neighbors, which was introduced in Graph 2.

Westbrock said he saw the fire after hearing a loud banging noise. When he realized the danger, he pulled the fire alarm and knocked on doors to alert others.

Graph 7 adds insight into Westbrock's thinking and repeats terms of "fire" and the theme of alerting residents.

"My dad was a volunteer firefighter, so I've seen all the videos growing up," he said. "I've gone through all the drills with him. I used to be a lifeguard in high school…everything just kicks in to be calm, collected and try to be levelheaded. Some type of instinct told me to run and grab the fire alarm and knock on people's doors."

The short graph 8 gives readers more information: The building has not been cleared for residents to return.

He has not been able to get back into the building to see if anything else is left.

Graph 9, also short, returns to the wedding theme.

The wedding is set for early next year.

Graphs 10 and 11 broaden the story to the fire and its impact on others besides Westbrock. Similar language appears: blaze, fire, apartment building, people.

> Damage to the apartment building has been estimated at more than $750,000. Dozens of people were displaced by the blaze.
>
> Fire officials say they cannot determine the cause of the fire, but Fire Department Capt. Dan Freeman said officials do not consider it suspicious.

Writing is a series of choices—choice of language, pertinent facts, introductions, organizational pattern, tone, quotes, and topics—to unify copy. All need to be made in an informed way, based on what writers know about their audiences.

Books and other writers can give you tips on how to organize your writing. The best way to learn is to apply the techniques through your own efforts. Do not let organization just happen. Remember the stages of writing. Make an outline. Consciously apply a certain organizational style to your writing. Let someone else read your piece to see whether it makes sense.

Good organization helps you reach your audience. Return to the Associated Press drug bust story on page 83 in Chapter 4. The reporter uses all the strengths of simple writing, repetition for unity, and quotes as transitions to pull readers through an emotionally compelling story that could have been just another routine drug bust story. The following chapters will guide you further in knowing your audience and writing for it.

Exercises

1. You are a reporter for *The Cityville Chronicle*. You have picked up the following police report—written last night—from the town police department. Write a message with a summary lead, then develop the message in chronological order.

> Report: Tony's Restaurant Robbery
>
> Investigating Officer: Sgt. Rodney Carter
>
> At 10 p.m. a robbery at Tony's Restaurant was reported. Owner Tony Hardy said he was working late preparing the payroll when a man wearing a stocking mask entered the back door of the kitchen at about 8:40.

Hardy said the man told him to go into the office and open up the safe. Hardy took almost $3,000 out of the safe and put it into a blue, waterproof sack.

The restaurant closes at 9 p.m. Hardy said he thought the robber knew he was there alone, but he didn't think the robber was a Cityville resident.

Hardy said he got a good look at the man: a stocky white man, about 5'6", and round-faced. He estimated the man's age to be 24. Hardy said the man's shoulders were so broad that he might have been a weight lifter. Hardy suggested that if the thief wanted to lock him up somewhere, the storage closet off the kitchen was as good a place as any. The thief agreed and locked him up there. The thief wrapped a clothes hanger around the door. He told Hardy he had a partner, and that Hardy wouldn't live to see his family and relatives if he came out of the closet before 15 minutes had passed.

Hardy said he waited the 15 minutes even though he didn't believe the story about the partner, or at least a partner who would be stupid enough to hang around for 15 minutes. He had no trouble getting out and then called the Cityville police.

We have some leads on the suspect and the investigation is continuing.

2. From the following information, write a summary lead for *The Cityville Chronicle* that focuses on *who, what, when,* and *where,* plus human interest. Then develop the message in hourglass format.

From the Cityville police chief, Alston Powers, you learn the following:

Two sisters were playing at a Laundromat about 5 p.m. yesterday. The girls are the daughters of Nancy and Phillip Childs of Cityville. The girls were with their aunt, Janice Childs. The 3-year-old, Jennifer, climbed into one of the washing machines. Her sister, Elizabeth, 7, closed the door. The machine started filling up with water. When she realized the washer was running, Elizabeth ran to get her aunt. Ms. Childs tried to open the washer door but could not, because the washers are equipped with automatic locks on the doors.

Powers said the girl was trapped in the washer for more than five minutes before she was rescued. He said a customer had put coins into the machine before the little girl crawled inside, but the customer hadn't used the machine because he thought it wasn't working.

On the telephone you talk to Chris Gibson, of 124 Basketball Lane, Cityville. He was on his way home from work and stopped at the Glen Rock Shopping Center to buy groceries. He heard screams coming from the Glen Rock Laundry and Dry Cleaner. He ran inside the Laundromat to see what was going on. Ms. Childs ran up to him and asked him to save the child. She asked if he had any tools, so he ran back to his toolbox in the back of his truck and got a hammer. Gibson said he took the hammer back inside and smashed the glass in the washing machine door. He then reached in and pulled her out.

A Cityville Hospital spokesperson said Jennifer was admitted yesterday afternoon and was listed in good condition. Her parents could not be reached for comment.

3. You are a reporter for *The Cityville Chronicle*. You are to write a story from the following information. Focus on a summary lead with a local angle. Organize the story in inverted pyramid.

A group of 55 cyclists from the United States arrived in Ho Chi Minh City in Vietnam yesterday. They ended a 1,200-mile course through Vietnam. The trip took them 20 days. The course was fairly grueling through some of the country's mountainous areas as well as flat parts. The group camped and stayed in villages along the way.

The U.S. Cycling Federation, which arranged the tour, said it planned to organize another event next year. Officials said the tours are a way to allow U.S. residents to get a close-up look at the country and their people.

When the group arrived it was greeted by firecrackers, flower necklaces, and cold towels. Bob Lester, 33, of Cressett, was one of the cyclists on the trip. He said, "This trip was the most amazing thing I have ever done in my life. I would recommend the experience to anyone who can pedal a bike." The cyclists are expected to return to the United States in two weeks.

The tour was part of an effort to open up Vietnam to outsiders and to present a different picture of the country than people had come to expect from the Vietnam War.

Among the cyclists were seven Vietnam veterans and three Vietnamese Americans, all from the United States. The 55 cyclists were from 23 states.

Several of the Americans said the journey had erased any doubts they might have held about Vietnam and its people.

4. You are to write a story for the next issue of *The Cityville Chronicle*. Write a summary lead, then organize the story point by point. Make sure to unify your writing. Your audience is Cityville residents.

LuAnne Neal, director of public affairs for the state Department of Commerce, tells you today the state is launching a three-part train safety program. The state has had its share of train crossing accidents, one recently in Johnston County where a man was injured when his car was hit at a crossing. The worst accident occurred five years ago when an engineer was killed and more than 350 people injured when a train derailed after hitting a truck near Haysville.

First, the state is asking that state highway crews work in cooperation with the Department of Commerce to inspect train crossings in the state. Engineers who ride the trains will spend the next month noting intersections that don't have lights or warning signals that possibly might need them. Highway workers can do the same in their jobs.

Second, the state is compiling statistics on the most dangerous railroad crossings in the state, that is, the ones with the most accidents. That way officials will know where to focus state and federal monies in improving the most dangerous crossings.

Third, a public education program will caution drivers on crossing railroad intersections. Too many times an accident was caused because a driver tried to beat the train to the intersection. That kind of action endangers not only the driver but everyone on the train, whether it is a passenger train or a freight train. The state will put flyers at drivers' license offices and in license renewal tag offices around the state. The flyers will be distributed to all students taking drivers education. Notices will be sent to all people who are renewing their automobile or truck license tags.

References

Jacqueline Farnan and David Hedley, "The Mapped Format: A Variation on the Inverted-Pyramid Appeals to Readers." Paper presented at the Association for Education in Journalism and Mass Communication Conference, Atlanta, GA, August 1993.

Fred Fedler, *Reporting for the Print Media*. New York: Harcourt Brace Jovanovich, 1989.

"Newswriting for the Commercial Appeal," produced by Lionel Linder, editor, and Colleen Conant, managing editor, 1989.

William Zinsser, *On Writing Well*. New York: Harper & Row, 1976.

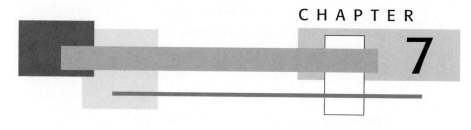

Producing Online Content

Most writers who work for media today produce copy with an eye and ear toward their companies' online sites. As the audience for online news continues to grow, traditional print and broadcast news sources are moving more breaking news coverage and other features to their Web sites. Technology companies like Yahoo!, AOL, and Microsoft dominate online news consumption in the United States. And millions of people who could never afford to print a newspaper of their own have become amateur reporters or commentators with their own blogs that cost nothing to publish online.

Increasingly, editors expect entry-level reporters as well as experienced staff to be more than just writers or photographers. Reporters today must be able to choose the right medium to tell each story, and they must be able to use the tools necessary to collect and edit information whether it is text, still images, video, audio, or animated and interactive graphics. You might have a job as a reporter who gathers audio and video along with notes. An editor might re-edit your story for multiple media, or you might do it yourself.

Professional communicators are trying to reach audiences in new ways. They are distributing news headlines via e-mail, mobile phones, and online social networks. Even in a multimedia world, writing remains the critical skill. Understanding and knowing audiences is also crucial, particularly in a media environment where newspapers, television stations, and Internet sites are competing for readers' and viewers' attention. Information that is relevant, concise, accurate, and complete is just as important for online content as for any other medium.

In this chapter you will learn

- how historical and other developments have led to a world of online information,
- the components of a news Web site,

- specific writing formats for online news stories,
- the effect of online audiences on news values,
- how to integrate a written story with multimedia elements, and
- challenges and opportunities facing future professional communicators.

The World Goes Online

The growth of the Internet as a communication tool ranks as one of the most important revolutions in publishing. Like the revolution set off by Johannes Gutenberg's invention of the printing press in the early 15th century, the growth of the Internet in the final decade of the 20th century made the publication and distribution of the written word much cheaper for publishers.

But the Internet, which has distribution methods from e-mail to instant messaging to the World Wide Web, has become more than a tool for cheap publishing. Its multimedia capabilities allow for video, audio, photos, and animations to be distributed without the expense of broadcast towers or government licenses and even without the delay of mailing a videotape. More revolutionary than the Internet's multimedia capabilities is its reliance on "hypertext" that links one page to another in an endless trail of footnotes and citations. Hypertext changes the way people consume and evaluate information. It has also led to changes in the relationship between publisher and reader.

Before the Internet, consuming a news medium such as a newspaper, magazine, or television newscast generally was the same for every member of the audience. A subscriber to the local paper received basically the same content at basically the same time of day as every other subscriber. Viewers of a television newscast saw the same program at the same time of day as every other viewer of that newscast. But with the advent of the Internet and other digital technologies, readers now have much more control over what news they read and the time and place they read it.

Although the explosion of the Internet as a news source in the United States dates only to about 1996, the concepts behind the Internet go back to about 1945 when Vannevar Bush, the director of the Office of Scientific Research and Development under presidents Franklin Roosevelt and Harry Truman, wrote an article called "As We May Think" in the July 1945 issue of *The Atlantic Monthly*.

In the article, Bush suggested that scientists whose ingenuity had been focused on war efforts turn their attention to the organization of the vast and rapidly growing collection of human knowledge. Bush proposed a tool called the "memex" to aid in the organization of the world's information. He described it as "a device in which an individual stores all his books, records, and communications, and which is mechanized so that it may be consulted with exceeding speed and flexibility." He said that its "essential feature" would be the ability of its users to connect information through a series of "trails."

Twenty years later Theodor Nelson, a sociology professor at Vassar College, began widely using the term "hypertext" to describe the information trails imagined by Bush. A reporter covering one of Nelson's lectures that year described hypertext as a "non-linear presentation of material on a particular subject." Just a few years after that, the U.S. Department of Defense began building a network of computers that would become the precursor to the Internet.

The networking technology that underpins the Internet remained the domain of the government for the next two decades. Internet didn't become widely available to the public until late 1990 when computer scientist Tim Berners-Lee created a new system for physicists around the world to share data. Berners-Lee called his set of computer programs "the WorldWideWeb project," and he made the code generally available for others to use for free.

In 1993 a group of professors and students at the National Center for Supercomputing Applications at the University of Illinois at Urbana-Champaign developed Mosaic, the first Web browser. The Mosaic computer program made it easy for a person who didn't know computer programming to read text and view images stored on a remote computer that connected to the Internet. Unlike many computer programs, Mosaic was also available for free to most users.

Newspapers made their first foray into online publishing by posting stories to gated online services, such as CompuServ and America Online. They began migrating to the Web in the mid-1990s, and visits to newspaper Web sites quickly increased for the first time as people stormed the Web looking for election returns in November 1996.

The Internet exploded as a source for news during the last decade of the 20th century. In 1996, 12 percent of Americans went online to get information on current events, public issues, and politics. News events such as the Clinton-Lewinsky scandal, the Super Bowl, and the terrorist attacks of September 2001 each led to a higher plateau in the numbers among the online news audience. By 2000, one in three Americans went online for news at least once a week. In late 2007, more than seven in 10 Americans said they went online for news. During the same time period, audiences declined for daily newspapers, television news, and radio news.

Electronic Media Then and Now

New media always bring about new ways to reach audiences. In preparation for discussing online communication, significant developments in electronic media, as shown in Box 7.1, deserve some attention: the telegraph, the telephone, radio, television, and the Internet.

BOX 7.1	Highlights in Electronic Media History
1844	Samuel Morse introduces first U.S. telegraph line
1861	Telegraph used, along with Pony Express, to report news from Civil War battlefronts
1877	Alexander Graham Bell patents the telephone
1878	First telephone exchange installed, allows one telephone subscriber to call another
1906	First experimental broadcast of AM radio
1912	RMS Titanic sinks; distress signal and news of disaster is transmitted worldwide via telegraph
1920	KDKA in Pittsburgh broadcasts the results of the presidential election
1922	First radio advertisement broadcast on WEAF in New York, lasts 10 minutes
1927	Radio Act provides government with authority to issue licenses and assign frequencies to radio stations
1933	President Franklin D. Roosevelt addresses the public via radio in a "fireside chat" meant to alleviate anxiety during the Great Depression
1933	"War of the Worlds" broadcast results in mass hysteria
1940	FM radio is introduced
1948	Demand for television increases; 975,000 televisions manufactured, up from 179,000 in 1947
1950	CBS gives the first demonstration of color television
1964	First television correspondent arrives in Vietnam to cover war

1971	First e-mail sent by computer engineer Ray Tomlinson
1973	First call made on a handheld mobile telephone
1983	FCC approves the first mobile phone for civilian use in the U.S.
1991	British scientist Tim Berners-Lee introduces the World Wide Web, the system of hyperlinked documents held on the Internet
1995	First web-based mail software released to public
1999	Google launched by Stanford University classmates Larry Page and Sergey Brin
2001	XM Satellite Radio launched
2006	Western Union sends its last telegram

Telegraph: Quick, Short, and Sweet

Introduced by Samuel Morse in 1844, the telegraph provided a solution for East Coast to West Coast communication. This new technology allowed an operator to transmit written messages as signals (Morse code) across wires so news could travel from city-to-city, then state-to-state, and eventually across the country at a faster rate than ever before.

The telegraph played a key role in the Civil War, as newspaper editors in the North and South sought to gather and report news as quickly as possible. By 1912, messages could be sent by wireless, and distress signals were telegraphed to nearby ships when the Titanic sank after striking an iceberg. Distant wireless operators reported rescue operations to news organizations, and by early morning, the entire world grieved simultaneously the loss of more than 1,500 passengers. Such instant communication paved the way for a consolidation of news organizations now known as the Associated Press, formed by U.S. newspapers in hopes of pooling resources and saving expenses through telegraphic news delivery. Consolidation provided for a standardization of the news. *The AP Stylebook*, a staple in today's newsrooms, emphasizes uniform styles of punctuation, spelling and language use.

Telephone: "Talking with Electricity"

In 1877 Alexander Graham Bell patented the telephone, a result of efforts to improve the telegraph. The telephone represented a dramatic change in communications, permitting voice transmission or "talking with electricity" and not requiring an operator skilled in Morse code.

In the early 1900s, about one in every 250 people in the United States had a home telephone. But by 1970, more than 90 percent of U.S. households and virtually all businesses subscribed to telephone service. In the 1990s, fixed-line phones gave way to today's cellular phones. The ability of handheld computers to play music and video and to store text has led many people to favor phones that combine computing and telecommunications with data storage capabilities.

Radio: Communicating through a Box of Wires

Radio at first was the purview of boys who built crude crystal sets so they could listen to a blend of talk, music, and, inevitably, static. By the late 1920s, people could purchase bulky receivers for their homes, and by the 1930s, radios were in 50 percent of U.S. households. Eventually, the radio became a household fixture, much as home computers did in the 1990s.

One of the first radio stations, KDKA, broadcast the results of the 1920 presidential election, and in 1925 news and special events became a regular part of programming. The number of radio stations grew rapidly, and by 1930 radios came installed in automobiles.

As the influence of radio increased, a single broadcast demonstrated the profound effect the new medium could have on public attitude. On October 31, 1938, Orson Welles broadcast an adaptation of H. G. Wells' *The War of the Worlds.* The program used simulated news flashes to suggest that Martians had invaded Earth. Despite frequent announcements that the Halloween program was fictional, mass hysteria resulted. In the aftermath, politicians called for more oversight of radio programming.

During the Great Depression, President Franklin Roosevelt broadcast a series of "fireside chats" in which he reassured an anxious public. Until television displaced it, radio was the dominant medium for information and entertainment in U.S. households and automobiles.

Television: Communication Heard and Seen

The technology required for radio paved the way for the introduction of television. Reporting a 1927 demonstration of television by Bell Laboratories, *The New York Times* said it was "as if a photograph had suddenly come to life and begun to talk, smile, nod its head and look this way and that." The development of television was suspended during World War II. In 1947 manufacturers produced 179,000 televisions; in 1948, the number jumped to 975,000. By the 1960s, 87 percent of American households had at least one television set and in 2003, 98 percent.

Subscription-based cable television introduced more choices and "premium channels" starting in 1972. Not until the 1990s did 24-hour broadcasts become common. Today, more than half of U.S. households receive their television signal via broadband, a form of high-speed Internet access. While television long ago replaced newspapers and radio as the dominant source of news and entertainment, TV viewership appears to have stabilized even as more young Americans turn to the Internet.

Internet: High(est)-Speed Communications

The Internet has perhaps had the greatest influence on modern lives, from the way people conduct business, participate in the political process, shop, and learn about distant people and places. Using the Internet, people all over the globe can communicate via e-mail, instant messaging, blogs, and even in real time, transcending the boundaries of time and geography.

The Internet represents a media environment combining text, video, and audio. News organizations can edit and update stories instantly and augment traditional print/text stories with digitized video interviews or photo galleries for which the print edition would not have adequate space.

Internet technologies allow for "citizen-journalists" who can report or post items they believe to be interesting or newsworthy. The Internet requires users to exercise news judgment or editorial skills because they often must determine the reliability of information found online. Today, going online is a routine activity for Americans in search of news, information, entertainment, and social networking.

Technological innovations affect how you reach your audiences. The access and depth of the Internet allow a diverse audience to watch or read the content you generate, perhaps well beyond the group for which your information is intended. Prospective employers assume today's college graduates will be comfortable creating content in multiple forms—and using new technologies to send it.

The Audience Begins to Participate

Beyond growing as a source for news, the Internet also brought about changes to the types of people who published news. Technology companies, such as Yahoo! and Microsoft, became major sources of news while the audience itself began publishing all sorts of information on the Web. Using hypertext technology, individuals no longer passively consumed news—they shared it, commented on it, and added new information to it. With access to the World Wide Web, anyone could become a publisher.

Perhaps the biggest contributor to the rise in amateur journalism has been the advent of blogging tools that made it easy for people who didn't know hypertext markup language (or HTML) to create Web pages for themselves. The first widely used blogging service was created in 1999, accompanied by other self-publishing tools that made it easier for someone without technical expertise to publish photos, videos, audio, or just about any combination of media online—often for free. Technorati, a company that tracks blogs, keeps an eye on more than 112 million bloggers.

Most bloggers don't consider themselves journalists who report facts to a broad audience. Most blogs are a type of personal diary that mixes opinion and first-person accounts for a small audience of friends and family. Others, however, are tied to media companies and contain news tidbits or staff observations.

As Internet access becomes faster and more pervasive, media consumption habits will continue to change. Many news organizations in the United States are beginning to think about how people will read news and information on mobile phones and other portable devices connected wirelessly to the Internet. The boom in unedited and unverified content that appears alongside accurate information online has made it even more challenging for people to organize, sift through, and validate vast amounts of information.

Online News Is Always On

Online news values are pretty much the same as for any other medium, but the continuous nature of online news can create a new struggle between the value of immediacy and other news values, such as prominence and proximity. Newspaper writers must stop collecting and organizing information at some point so the paper can be printed and delivered. And when it's time to go on the air, even live broadcasters are forced to stop writing and editing so they can present the information to their viewers. But the Internet never goes to press, and the cameras are always rolling.

While continuous news has been around since the advent of CNN, the nature of news is a bit different online than on broadcast. Because broadcast is a linear medium—meaning its delivery of the news moves continuously and in one direction through time—currency or timeliness almost completely trumps all other news values. Small developments in a story line are given exaggerated importance—whether the time horizon of the story is one day, like a refinery fire, or more than a year, like a presidential campaign. Broadcasters who always have air to fill often fill it with repetition, speculation, and analysis. They emphasize immediacy. And they have no choice but to keep talking—about something.

Online writers, however, have a choice about whether and when to move the story forward rather than the obligation imposed by broadcasting. Most online news sites (with the notable exceptions of sites with a blog format) do not emphasize immediacy to the detriment of all other news values. Online news readers choose which stories to read, at what time of day, and in what order. This advent of on-demand news puts a larger burden on the online news writer to balance currency with proximity, prominence, and impact.

Imagine, for example, you are the daytime editor for a news Web site. It's 10 a.m., and the president has just announced a new economic stimulus package. Or the mayor has just announced she won't run for re-election. Certainly both are news, but so is the investigative piece you posted at 6 a.m. about the landfill's contamination of the local watershed. And so is the analysis piece you did of the increasing political importance of Latinos in the upcoming local election.

The two in-depth pieces had been leading the site. But what do you do now? And if you decide to lead with the breaking news, when—if ever—do you put the in-depth pieces back atop the site?

This kind of tension doesn't just happen at the macro, site-wide level. It happens at the story level as well. Do we add the latest news from the campaign trail to the lead, or do we lead with the most prominent?

These decisions have always been a challenge to some extent for wire services, but the additional uncertainty of writing for online is that editors don't know when a reader is going to come back. Newspaper editors know they will get a chance to talk to their newspaper readers tomorrow morning, at a fairly certain time. The broadcast audience will tune in at the top of the next hour. But how often is the online audience coming back? Without the answer to this question, it's tough for online writers to know whether the audience seeks incremental updates or in-depth analysis. Surveys by the Pew Internet and American Life Project indicate that members of the online news audience are slightly more likely to say they read news online for its immediacy than to say they read online news for its depth or breadth.

Online News Is On-Demand

While writers use news values in structuring content, online editors use news values to determine where to place content. Editors of a news site may place one set of stories on the homepage in the morning because they think those are the stories that are the most important for readers to see. By the end of the day, computer records often show the stories that received the most audience attention were completely different stories scattered deeper in the site. Audiences are using their news judgment to decide what to view—often in conflict with what editors think.

Readers have more tools than ever before to disregard the news judgment of editors. They use e-mail, RSS feeds, blogs, and social networking sites to "re-mix" stories from a variety of sources into a news site made just for them and perhaps a group of friends or colleagues.

Readers use their own news values to search for information, and those might differ from what journalism students learn in newswriting classes. Searching is second only to e-mailing in its frequency among all online pursuits. For example, on a day when snow threatened the suburbs near Washington, D.C., "Fairfax county public schools" was one of the most popular search terms on Google Trends. And on the day Lindsey Paulat was arrested for firing a gun in the home of Pittsburgh Steelers wideout Cedrick Wilson, her name quickly appeared as one of the most popular search terms on the Web.

With the Internet, audiences can choose what information they consume and when they consume it. TiVo and other digital video recorders have made "time-shifting" more prevalent among television audiences who literally move programs from the time a broadcaster sends it to another time that is more convenient for them to watch it.

Apple's iPod and other portable digital audio players have done the same thing for "place-shifting" news reports. National Public Radio's news reports, once available to an audience only at the top of the hour, are available anytime via NPR's podcast.

Audience behavior is affecting news judgment in at least one way. News outlets from Yahoo! to *The Washington Post* to *The News & Observer* display lists of the most read, most e-mailed, most discussed, or highest-rated news stories.

Prominently featured, these stories become self-fulfilling prophecies, driving still more readers to them.

For the editors of many sites, watching real-time consumption of news is becoming a factor that determines which stories they cover further, play higher, and explain more deeply. Popularity is becoming a more predictable element of news judgment among professional journalists.

A quick glance at social news sites such as Digg.com shows that the stories most likely to be shared by readers are stories that are remarkably original—some even too good to be true, no doubt. This fact means that, in a world where more people are reading news online, writers must work much harder to differentiate their stories from all the other similar reports across the Web. With so many choices for readers, news writers need to seek unique angles, target specific audiences, and dig deeper for uncovered facts. News values of impact, magnitude, and human interest are just as important online as in traditional media.

What's Different about Online Content

Writers have three primary advantages when they publish online.

1. Online news can be multimedia, incorporating not just text and still images, but audio, video, animation, and audience interactivity.

2. Online writing can be made more relevant, either by publishing news faster or by customizing the content of the story for specific audiences.

3. On the Web, space is virtually unlimited, so writers can explain many more details than in print. Online writers must remember, however, that the audience still has limited time, so long-format writing must be compelling from the first paragraph to the last.

Although online writers can enjoy these three benefits of the medium, professionals know that not every storytelling technique is suitable for every story. For example, a piece about new enrollment figures at the local college might include many numbers, making it appropriate for a long, explanatory text story but not necessarily video. A human interest story about a local personality, however, might warrant using video to show readers the face and behaviors of the story's subject. More and more, professional writers need to practice not just news judgment, but also media judgment—the ability to know which storytelling techniques to use for a particular story.

Multimedia Aspects

In 2007, *Washington Post* columnist Gene Weingarten won a Pulitzer Prize for a piece he wrote about the reaction of subway riders to violin virtuoso Joshua Bell. Weingarten's words won him journalism's most coveted award, but he also used *The Post's* Web site to tell the story with video—a technique that worked well because the audience could see and experience the scene Weingarten artfully described with his words. Without the words, the video would have been curious, and it would have lacked context. The words without the video would have left much to the readers' imaginations.

Just as photographs enhance stories in print, video and audio can make human subjects more compelling, and they can help readers visualize unusual scenes. Video often works well for stories dominated by the *who, what* or *how* news elements.

Weingarten's use of video allowed audiences to experience Bell playing in a subway station at any time—they didn't have to be there when it happened. Audiences could view the video on demand. But many online communicators are also streaming live video over the Internet. The White House streams its daily press briefings, and many local newspapers stream high school football games on Friday nights. Both take advantage of the medium's ability to provide immediate information.

Relevance of Online News

Online writers can also use the medium to make their stories more relevant to individual members of their audience. Perhaps one of the biggest challenges for writers in traditional media is the choice of which facts to include in the lead of a story. They must choose facts that are most compelling to a broad general audience. Online writers with some computer programming skills are beginning to look at new ways of telling stories that allow individuals to begin with information most relevant to themselves.

One example might be a story about the local housing market. In print, the lead of such a story might focus on a statistic—perhaps the average sales price or the aggregate sales volume in a market—that characterizes a broad area. But within those broad statistics are often outlying neighborhoods where home sales are bucking the trend. Online, a writer might be able to create a database so that each member of the audience could look up home sales in a specific neighborhood or the sales of homes of a certain size.

Even with this ability to customize information, the writer's job is to put the numbers in context. Understanding data without historical background, or information about an overall trend, requires more effort from the audience. Professional writers know how to make data relevant, help readers process that information, and put it in some usable form.

Another way online writers make their stories more relevant is engaging the audience in online conversation. This dialogue can take the form of a live chat, a list of reader comments on articles, or discussion boards on a general topic.

Writing in these interactive conversations with the audience can have its own style or drawbacks. On one hand, they can take a more conversational tone that inherits some style from broadcast media, such as call-in radio talk shows. Or, because the text lives forever, an awkwardly phrased sentence or inaccurate statement by a writer might give the audience the impression that the writer might not have a strong grasp of the subject or of written language. Writers in online chats must be able to think quickly and clearly on their feet.

The Components of a News Site

To understand how to produce online content, writers must know the structure and organization of Web sites. News Web sites are organized differently than a newspaper, although they have some important similarities. First, Web sites are comprised of two types of pages: index pages that guide viewers to content and the content pages. Newspapers, on the other hand, have only one kind of page that serves both purposes. The headlines that help readers find a story are found on the same page as the body of the story.

Among printed media, the structure of magazines most closely resembles the structure of news Web sites. At the front of most magazines—and on the covers of many—an index catalogues the stories found deeper in the magazine. In a print magazine, the content indexes provide some enticing information about the story and tell readers on which page the story can be found. On news Web sites, index pages also contain enticing information about stories deeper on the site. But the information about where the audience can find the story also contains the computer code the audience doesn't see to link to the specific content.

For example, the contents page of a print magazine might have this summary:

62 Parents Battle High Costs of College

This year's freshman class will take out more college loans than any group of college students in history.

The "62" before the text of the headline tells readers that the story can be found on page 62.

On the magazine's Web site, readers might see the same words but without the number 62. Instead, readers would click on the headline and activate the computer code that makes the story appear.

It is important for writers to understand how audiences use index pages differently than content pages so they can use the language (see Box 7.2) and style appropriate to each purpose. Audiences use index pages to skim quickly for information relevant to them. They often spend just a few seconds on an index page, and they rarely click on every piece of content to which items on the index page link. Writing on an index page needs to be brief and informative.

BOX 7.2   Glossary of Web Terms

Home page: the page typically encountered first at a World Wide Web site that usually contains links to the other pages of the site

Web site: a group of World Wide Web pages usually containing hyperlinks to each other and made available online by an individual, company, educational institution, government, or organization

Web page: a single page of data within a Web site, often written in HTML and ending with either ".htm" or "html"

Tag: Identifiers that go around each type of text on a page. The tags may identify links or even text as a headline, such as: <h1>News Alert: Airplane Crashes on Freeway</h1>.

Cascading Style Sheets or CSS: Another type of code that tells a computer how to display items on a screen

Homepages are a type of index page, although not all index pages are homepages. A homepage is the "top" or "front page" or the "cover" of a news Web site, and there editors place the information they most want readers to see. The homepage often is the single most-read page on a Web site.

Other kinds of index pages may be found deeper in the site and often are indexes of only one particular category of information. They can be thought of as "section front" pages or "topic" pages because they contain links to content that is all on the same topic – for example, sports, politics, or entertainment. Some index pages are very broad in their scope while some are incredibly narrow, even down to the point where they are only about a single person.

If the information shown on the index page is relevant to the audience member's needs and if it is presented well, the reader will click on the link for that story. Then he or she arrives at content pages or destination pages for the audience. There the reader will likely spend more time delving deeper into the story. Many content pages on news Web sites follow the format and style of a news story in any other medium.

Leads and Blurbs

From earlier chapters in the text, you are already familiar with the characteristics of a good lead: short, to the point, attention-getting. Such leads are essential when writing for an online audience. Online leads should be brief and full of information for several reasons:

1. Online audiences often quickly skim information and are unlikely to have the patience for any type of lead that delays presentation of the essential *who*, *what*, *when*, *where*, and *why* of the story.

2. Web publishing systems used by many professional news and information organizations often extract the lead and distribute it to index pages or even to other Web sites as a stand-alone piece of content. Leads that don't contain the essential information often seem like heads without a body.

3. Search engines scan Web pages by starting with the text at the top of the page. Online leads should contain any key words a potential reader might use to find the story. Sometimes search engines display the first few words of a story on the search results page.

When writing leads for the Web, writers should emphasize nouns over verbs and especially nouns over adjectives because people are much more likely to include nouns in their search terms. They are more likely to search for the *who*, *what*, or *where* of a story than for the *when*, *why*, or *how*.

Search engines also emphasize the traditional value of tight leads. While the average lead in a newspaper or wire service story is between 20 and 40 words, search engines often display on their results pages only the first 20 to 25 words in an article.

Writers and editors must remember that leads should be written primarily to be read by humans and only secondarily to be read by computer programs, such as search engines. But very often good techniques for search engine optimization are also good techniques for writing a more clear and concise story.

While summary leads are popular online and well-suited to the Web, they are not the only kind of summaries a writer or editor might need to write for an online story. The summary information found on index pages are called "blurbs," and they require a slightly different writing style from the style used in a summary lead.

Remember, index pages are collections of stories, and the audience quickly skims these pages. Blurbs, therefore, need to be very brief and full of information. But they should also be more evocative—or even promotional—in their tone.

For example, compare the headline and blurb on the washingtonpost.com homepage to the headline and lead on the associated story. The homepage blurb had this text:

After Iraq, the Battles Continue

Mixed martial arts star Brian Stann has a story that sells and an undefeated fighting record.

The story had this headline and lead:

The War Is Over for Stann, but the Battles Continue

Before each fight, Brian Stann walks into the cage knowing that whatever happens, nothing will compare to the hell he survived in Iraq.

While both the blurb and the lead are written to tease the reader deeper into the story, the blurb on the homepage conveys more information and has about

30 percent fewer words. The lead on the actual story doesn't tell the reader why Brian Stann is walking into a cage for a fight, but the blurb tells readers right up front that he is a mixed martial arts star. On the homepage, the word "Iraq"—a popular news topic among readers in mid-2008 when the story appeared—is prominent in the blurb's headline. In the story's lead, Iraq is saved until the end for dramatic effect. The blurb aims to draw the reader in by directly promising "a story that sells," while the lead hints at cage fights and a portrait of "hell."

Because they usually appear directly below a headline for the story, it is important that headlines and blurbs are written to work well together, avoiding redundant information where possible. Look at this headline and blurb from the homepage of NYTimes.com:

McCain Camp Says Obama Is 'Playing the Race Card'

The statement was in response to remarks Barack Obama made warning that Republicans would try to scare voters.

In this blurb, "the statement" is ambiguous without the headline. But alongside the headline, it clearly refers to the comments from McCain's presidential campaign.

Updates to Breaking News

Because of the "always on" nature of online news, information updates must be made quickly when new facts are available. When filing breaking news for the Web, it's important for writers to write a story quickly with as much information as they can verify, even if it is clear that more is coming. This pattern follows on the long tradition of broadcast news, when networks would interrupt their regularly scheduled entertainment program with short news briefs in the event of big news.

For example, a local newspaper might receive word about a shooting at a local high school. Reporters know that concerned parents who can't get through the jammed phone lines on campus will likely turn to the newspaper's or TV station's Web site for updates. It's possible that no one was injured, but it's also possible that several students were killed. A reporter working on this story for the next day's paper would want to wait to obtain the essential information before writing the lead or determining how much prominence it should be given in the next day's paper. But the interest of public safety demands that a journalist post even this cursory information online as fast as possible.

An early version of the story might be a single paragraph that includes only the *what*—that a shooting has occurred. And it may directly acknowledge which important news elements remain unknown. It might read something like this:

> Shots were fired at Central High School shortly after 11:30 a.m., according to police reports. It's unknown whether anyone was injured in the shooting or exactly where on campus it took place.

While the reporter is still waiting for more news, the story could then be fleshed out with background about Central High School or school shootings across the country. A second paragraph may look like this:

> Central High School is no stranger to violence. Last year, two students were sent to the hospital after they were stabbed in a gang-related brawl.

Later, the reporter might hear that a former student is in police custody in the shooting. Where should that information be placed in the story? Rather than add it as a third paragraph, that important information could be worked in to the lead.

> Following a shooting at Central High School this morning, police are holding a former student in custody in connection with the incident. It's unclear whether the student is a suspect, and it is also unclear whether anyone was hurt. Police reported that shots had been fired on the campus shortly after 11:30 a.m.

The story now has some information about *what, where, when* and *who* was involved. But it's far from complete. The most important information to the news site's audience will be whether anyone was injured. When the reporter receives this news, the lead will need to be rewritten entirely, perhaps like this:

> Three students were killed this morning in a shooting at Central High School. The names of the victims have not been released, but police identified them as two girls and one boy. Police are holding a former student in custody in connection with the shooting that took place shortly after 11:30 a.m.

The lead news element shifted from the *where* and the *when* used in the original lead to the *who*—albeit an incomplete version—in the latest variation of the lead.

Each of the new versions of the story replaces the previous one at the same Web address. This technique is important so that readers who found the initial story can easily come back to the same place to find updates. If each version were published at its own unique address, the audience might never know the story had changed. Most news organizations also print at the top of the page the time the story was updated so readers can gauge the currency of the information.

Each of the changes to the story has been an update. In other words, new information prompted a change in the story. This process would also follow if the death toll increased from three to four, for example. Because the Web allows for information to be changed, it is okay to publish facts that may eventually change.

Structuring Messages

Today, the limitation that writers must grapple with is the time of the reader. The online audience tends to skim news at a much faster pace than the print news audience. A reader not quickly hooked with a compelling and complete lead is a reader likely to click on to the next site.

The Inverted Pyramid Online

On the Internet, which was designed for reliability and where the space is practically unlimited, the inverted pyramid remains one of the best-suited story forms. The inverted pyramid has even become a metaphor for the structure of news sites themselves. The homepage of a news site contains the essential information about a broad range of stories, and as visitors to a site delve deeper, they gain more and more details. From the home page, a reader is likely to click to a news story. From that news story, a reader might click on one or more links to related stories from the archives, primary source documents, or other in-depth information on the topic.

Links are an important tool of online news writing, but they must be used with care. Done well, they can improve the transparency of the reporting and build the audience's trust. Done poorly, they can erode confidence in the reporting as much as any misplaced comma or misspelled word.

Incorporating links into a story allows a writer to omit nonessential details that might interest only some readers. Links can be especially helpful to readers who might be skeptical about the information in the article or to readers with immediate or deep interest in the topic.

A writer might add different types of links to a news story online:

1. Primary source documents, such as town budgets or long government reports cited in the story.

2. Audio or video of full interviews with a source quoted in the story.

3. Older news stories on the same topic.

4. Other sites that contain detailed biographical or historical material related to the story.

5. Other sites where a source may make a longer or more nuanced argument in support of a position noted briefly in the news story with a quote or paraphrase.

Any link that allows readers to examine a writer's reporting methods is a good link because it builds trust with the audience. But writers can also erode trust if they don't use links correctly. Writers who include links in their stories must be aware of two pitfalls:

1. While links to other Web sites are not explicit endorsements of the information found on those sites, they imply a level of validity from the writer to the reader. Linking to another Web site that contains false or defamatory information can tarnish the writer's reputation.

2. Broken links that lead nowhere or to the wrong page can also erode trust. If possible, writers should check their links before they are published. If that's not possible, they must verify their links as soon as possible. Such checks are part of the online editing process and are as important as checking for spelling and grammar.

Editors use two ways to link from a story. "Inline" links are made from words inside the body of the story. "Sidebar" links stand alone, often in a bulleted list, in a separate space adjacent to the story.

Inside the story, editors must choose which words to link so the audience understands where they will go when they click on the link. Here are some guidelines:

1. Link no more than three words in a row. Longer links often are difficult to read on a computer screen.
2. Choose nouns or verbs that describe the destination of the link. For example, if linking to a police report, look for the words "police report" to choose as the linked text.
3. If multiple places in the story reference the destination page, place a link only on the first reference.

When placing links adjacent to the story, here are some guidelines:

1. Write three to five descriptive words as the text of the link. Emphasize nouns and verbs, such as "action unfolds at Olympic venues."
2. Use single word descriptions to tell the reader important information about the medium or style of the destination link. For example, if the link goes to a video of the high school football game, good link text might be "Video: Friday's Game Highlights."
3. Readers have a difficult time choosing from more than three to five links. If your news organization has thousands of archival stories on a topic, don't link to all of them from the space adjacent to the story. It is better to place a long collection of links on a separate page.

The Blog Format

Starting in 1999 with the widespread adoption of the first Web-based, free publishing system called Blogger, the Web has exploded with sites laid out in the blog format. Blogs—short for "Web logs"—grew in popularity first as a tool for amateur diarists to publish text to the Web without the need to know HTML code.

Since then, some of those bloggers have become semi-professional or full-time professionals as diarists, commentators, or even news-breaking reporters in every niche category imaginable. Blogs are now stand-alone columns or even attached to local news. Thus the format has become widely adopted at traditional news organizations like *The Washington Post* and *The New York Times*, where editors once shunned it. Most bloggers, however, are amateurs who do not consider themselves journalists, do not adhere to a tradition of professional ethics, and do not write for a general audience.

Blogs generally have these characteristics:

1. A blog consists of "posts," which can be of varying length. Posts, like news stories or articles, are about a single topic or event. But unlike articles or news stories, they do not necessarily follow the same inverted pyramid structure.

2. Posts are laid out vertically on a blog's homepage in reverse chronological order. The most recent post is at the top of the page and the oldest at the bottom.

3. Professional news blogs are almost always on a single topic. In newsrooms, those topics often are called "beats." Music, schools, parenting, technology, politics, a certain sports team, or a specific television show are all common topics for a blog.

From these basic similarities, blogs can take on all sorts of optional forms. They can be filled with straight news or pure commentary and often are a mixture of both. They might contain dozens of participants' views on an event, such as the hometown supporters who attended the 2008 Olympics. Many allow their readers to comment on each post. Most are written by a single author, but many news blogs have several reporters who post to them. Most bloggers make prolific use of links within their posts to footnote their commentary or to demonstrate transparency by allowing readers to view original source material.

Because of their layout that places the most recent post at the top of the page, blogs are good tools to use for breaking news situations. When a gunman killed 32 people and himself at Virginia Tech University in Blacksburg, Virginia, in 2007, student journalists on that campus and professional reporters at the nearby *Roanoke Times* both turned to a blog format to publish breaking news updates to the Web.

Here are the first four updates on the shooting from *The Roanoke Times*. Note how the newer posts at the top avoid repeating information in older posts—this aspect of the blog format makes it different from updating a breaking news story written in a traditional, inverted pyramid style.

11:53 a.m.

Scott Hendricks, an associate professor of engineering science and mechanics, said he was on Norris Hall's third floor this morning around 9:45. "I started hearing some banging and some shots, then I saw a student crawling on the ground."

Hendricks said he was not sure if he saw any of the casualties, but "I saw a bloody T-shirt."

Hendricks said he went into a classroom with students, closed the door and waited until things were quiet before leaving the building.

11:49 a.m.

The Associated Press is reporting eight to nine casualties, attributing the information to an unnamed official source.

Virginia Tech's Newman Library became a shelter as university staff urged students and passersby to come in from the sidewalk. Library staff estimated that hundreds of people are in the building now, far more than would be usual at this time of day.

Sarah Ulmer, a freshman from Covington, sat on the floor and recounted how she'd been walking between buildings this morning when she saw police officers near McBryde and Norris halls.

"The police said, 'Get out of the way, get out of the way,' and then they said 'Run,'" Ulmer said. She couldn't return to her dorm room in East Ambler Johnson hall because it was near one of the shooting sites, so she headed toward Newman.

"I figured it was safe," she said. "It was the library."

Watching police from the library's fourth-floor windows, David Russell, a sophomore from Montgomery County, Md., echoed a common sentiment, comparing today's events to last year's manhunt for accused murderer William Morva.

"This year with Morva, the bomb threats and this now, it's crazy. It's not really what you'd expect from a small farm school."

Updated: 11:06 a.m.

The Associated Press is reporting there is at least one person dead as a result of multiple shootings on the Virginia Tech campus this morning. Wounded have been removed from buildings. Tech student Steve Hanson was working in a lab in Norris Hall at 10:15 a.m. when he heard what he thought was loud banging from construction. Hanson was soon scrambling out of the building and he said he saw one person who was shot in the arm. At Pritchard Hall, a dormitory near one of the shooting sites, students were being pulled into the buildings and told to stay away from windows and off the phone.

Updated: 10:17 a.m.

Multiple shootings have occurred at Virginia Tech this morning involving multiple victims. The second shooting happened in Norris Hall, the engineering building near Burruss Hall. Police are on the scene and rescue workers have set up a temporary treatment facility. The campus is on lock down. All classes and activities have been cancelled for the day.

Montgomery County public schools are all on lock down. In Blacksburg, no one is being allowed in any school building without approval by the school administrators, said Superintendent Tiffany Anderson.

The university has posted a notice of the incident on its Web site and is urging the university community to be cautious and contact Virginia Tech police at 231-6411 if they notice anything suspicious. No further details were available. The Roanoke Times will update with new information as it becomes available.

Ryan Teague Beckwith, a political reporter who writes the "Under the Dome" blog for *The News & Observer* in Raleigh, North Carolina, also uses this format to update fast-moving stories. But his writing style is more similar to the style audiences might find commonly used by news or sports columnists in a newspaper. In a word, the style is more "conversational" and less formal in its adherence to grammar and more likely to include subjective adjectives like "finally" or "only." Despite these differences in style, verified factual reporting remains the driving force behind his posts. An example of how he covered a tussle in 2008 between the John Edwards presidential campaign and a journalism student at the University of North Carolina can be found at http://projects.newsobserver.com/tags/carla_babb.

It is important for professional communicators to remember that blogging is merely a format, just as the inverted pyramid is just a format. Blogs can be filled with any sort of content—truth, lies, opinion, gossip. Anyone who wants his or her blog to be broadly read and respected must adhere to high standards of accuracy, but writers who are considering using a blog as a source in a news story must remember that many people do not adhere to those standards.

Correcting Online Copy

Because the stories live online long past the time when the story is news, it is also important to correct quickly, permanently, and transparently any error of fact that might make its way into publication. What happens if a reporter has to change a story because a fact is wrong? That is when it is essential to print a correction.

Perhaps the reporter misunderstood the police department spokesman who told her the gender of the victims. Or perhaps the spokesman got it wrong himself. The story of the text must be corrected, and the correction must be clearly described elsewhere on the page. Without a description of the correction, a reader who returns to the story might see the changed information and become confused about whether the old information or the new information is accurate.

Both *The Washington Post* and ESPN, among other news sites, keep collections of the corrections they run in all media. For current examples of the wording of online corrections, you can type either "washingtonpost.com corrections" or "ESPN corrections" into a search engine.

Corrections need not always be formal. Some opinion columnists and bloggers use a more informal tone to alert readers to their errors. For example, *U.S. News & World Report* columnist Michael Barone posted this correction to his blog in 2005:

> In my August 25 post I made a mistake.
>
> *Austin Bay, syndicated columnist, novelist, blogger, and reserve Army colonel who has served in Iraq, is always worth reading. Here, in response to a challenge by blogger Jeff Jarvis, he argues that the Bush administration should try to engage the mainstream media, despite its bias and hostility, rather than engage in what he and Jarvis agree is a policy of "rollback."*
>
> The blogger I cited was not Jeff Jarvis, of www.buzzmachine.com, but Jay Rosen, of New York University. Since I linked to the correct post, many readers

may well have caught the error and therefore were not materially misled. Still, I'm sorry for the sloppiness, and I apologize to Jay Rosen and to Jeff Jarvis. In his courteous E-mail pointing out my mistake, Rosen notes that many people confuse him and Jarvis and wonders why. My reply was that both have first names starting with J and both seem (to me anyway) to specialize in intelligent press criticism not from a right-of-center perspective—a small category, I think.

Regardless of the tone, placement, or content of corrections, professional writers aim to make them rare. Errors of style, grammar, or fact compromise the trust a writer has established with the audience.

Professional writers should never report information that has not been vetted and verified as fact. Unconfirmed rumors—even those from a usually reliable source—have no place in news writing in any medium.

Challenges and Opportunities

The Internet—and other emerging digital and networked communication tools—are changing the way we share stories about the world in which we live. Writers in all media must be aware of the threats and opportunities that new media present to traditional formats and rules of news.

Perhaps one of the biggest changes is the rush of new publishers to the Internet, from personal diarists to technology companies that have no tradition of journalistic ethics or values. In a world where publishing information is easy, a writer's message must be heard among the chatter and clutter.

Influences to Monitor

Because of the proliferation challenge, news writers might begin to cater their efforts to the audiences' behavior in an attempt to predict the audiences' interests and tell stories that meet those interests. But audiences will always have a need for unexpected news and information. After all, oddity is an important news value. Good writers will need to find ways to bring new information before audience members who increasingly filter out information they consider irrelevant or uninteresting. New information, new ideas, and new voices are needed to provide democracy with constant rejuvenation.

Some professional communicators are also concerned about an emerging "digital divide" between people who use new communication technologies and people who continue to rely on traditional media. While home computers, broadband Internet access, and mobile phone use has exploded over the last decade, many Americans cannot afford the latest gadgets. When considering their audiences, writers need to decide whether they want to reach a broad audience or only the most sophisticated and affluent people.

As technology develops and use expands, today's media world remains somewhat of a Wild West in terms of ethics and values. Writers must proceed with caution in adopting each new information format so they don't unwittingly violate audience trust. Standards and expectations—and sometimes the laws—of privacy, transparency, and professionalism continue to change not only in the United States, but in cultures around the world that have the same access to a small-town newspaper Web site as town residents. Most immediately, news writers today face increased pressure to publish information quickly, sometimes at the potential expense of accuracy.

Media companies have had to consider their liability when readers post story comments directly to the news site. Some postings contain language considered by some to be offensive, vulgar, or profane. While federal law protects online sites from libel in such postings and readers are encouraged to respond, media managers on occasion have opted to shut down and prevent postings, but more for ethical than for legal considerations.

The way writing reaches audiences—literally—through new delivery outlets is also changing. While newsstands and street-corner vendors or living room television sets and cinema newsreels might have been familiar forms of media distribution in the past, the future may be dominated by search engines like Google, online service portals like Yahoo! and MSN, or even hybrid content delivery companies like Apple's iTunes or Amazon.com.

This change in the distribution system of news and information is also changing the business models of many traditional news media companies that behaved according to a long-established standard of ethics and values. Will writers pay to have their articles displayed on popular locations? Will Web sites or mobile phones pay to make unique news and information available exclusively to their audiences? Will telecommunications companies that provide Internet access begin to sell advertising? Will advertisers that used to pay for placement in newspapers and on broadcast stations start paying for placement across a network of amateur blogs? Will readers who want high quality information start paying premium prices for immediate or customized news alerts? All of these changes to the media economy may affect writing styles of future news professionals.

Audience Consumers and Producers

New media provide many new opportunities for writers to make their work relevant and memorable to audiences. As more and more Americans work at desks with computers connected to the Internet, the daytime audience for news has grown remarkably over the last decade. Newspapers and broadcast shows that could reach audiences only once a day now can deliver important information to people all day long.

Breaking news throughout the day is training the news audience to demand more relevant information. They are using databases, search engines, and complex algorithms to find only the stories most relevant to them. For example, people suffering from a rare disease don't need to wait for a new study or drug trial to put that disease in the news. They now can quickly turn to specialty Web sites at any time to see the latest information from the Centers for Disease Control and Prevention or from the American Medical Association.

And it's not just official government or industry sources from which people are seeking on-demand information. They are also turning to each other, and professional communicators are just now learning how to engage with their audience in a conversation that leads to more relevant and enlightening news.

In some cases, news writers are turning to their audience to help them find new information and write more complete reports. As professional news organizations employ fewer reporters, the reporters are asking the audience for help sorting through vast amounts of data—such as campaign finance reports—and helping them be their eyes and ears, watching for everything from potholes on neighborhood streets to drink specials at the local bar.

Many of the best opportunities for writers are probably yet to be imagined, but professional communicators of the future will need to remain alert for new ways to reach audiences with the same high standards of accuracy, completeness, transparency, and relevancy that have won audience trust in traditional media. The rapid changes in communication technology seem likely to increase the pace and broaden the scope of these challenges. However, if history is any guide, writers who remain committed to providing precise and concise information to their audiences will surf the waves of change most successfully.

Exercises

1. Compare the news articles on the front page of a national newspaper's Web site with the news articles on the front page of Digg.com and the front page of a national television news site. Which news values are most commonly reflected in each site's story choices? Why might that be the case?

2. As a writer with a story to share with the world, how would you use social news sites?

3. Look at search trends and social news sites. Compare the stories to those found on a traditional news site. Write a story proposal for your editor about a potential article you could write. Base the idea on your survey of the search and social sites. What news values are found in your story pitch?

4. You are an online editor for your newspaper's Web site. You have the following lead from the print edition. Write a blurb for the home page. Then rewrite the lead so the important keywords would appear in the first 20–25 words in the online story.

> When Carmen Alvarez planned her Christmas decorating, she knew she wanted to string lights across the front of her two-story house. She bought icicle-type lights on sale, then last Saturday morning she hauled the family's ladder out of the garage, set it against the wall by the front porch and began to climb. As she reached the fifth step, the ladder collapsed. Alvarez fell on the concrete front porch steps, broke her collar bone and suffered an upper-back injury. Her 12-year-old son heard her scream and called 911.
>
> Alvarez's accident is quite common. More than 500,000 ladder-related injuries are reported each year, and about 500 people die. Organizations, such as the American Academy of Orthopaedic Surgeons, publish information about how to inspect ladders and do home chores without injury. They sponsor a program called "Climb It Safe."

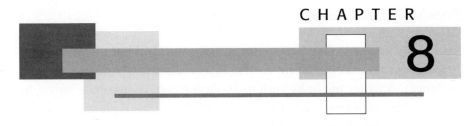

Beyond Breaking News

Media messages are written for many reasons: Some messages break urgent news stories or give consumer information; some explore newsworthy personalities or places; others present opinion, analysis, or criticism. The reason or purpose of a message can determine the format. A story about a hotel fire, for example, will use a different format and tone from a profile of an award-winning teacher.

Each day audiences find a range of stories in their favorite newspapers, magazines, online sites, or television shows. Writers might follow one of the organizational formats outlined in Chapter 6 or develop a combination that works for the specific piece they are writing. For example, a breaking news story will have a summary lead, background, and chronology. Consumer stories might use an anecdotal lead followed by specific tips. What works for a bank robbery will be inadequate for longer pieces that must communicate more complex information.

Entire textbooks have been written on how to research and construct specific story types, such as features. Web sites such as www.poynter.com and publications of journalism organizations also give tips. No basic text can cover in depth all story types and how to write them. Beyond breaking news, among the more common story types that writers develop are features, obituaries, and speech stories.

In this chapter, you will learn

- the difference between features and news,
- feature leads and organizational formats,
- the parts and style of obituaries, and
- the basics of writing speech stories.

News versus Feature

Apart from breaking news, most articles today are news-features or features. Features can be developed on any subject for any reason and inform or entertain audiences. A writer might be curious about the craft of making a basket he bought while on vacation in Charleston, South Carolina, or the sudden sound of cicadas around his home at night.

Increased reports of domestic violence might prompt a reporter to write a lengthy article on one woman's recovery. Just as with any story, features must be complete, clear, accurate, and fair. Some features will be more concise than others. Features use quotes and adequate attribution, and they mix indirect with direct quotes. Features carry the same news values as news stories—prominence, conflict, oddity, proximity, and especially human interest.

Traditionally, writers have used one value to distinguish news from features: timeliness. Features have a timeless quality. They can be published at any time and remain useful and entertaining. News, however, must be printed immediately. The death of a nationally known fashion designer is news; a story about fashions is a feature. In sum, *news tells*, a *feature shows*.

Some features, however, are linked to news stories. When actor Heath Ledger died, related or sidebar stories focused on abuse of prescription sedatives and antidepressants and the dangers of combining such drugs in potentially lethal quantities. Such sidebar stories can stand alone, that is, they are complete stories themselves but have been written because of a news event.

Adding the Visual

To the traditional distinction of timeliness, writers must add another consideration: How much did the reader see? In other words, did the story take the reader to the scene? Did the writer make the reader feel he or she was there? It has been said that journalism becomes literature when it tells the reader not just what happened but what it was like. Erik Lawson wrote in *Isaac's Storm*, his book on the hurricane that struck Galveston, Texas, in 1900:

> *The wind neatly sliced off the top floor of a bank, leaving the rest of the building intact. It stripped slate shingles from houses and turned them into scimitars that disemboweled men where they stood. Atmospheric pressure fell so low, a visiting British cotton official was sucked from his apartment trailing a slipstream of screams from his wife.*

More than 100 years later, feature writing must still carry the visual impact. Because electronic media more and more have assumed the role of breaking news, newspapers and magazines have taken on a visual aspect seen in more description, in analogies and metaphors, and in more explanation or analysis. The feature story's job is to flesh out the headline and to provide the substance and follow-up—even with the magnitude of a news story like Hurricane Katrina.

Feature stories that appear in a newspaper might also appear on the newspaper's Web site. Because of the multimedia capability of the Internet, an editor could add to the text a slide show with a voiceover or a video where readers see the person and hear her voice during the interview. Additional information might list, for example, agencies that work with battered spouses or the phone numbers for the state's Congressional delegation. Television stations also refer viewers to their Web sites for more detailed information on feature spots.

At the heart of today's feature writing is what Gene Roberts, retired executive editor of *The Philadelphia Inquirer* and managing editor of *The New York Times*, expected of his writers. His expectations are aptly described in the text for the Eugene L. Roberts Prize awarded to qualifying students at the School of Journalism and Mass Communication at the University of North Carolina at Chapel Hill:

> The Eugene L. Roberts Prize is meant to encourage and is dedicated to
> the story of the untold event that oozes instead of breaks; to the story that
> reveals, not repeats; to the reporter who zigs instead of zags; to
> the truth as opposed to the facts; to the forest, not just the trees; to
> the story they'll be talking about in the coffee shop on Main Street;
> to the story that answers not just who, what, where, when and why,
> but also "So what?"; to efforts at portraying real life itself; to journalism
> that "wakes me up and makes me see"; to the revival of the
> disappearing storyteller.

The "so what" aspect that Roberts notes is critical for any feature writing. Just as in news stories, many features have a nut graph or news peg. Readers need to know why the story has been written. As noted in Chapter 6, the nut graph might be found after five or six graphs. In a feature story, readers might have to look a little longer, but the nut graph should be clear. Consider this lead from *The Seattle Times:*

> Sally Garcia, a 53-year-old lawyer disabled by multiple sclerosis, was torn.
>
> A new-generation medication, Copaxone, was really working for her. After two decades of being in and out of hospitals, Garcia was taking steps to work again.
>
> Her wallet, though, was in severe distress. Under her Medicare prescription plan, Garcia's share of the expensive drug was $330 per month. All together, medications were taking a third of her disability payments—her only income—and she couldn't swing it.
>
> Copaxone, Enbrel, Remicade: For some patients, such new-generation drugs, often called "biologicals" or "bioengineered" when they are created by genetically modified living cells, have performed magic. In some cases, they work when other drugs have failed, or for diseases that previously had no drug treatments at all.
>
> But they cost a lot—often $2,000 to $3,000 per month.
>
> And in a double whammy, some insured patients who previously paid a fixed amount—likely $30 to $50 even for the most expensive, brand-name drugs—are suddenly finding the rules have changed.

Health reporter Carol M. Ostrom uses an anecdotal lead to set up the story. The fourth graph is the nut graph where readers begin to learn the point of the story: Bioengineered drugs are helping many people. But then graphs 5 and 6 complete the point: These wonder drugs are also priced beyond what many people can afford and what insurance companies will pay.

Writing the Feature Lead

Lead types covered in Chapter 5 apply to writing features. Writers have the freedom to use direct address, descriptive, question, or other leads to attract readers to stories. For example, reporters writing stories in advance of the state fair might lead with:

> Come one, come all, to this year's state fair.

Or:

> Food. Rides. Ribbons. Pigs.
>
> That's what brings Martha Bryson to the state fair each year.

Or:

> For Matt Rutger, vacation is 10 days at the state fair where he has operated his family's foot-long hot dog stand for 20 years.

Whether topics are light or serious, most features do not use summary leads in the same way news stories do. A summary lead might be used in a sidebar or supplementary story in a package of feature stories. Rather than the straightforward *who-what-when-where* news summary format, the summary feature lead might tally reaction in an informal poll or synthesize data. For example, a story that uses an anecdotal lead to introduce an economic story about downsizing of the furniture-building industry in the state might have a sidebar story giving the latest unemployment figures and trend data. The lead might read:

> The state's unemployment rate reached 6.2 percent in June, its highest since August 2004, according to statistics released today by the state office that tracks such data.

The lead summarizes other economic woes in the state.

Probably the most common leads for feature stories are descriptive and anecdotal. Many news-features use those lead types to set up stories grounded in a news event. When reporters use an anecdotal lead, they must remember to carry that example throughout the story. For example, if a campus reporter writes a news-feature about the increased cost of textbooks, she might use one student's experience as a lead into the story. The body of the feature would cover the increased costs, why textbook prices are going up, what percentage the campus bookstore gets, and comments from the student in the lead, as well as from other students. The end of the story would use a quote from the student introduced in the lead.

The Wall Street Journal has utilized this approach to the point that it is often called *Wall Street Journal* style. It takes the reader through the hard facts of the story—the background, analysis, and details that form its hard core—but focuses on an individual, a project, or a family. Look for the features on the *Journal's* front page to study this writing style.

Feature Formats

No single format defines a feature story. A feature might be as simple as the local reaction to a well-known high school athlete's death: A summary lead followed by a unified telling of family members' and school friends' recollections. Or, some reporters might spend months investigating and writing a series of articles to run in a one-day package or be spread out over several days.

Most writers agree that a feature has a beginning, a middle, and an end. Within that framework, a writer uses description, quotes, unifying elements, and tone to pull readers through the story. Narrative devices, such as suspense and action, can also capture readers.

The purpose and content of a feature story might dictate a format. For example, a how-to feature on improving study habits will describe why study habits are important, then outline where to study, when to study, how to organize notes, how to review, and how to gauge success. A feature on reducing the risk of heart attack might begin with an anecdotal lead, focusing on a heart attack survivor, then outline in a mapped format three criteria—lack of exercise, poor diet, and smoking. A story on a retiring faculty member might use chronology as a primary format for chronicling the teacher's career.

Feature Organization

Writers often look for fresh ways to portray a subject covered time and time again. At the retirement of a living-legend baseball star, a writer assigned to the story with a horde of other reporters noticed the star's wife standing several feet behind him, and to the side. The writer told the story through her reaction to the tributes offered to her husband and his farewell words. At a routine story of children going off to camp, a writer noticed that one child's parents had a hard time saying goodbye; they'd kiss the child, send him off toward the bus, then call him back…again…and again…and again. The writer told the story from that family's perspective.

Writing formats change. Newspaper reporters, for example, have adopted more narrative styles of writing, using anecdotal and descriptive approaches. Some editors believe that style attracts more readers; others say the style will pass. Time will be the test of whether new formats attract and retain audiences.

Types of Features

As noted earlier, feature stories are written simply to entertain or inform, standing on their own or complementing news stories. While feature stories contain similar elements, such as description and quotes, they sometimes can be classified by type.

- **How-to** features are included among consumer features that instruct readers or viewers. Experts give tips on topics ranging from how to build a coffee table, make strawberry jelly, find day care, or get a date. Stories should include additional resources and step-by-step guidelines. The story might use bullets to list information, such as specific ingredients and where to buy them for a specialty recipe.

- **Personality** stories can be two- to three-page pieces that focus on one aspect of an individual's life or a 60-inch profile that gives an in-depth look at a person. For example, when the president presents a Cabinet or U.S. Supreme Court nominee, the media will write extensive profiles on the individual's professional—and sometimes personal—career.

- **Historical** features recount events in an earlier time. Often, the anniversaries of events, such as the Battle of Gettysburg, generate such features. When the Discovery shuttle was launched after more than a two-year hiatus, historical features gave an overview of the U.S. space program. Researching these stories might mean looking at archives and other historical records as well as getting oral histories from people who remember.

- **Place or travel** features tell readers or viewers what they will find at a particular destination. Such stories can also be how-to articles, containing information about where to stay or eat and what to see. Detailed description sets the scene so audiences can see the place in their minds—beyond the accompanying photos or other visuals—and be enticed to visit. As a note, most publications will not publish a travel feature if the writer has had his or her expenses paid by a business or group.

- **Color** features are just that: They describe in great detail a colorful event. For example, a reporter assigned to cover a street festival would use language and description that relate to all the senses: sound, taste, smell, touch, and sight. Writers must be careful to use original and fresh description and avoid clichés or superficial language.

- **Brights** are often news stories that can be a short news-feature, generally no longer than six to seven paragraphs and with a twist at the end. Such stories must be well crafted and succinct. Consider this bright, including the end quote, from the Associated Press:

SHANGHAI, China—These pigs run, jump and swim—almost anything but fly. Thousands of Shanghai residents turned out to a city park to watch a herd of pigs compete in what organizers are calling the Pig Olympics.

They run over hurdles, jump through hoops, dive and swim in shows twice a day, according to the Shanghai Daily newspaper.

The pigs, a midget species from Thailand, begin training soon after birth and can start performing after they are 12 months old.

"These lovely pigs are a special species that is good at sports by nature," said Yang Ying, a manager with promoters Bluesea Broadway Co. Ltd.

Pig races are common in many places, but heavily urban Shanghai offers few opportunities to see farm animals in action.

"It's incredible," said 8-year-old Tan Yizhou, who presented a gold medal to one of the winning pigs. "I never thought that a pig could be so clever."*

Putting It Together

Look at this feature by Associated Press writer Kathleen Hennessey. Her story has all the attributes of good feature writing: quotes, description, prominent characters, suspense, and humor. She uses simple language and varies sentence types.

LAS VEGAS—Tempest Storm is fuming. Her fingers tremble with frustration. They are aged, knotted by arthritis and speckled with purple spots under paper-thin skin.

*Copyright 2005 The Associated Press. Reprinted with permission.

But the manicure of orange polish is flawless and matches her signature tousled mane.

She brushes orange curls out of her face as she explains how she's been slighted.

She is the headliner, you know. She is a star. She is classy.

"I don't just get up there and rip my clothes off," she says.

Indeed, the 80-year-old burlesque queen takes her clothes off very slowly.

More than 50 years ago, she was dubbed the "Girl with the Fabulous Front" and told by famous men she had the "Best Two Props in Hollywood." Since then, Storm saw the art that made her famous on the brink of extinction. Her contemporaries—Blaze Starr, Bettie Page, Lili St. Cyr—have died or hung up the pasties.

But not Storm. She kept performing. Las Vegas, Reno, Palm Springs, Miami, Carnegie Hall.

Her act is a time capsule. She knows nothing of poles. She would never put her derriere in some man's face. Her prop of choice is a boa, perhaps the occasional divan.

It takes four numbers, she says adamantly, four numbers to get it all off. To do it classy.

But the producers of tonight's show, just kids, they want her to go faster. She gets just seven minutes.

They gave her trouble last year, too. They even cut her music before she finished.

There may not be a next time for this show, she says. The threat lasts just minutes.

"No, no. I'm not ready to hang up my G-string, yet. I've got too many fans that would be disappointed."

Famous friends

Stardom and fandom feature prominently in Tempest Storm's life—and in her neat, two-bedroom Las Vegas apartment.

Visitors are greeted by photos of a young Elvis, her favorite rock 'n' roller and, she says, a former lover.

The relationship ended after about a year because Elvis' manager didn't approve of him dating a stripper, she says.

But she could not change who she was. Stripping already had made her famous.

It put her in the room with Hollywood's heavyweights. Frank Sinatra, Dean Martin, Mickey Rooney, Nat King Cole.

She dated some, just danced for others. The evidence is framed and displayed on tables and the living room wall.

That's Storm and Vic Damone. Storm teaching Walter Cronkite to dance. Storm and her fourth and last husband, Herb Jefferies, a star of black cowboy films who swept her off her feet in 1957 when such unions were instant scandals. They divorced in 1970.

"When I look at this picture I say, 'What…happened between this gorgeous couple?'" she says.

Storm is rarely wistful. She has no doubt she still is what she once was. Although she performs just a handful of times a year, she would do more, if asked. She chides those who think age takes a toll on sex appeal.

"Ridiculous," she says.

There are just as many recent photos in the room: Storm and her daughter, a nurse in Indiana. Storm and her fiance, who died a few years ago. Storm and a beaming older gentlemen, just a fan who approached her for a photograph.

"That stage saved me," she says as she leaves a sound check hours before the night's performance.

She had been expecting a much smaller space, and she is relieved. She's a "walker," she explains. She needs room to move.

It is a direct and once-racy style, the signature work of Lillian Hunt, the choreographer at the Follies Theater in Los Angeles where Storm became a star.

She was Annie Blanche Banks then. The 22-year-old sharecropper's daughter had fled sexual abuse, two loveless marriages and poverty in small-town Georgia, she says.

She was working as a cocktail waitress but wanted to be a showgirl. First, she needed her teeth fixed.

"Do you think my bust is too big for this business?" she asked Hunt at her audition.

Hunt put her in the chorus line, told her not to gain a pound and called a dentist.

In Storm's telling, she didn't stay long in the background. She got a new name. ("I really don't feel like a Sunny Day.") She took to the spotlight quickly.

No reason to stop

On Sundays, Storm tunes in to a televangelist who tells her anyone can overcome odds. It's the only religion she's ever taken to.

She believes this is the lesson of her life. Be a survivor. Never stop doing what you love; it makes you who you are.

"If you want to get old, you'll get old," she says.

There have been men who disappointed her, financial strain, brain surgery.

After it all, she sits on her couch and exercises in front of the television on a small stationary bike. She doesn't smoke or drink or eat much.

"I'm just blessed, I think. And I know when to push myself away from the table."

If some might see all this as chasing after lost youth, she says she cares little. Younger dancers tell her she is an inspiration to them, and she has no reason not to believe them.

"I feel good about myself. And I enjoy it," she says. "I have fun when I'm on-stage, and the audience loves it. Nobody ever said it's time to give it up. Why stop?"*

Obituaries

When people die, reports of their deaths usually appear in local media. Those stories, called obituaries, often are among the most-read articles in the paper. They chronicle an individual's life and follow a specific format set by the particular medium. Obituaries generally are two types: news obituaries or paid death notices. The news obituary is written by a member of the news

*Copyright 2008 The Associated Press. Reprinted with permission.

staff and published in a news section. The paid death notice is handled by the advertising department, might appear in a smaller type size than news columns, and can be written by a family member. Media publish obituaries, whether news or paid, in specific locations familiar to audiences.

Major media, such as *The New York Times*, have obituary files on prominent individuals as do the major news wire services, such as the Associated Press. Background information, photos, and even articles are stored, ready if the person dies unexpectedly—or not. When U.S. Sen. Jesse Helms died in 2008, the media were prepared. They had known he was ailing and had compiled extensive material. Along with the main news story reporting his death and funeral services, media included articles on his political career, a history of his votes in Congress that earned him the nickname "Senator No," and stories on his family. Biographical material was ready even for younger celebrities, such as actor Bernie Mac who died at age 50 and songwriter-singer Isaac Hayes at age 65. Media were able to produce complete reports of each man's careers within hours of the news he had died.

Basic Information

Obituaries contain the news elements and the résumé of an individual. Each obituary should note the complete name of who died, when he or she died, where, how, and why. (The "what" is that the individual died.) "How" someone died, such as unusual or tragic circumstances, might make that death a news story, such as a teen mauled by a tiger. Often why a person died will not be revealed based on the family's request. In the 1990s, media grappled with reporting that a person died from complications of AIDS. That cause of death is now included. Many media do not include the cause of violent death unless it can be attributed to a medical examiner, particularly in the case of a suicide.

Obituaries also outline a person's life, particularly career details, accomplishments, contributions, volunteer work, organizational membership, or other personal information. For a prominent individual, a reporter might interview coworkers, family members, or others to have quotes in the obituary. Clips from speeches or other appearances might be included. The notice will also list funeral arrangements, visitations, survivors, and where to send memorials or contributions.

For survivors, immediate family members are included. Ex-husbands and ex-wives are not, unless you are writing an obituary of someone who has had a number of spouses. Their names would be part of that person's life story.

Funeral homes provide most information for obituaries. Some media will not accept obituary information from family members. People have played practical jokes on friends by placing a death notice when the person turned 40 or 50 years old. Reporters who are writing news obituaries will get information from résumés, place of employment, interviews, biographical sources, the Internet, and government documents. For obituaries written in advance of a person's death, an interview with the individual might make up part of the file.

Accuracy is critical in obituaries. Often families cut out obituaries and keep them with family records or in a family Bible. In a time of mourning, a family's sadness and stress increase when an obituary reports the wrong age or misspells a name. In compiling information, reporters must ensure the information is correct. They should get the birth date and calculate the person's age. Pitfalls of research are discussed in Chapter 9.

Format and Structure

Each media outlet has a format it uses for writing obituaries. For example, the obit might simply state:

> Kevin D. Smith, 33, New Orleans, Saturday. Funeral: 10 a.m., Tuesday, Jones Funeral Home. Surviving: wife, Katherine; children, Thomas, Renee, Gretchen of the home.

In paid death notices, the family pays according to the length, generally measured in column inches. The family can write the notice as long as it wants, including such detail as the person's parents and grandparents, career path, organizational membership, even personal information, and where to send memorials.

In a news obituary lead, a writer would focus on *who*, *what*, *when*, and *where*, along with *what* the individual is known for, such as a professional career or volunteer efforts. Consider this Associated Press lead when Isaac Hayes died:

> Isaac Hayes, the baldheaded, baritone-voiced soul crooner who laid the groundwork for disco and whose "Theme From Shaft" won both Academy and Grammy awards, died Sunday afternoon after he collapsed near a treadmill, authorities said. He was 65.

A dateline would tell where the person died, but where the person lives should be included as in this lead from *The New York Times:*

> Dr. Michael E. DeBakey, whose innovative heart and blood vessel operations made him one of the most influential doctors in the United States, died Friday night in Houston, where he lived. He was 99.

From the leads, readers learn *who* died, *when, where,* and *why* they will be remembered. The body of the obituary will put the events of the person's life in order, usually chronologically. The general format for obituaries is the lead, contributions, career and life, survivors, funeral services, and memorials or donations. Norma Sosa, a former obituary writer for *The New York Times,* notes that the *Times* follows a specific format that has a kicker, when appropriate, as the last paragraph. She says:

> *Use a quote or anecdote that you feel reflects a stand-out aspect of a person's life, views, work, or contribution. It's the thought that remains in the reader's mind—what you, the researcher and writer, felt was the single most important or interesting thing you learned about the person. It could be something counter-intuitive, funny, sad, surprising, or poignant.*

Sometimes quotes from the individual as well as others can tell the story, as in the CNN obituary on former press secretary Tony Snow, who died as a result of colon cancer in 2008. Snow told reporters shortly after he was diagnosed: "Not everybody will survive cancer, but on the other hand, you have got to realize you've got the gift of life, so make the most of it. That is my view, and I'm going to make the most of my time with you."

The CNN obituary quoted President Bush: "The Snow family has lost a beloved husband and father. And America has lost a devoted public servant and a man of character."

The CNN story on Snow's death exhibited the depth the online format has in reporting. Links throughout the article took readers to gallery comments from politicians and journalists, to information about cancer, to video clips of Snow, and to a page where people could leave remembrances.

Speech Stories

Writing speech stories presents challenges to note taking and organization. Taking notes during a speech is much more difficult than during an interview. In an interview, you can ask an interviewee to wait a few seconds while you fill in your notes. During a speech, you cannot stop the speaker; you have to keep up with what he or she is saying.

Taking notes during a speech, however, is somewhat like taking notes for a professor's lecture: You want to have as much material to study as possible, and you may have the opportunity to ask a clarifying question after the lecture is over. You may find that developing a shorthand is the easiest and fastest way to get complete notes.

Also, when the speaker is telling a joke or an anecdote, use this time to review your notes and to complete sentences. Put quotation marks around remarks you know can be used as direct quotes—this tip helps when writing the story.

Good note taking means listening carefully to what speakers say. Ears can deceive. Consider the following errors made when writers did not listen carefully and then did not think when writing the story.

"Bureaucrats are never seizing in their efforts to keep information from the public," he said.

The speaker actually said "ceasing" not "seizing."

"Having a big hearth has nothing to do with how big your wallet is," said Mrs. Bush.

She actually said "heart" not "hearth."

"The creation of new toxic dumb sites has all but been eliminated," Browner said.

She really said "dump," not "dumb" sites.

She saluted American industry, small business, schools, and American citizens for banning together to solve the country's environmental problems.

The speaker said "banding" not "banning."

> People in countries have "the need to create extinct, stable governments," he said.

The speaker said "distinct," not "extinct."

> "Canada stepped outside its democratic laws to get the treaty written," she said.

The speaker actually said "diplomatic," not "democratic."

Sometimes writers hear the right word but misspell it. This error damages their credibility and can be embarrassing. For example, one writer called a school's lecture series the "Wheel" lecture when it is named the "Weil" lecture. Another referred to a river as the "Noose" River when it is spelled "Neuse." Consider these:

> "Investigators found millions of land mines sewn into the earth," Williams said.

The writer should have written "sown."

> "Our commitment cannot waiver," she said.

She said "waver."

> "Congress is trying to role back the progress of 25 years of environmental legislation."

It's "roll" not "role."

> "America should be neither a claste nor a classified society."

The speaker said "classed" not "claste."

> "Ronald Reagan was applicable with the press during his presidency."

The speaker said "affable."

> "After belaying a question about tithing, [Ronald] Reagan whispered to me,
> 'I should have taken your advice,'" journalist Helen Thomas said.

Thomas said "belaboring" a question.

"The accident does not pose any immediate treat to nearby residents."

The writer made a typographical error. The speaker said "threat" not "treat."

Tips for Writing about Speeches

- When you start to write the story, always look for the theme. Ask yourself: What does the speaker want us to know? In one speech the theme may be the importance of democracy, in another the value of higher education, and in yet another public service. It may be in the speech title, or the speaker may deviate and pick out a pet subject on which to elaborate. The theme will be a clue to the lead for your story. Generally, in the lead, a summary of what the speaker said will go first, and then attribution will end the first sentence. An exception is made for a prominent speaker, such as the president or a local government official. Then the name goes first.
- Rarely will the first paragraph be a direct quote. Few speakers summarize their comments in 20 words or less. The lead may use a partial quote.
- Write a lead that states what the speaker said. Use attribution verbs such as "said" or "told."
- Do not write a label lead that simply identifies the topic or theme of the speech. That means do not use attribution words such as "discussed," "talked about," "spoke about," or "expressed concern about." See the difference:

Label Lead:
Three members of the Broadcasting Board of Governors held a panel discussion on the future of international broadcasting on the university campus last Wednesday.

Summary Lead:
U.S. government broadcasts to regions all over the world can explain democratic values to people living in countries that have repressive governments, according to a panel of experienced broadcasters and journalists who spoke at the university last Wednesday.

- Have a second graph that follows and supports the lead.
- Do not have a second graph that burdens readers with background on the speakers. See the difference:

Graph 2:

The panelists were David Burke, chairman of the Broadcasting Board; Evelyn Lieberman, director of Voice of America; and Kevin Klose, director of the International Broadcasting Bureau, which oversees Voice of America, Radio and TV Marti, and Worldnet Television.

Better Second Graph to Follow the Summary Lead:

"By providing news and public affairs broadcasting, we can help them establish stable democracies," said Kevin Klose, a panelist and director of the International Broadcasting Bureau, which oversees Voice of America, Radio and TV Marti, and Worldnet Television.

The third graph would note the other two panelists and the qualifications that speak to their credibility. You do not have to include a complete résumé. If the panel had a discussion title, it would be included in graph 3. Writers would also summarize here the topics covered, such as

The panelists primarily focused on the role of U.S. broadcasts since the fall of the Berlin Wall, but they also discussed new technology and how to bring their organizations into the 21st century.

- Have a balance of direct and indirect quotes.
- Look for a direct quote as a good way to end a story. Or end the story with more background about the speaker.
- Make sure your story has adequate attribution, even if you cover only one speaker.

Writing the Actual Story

With the 2008 presidential campaign, people throughout the United States had many months of reading or listening to speeches or media coverage of speeches. The availability of speech texts online through campaign offices allowed voters to read the complete comments, no matter what the specific stories said.

Reporters today often do not write stories solely off the speech content itself, but they will include others' reactions to the speaker's comments, background information to give the speech topic some context, and sometimes references to previous speeches. The availability of transcripts allows reporters to double-check speakers' quotes and determine whether a speech is more of the same rhetoric or a departure. The posting of transcripts also means that reporters today must be especially careful in quoting speakers accurately because a vigilant readership will certainly check behind them.

Exercises

1. Find a news story that also carries a sidebar or companion story that is a news-feature or feature. Compare the language between the two stories. Identify how the sidebar story carries more description by highlighting the words. Look at the organization of both stories. How do they differ?

2. Based on the stories in Exercise 1, look at the publication's Web site for the same stories. How are the stories presented visually, such as photos or video? Can readers find additional information? What do these elements add to the stories' information or entertainment value?

3. Go to today's *New York Times* Web site, and click on obituaries. Look at a lead and how the writer has focused on the individual's life. Look at the last graph. How did the end (usually a quote) wrap up the individual's life? Compare *The New York Times'* obituary to an obituary on the same individual in your local or regional newspaper. How did the obituaries differ?

4. Prepare an advance obituary for a national figure, either in politics or the media. Using a search engine, find at least five online sources, for example, the state Web site for a governor, a campaign Web site for another politician, or a news station's Web site that includes employee biographies. Try to find an article by or about the individual so that you can use quotes. Write the obituary with all the information; leave the lead blank where date, time, place, and cause would be included.

5. Go to a political site, such as the home page for the Republican National Committee or Democratic National Committee. Check for transcripts from major speeches. Then do a search for news stories to compare how media covered the speeches. How were the leads different? The quotes used? Background? Additional information?

6. Check CSPAN's latest offerings of videotaped speeches. Select one and play the speech. Write a news story of 500 words, then do an online search to compare your story to coverage in media.

References

Norma Sosa, Lecture on how to write obituaries, Midweek Special, School of Journalism and Mass Communication, University of North Carolina at Chapel Hill, Spring 2001.

"Former White House spokesman Tony Snow dies," CNN, July 12, 2008, accessed Aug. 19, 2008 at http://www.cnn.com/2008/POLITICS/07/12/obit.snow/.

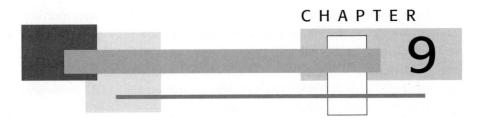
Research and Observation

Writing begins with an idea. During a trip to the ocean, a writer is fascinated with the porpoises that periodically surface and roll as they travel offshore. She wants to write about porpoises. But she needs more than just her observations to write a factual, accurate, complete, and entertaining article. She must learn more.

Gathering information is like detective work. As a sleuth, you start with a clue. Step by step you add pieces until you have enough information to reconstruct events and solve the case. As a writer, you add to your knowledge until you can create an accurate and complete summary of the topic.

Writers, like detectives, gather information from research, interviews, and observations. Also, like detectives, writers gather a broad array of information to ensure their searches are objective. Such work is called reporting. Research—or reporting—allows writers to study what others have already found out. That information might be in books, magazines, letters, statistical abstracts, encyclopedias, databases, blogs, or any number of other print or electronic sources. Writers can access thousands of documents using online Web search engines or commercial databases. More and more information is added to the free, easy-to-use Web every day. But it's important to remember that much of the best information in databases can't be found on the Web. Reporters often team with news librarians who have information-tracking skills to develop breaking news and long investigative pieces.

Armed with facts retrieved in research, writers can continue reporting by interviewing expert and relevant sources who add personal comment on the topic. Personal reflections give context and interest to facts, and interviews can confirm or verify online or library research. Interviewing, quotes, and attribution are discussed in Chapter 10.

Writers also take time to note their observations as part of their reporting. Student writers are sometimes reluctant to include their impressions for fear they will appear too subjective. They must overcome that fear. In the porpoise story, the writer would be remiss not to describe the rolling action of the sleek, gray mammals as they break water a hundred yards off the beach. Audiences want to know what the animals look like and how thrilled the author is at seeing a school of several dozen porpoises dotting the waves as they surface for air.

In this chapter, you will learn

- how to develop search strategies that will mine print and online resources,
- what specific sources to consider,
- the plusses and minuses in online and other research, and
- how observation is a part of gathering information.

Getting Started

Writers start out as generalists; they know a little about a lot of subjects. Some develop specialties or subject areas they prefer. Whether they are newspaper or electronic media reporters, public relations practitioners, or advertising copywriters—whether they cover general assignment topics or special beats, such as business, medicine, sports, or environment—writers need to do research as the first step in reporting. A medical writer may know medical terminology, but if he wants to write about autism he must become knowledgeable about the topic. A government reporter must learn about the newly elected members of Congress before she goes to the opening session.

Writers need to find information that is accurate, relevant, and up to date. Time is their greatest enemy. Most writers have deadlines and limited time to devote to research, particularly if they write for daily publications. So they need to find information quickly and efficiently.

Librarians can save you time, develop search strategies, and expand source lists. As the librarian at the School of Journalism and Mass Communication at the University of North Carolina at Chapel Hill, Barbara Semonche developed a dozen guides for students in the quest to find information. She notes:

You can be certain of two things: either you will find useful information efficiently or you will not. You will find too much information or too little. Your success will depend, to a certain extent, upon the quality of your search strategies. The other part is finding the best reference sources.

For UNC–Chapel Hill students, Semonche wrote a "first steps in basic research" handout that cautions:

> The resources available to students, scholars, journalists, and the general public are staggering in variety and amount. Nevertheless, not every question has a simple, direct, fast, comprehensive and/or accurate answer. Further, different reference books and resources offer differing responses, accounts, and statistics for the same or similar queries....It is essential that students develop a growing and diverse repertoire of reference/research sources and information strategies.

She recommends that students build their own personal set of reference materials. On her list are a dictionary ("the best you can afford"); a thesaurus; several style and usage manuals; the current year of *Statistical Abstract of the United States*; the current year of *The World Almanac of Facts*; the current year of *The Almanac of American Politics*; several books of quotations; a good atlas or gazetteer; and a good math textbook, "preferably one that does math the 'old' way." Students should also get into what she calls the "browse habit" and seek new, unfamiliar references.

Developing a Strategy

To be successful in research, you need a strategy to find information. Once you have defined your topic, you must make a list of questions, identify obvious sources, conduct searches for additional sources, review those sources for additional leads, refine your questions, and then interview.

Let's say you are a medical reporter and want to write a story on childhood immunizations. You first must make a list of the information you need to know, such as the following questions:

Initial Question List for Story on Childhood Immunizations

Who has to be immunized?
What are the state laws?
What shots do children have to have?
At what ages do children get which shots?
Are there any reactions to the shots?
How much do the shots cost at a doctor's office?
Can children get shots at public health clinics? How much do they cost?

Where are the clinics here? What are the hours for immunizations?
How many local children register for school and aren't immunized?
Is this a problem locally?
Have any other diseases surfaced locally?
Why are children not immunized?

Additional Questions after Research

What are the risks to children who aren't immunized?
Do children ever die from immunizations?
What are the reactions parents can expect after a child gets a shot?
How many children in the state aren't immunized properly when they start school?
How many immunizations are given each year in the state? In our county?
What childhood diseases are appearing again?
How much of the cost of immunizations does the government pay?
Do we consider some diseases eradicated?
Fifty years ago, children suffered from mumps, measles, and even polio. Now children can be protected against even chicken pox. Are we too complacent about a resurgence of diseases?
Are there any diseases left that children need to be protected from?
If a certain number of children are immunized, does that protect other children, as in the herd effect?
What factors prevent parents from having children immunized at the proper time?
What immunizations do college students need?

The obvious sources for answers to these questions would be newspaper and journal indexes, articles and information at online health sites, pediatricians, and local health department and school officials. You would also interview experts and agency officials.

Eventually your source list grows to include state health officials, state statutes that stipulate which immunizations children must have to enter school, officials at the Centers for Disease Control, legislators who allocate funds for immunizations, parents, and even children. You refine your list of questions for each source and prepare to interview your sources.

Your search strategy is similar if you are writing a story for your alumni magazine on a graduate whose first novel has been published. She is an assistant professor at a college in another state. Before the interview, you need to find information on the author. Most students and writers today go to the Internet first and use a search engine to find information. Such a search might reveal biographical information on her publisher's Web site. Check your library for *Contemporary Authors*, a biographical guide to current writers in fiction, journalism, film, television, and other fields.

If you can find no accessible biographical history, you will have to rely on a strategy that includes interviewing former professors, roommates, colleagues, friends, and family members. You might have to call the English department where she teaches and have someone fax her curriculum vitae. You might have to consult newspaper indexes in public libraries in her home state to find specific articles about her. If one source indicates an organization to which she belongs, you might need to look for references with that organization. Articles about the organization could include material about your up-and-coming author.

Basic References

As you search for information, your journey might include online searching as well as a trip to a special collections library to pore through historical documents. Many basic print sources are available online. You can find out which ones by exploring virtual libraries, such as the Librarians' Internet Index at http://lii.org. Librarian Barbara Semonche's basic reference list mentioned earlier in this chapter is an excellent starting point. Writers should always remember basic sources such as telephone books, city directories, and collections of people by occupation, political affiliation, or other activities. From there, more specialized references can tell you the meaning of certain acronyms, such as MASH for Mobile Army Surgical Hospital, or even real estate terms, such as escrow.

Today's researchers and writers use hundreds of sources and always must be sure sources are credible and updated. Listed here are some types of publications that writers traditionally have relied on for information. Remember: Most publications have Web sites.

Biographical Sources. Biographical references contain information about well-known people. Some are specific, such as *Who's Who in American Politics*. The information will include date of birth, parents' names, education, career, awards and achievements, and family data. Among other biographical sources are *Who's Who*, *Webster's Biographical Dictionary*, *Current Biography*, *Who's Who* *among African Americans,* and *Who's Who among Hispanic Americans.* More than 100 biographical dictionaries exist, each focusing on a special group or profession.

Statistical Information.   *Statistical Abstract of the United States* is one of the most widely used reference books and is online. It provides information from the number of police officers in Albuquerque, New Mexico, to the number of houses with indoor plumbing in Lincoln, Nebraska. Data are based on information collected by the federal government and other sources. *The Census of Population of the United States* is published every 10 years. Census information is available on the Internet at www.census.gov. *Editor and Publisher Market Guide* contains data on cities, such as a city's shopping malls and whether its water is fluoridated. Most states compile statistical books, particularly those dealing with vital statistics: births, deaths, marriages, and divorces. Writers can find information on states, counties, cities, and even sections within cities that is especially helpful if they are looking for the local angle on a story. For international information, writers can consult the *United Nations Demographic Yearbook.*

Political and Government Information.   *The U.S. Government Manual* contains information on departments and agencies in the executive branch. *Congressional Quarterly* publishes a weekly report that catalogues the voting records of Congress and major political speeches. States annually publish manuals that contain information about branches of government and legislatures, summaries of the state history, the state constitution, and biographies of major state officials. Information on foreign governments and leaders can be found in reference books, such as *The Statesman's Yearbook 2008: Politics, Cultures and Economies of the World* and other publications that focus on world leaders. Remember to check for online sites, too.

Geographic Data.   Writers might need to check on the locations of cities, towns, and countries. They can refer to local maps or the *Times Atlas of the World* and *Rand McNally Commercial Atlas and Marketing Guide.* Online sites, such as mapquest.com, will guide writers to locations and even provide maps and directions to get there. Writers can find up-to-date maps of continents and regions at sites such as World Sites Atlas at www.sitesatlas.com or National Geographic at www.nationalgeographic.com.

Business Information. Writers might need data on a company or an industry, and students might need information on a potential employer. Today's competitive companies usually have extensive and interactive Web sites. Research on companies could also be found in annual reports, on file in many libraries.

Information on thousands of companies can be found at the Securities Exchange Commission Web site at www.sec.gov. Incorporation records must list officers, addresses, and company descriptions, and these documents are filed with states' secretary of state offices. Many businesses fall under the purview of state regulatory agencies, such as the state insurance commissioner. Information on companies can also be found in reference books, such as *Standard & Poor's Index*. Also, for company information that can lead reporters to sources, check out the American Press Institute's site for business writers at www.businessjournalism.org.

Professional Sources. In any search for information sources, writers should consider professional organizations such as societies, guilds, and associations. These sources often have links or references to other depositories of information and can provide updates on media issues, contact names, and historical background and serve as a means to verify facts. Before writing about trends in real estate, reporters will want to look at NationalAssociationOfRealtors.com and at related sites for local and regional Realtors. Similar sites are available on thousands of organizations that serve particular interests such as medicine, law, construction, government workers, architects, and others.

For background on professional issues in journalism and mass communication, some sites worth checking are the Poynter Institute at www.poynter.org; the American Society of Newspaper Editors at www.asne.org; the Inter American Press Association at www.sipiapa.org; Nieman Reports at www.nieman.harvard.edu; Public Relations Society of America at www.prsa.org; American Advertising Federation at www.aaf.org; Association of Electronic Journalists at www.rtnda.org; Investigative Reporters and Editors at www.ire.org; and Society of Professional Journalists at www.spj.org. Journalism organizations and issues also are a focus of UNITY: Journalists of Color at www.unityjournalists.org.

Pitfalls in Research

The hunt for information can be complex. Librarian Barbara Semonche warns that not all information comes in a compact, convenient form. At the start of a search, students may discover people who share the same names as celebrities, such as basketball star Michael Jordan, television personality David Letterman, or even McDonald's mascot Ronald McDonald. Researchers must check to be sure that the person named on records or documents is in fact the same person they seek.

Information may be dated or incomplete. For example, early biographies of actor Brad Pitt would fail to include the correct number and names of his children. Students and other researchers must remember that not every reference includes every individual, and those that do may not have all the facts. Researchers must look at many sources, both print and online, to find complete information. Searching for information is rarely one-stop shopping. Using many sources helps uncover discrepancies and inconsistencies about information and ensure that information is as accurate as possible.

Writers should look continually for additional and alternative sources. The research game is a detective hunt. Names or sources mentioned in an article or in references can lead to nuggets of information elsewhere. The only constraints will be time and deadline pressure.

Government Sources

Local, state, and federal governments produce millions of pages of documents every year, ranging from official findings, such as federal Food and Drug Administration studies, to county tax records and the disposition of local traffic cases. Most government documents are open and accessible to the public. Many are free by mail on request, and others are available at the city hall, the county courthouse, a regional federal repository, online, or the Library of Congress. They provide a wealth of information for writers and curious citizens.

Government officials and others have taken advantage of the information age to put reams of material online. Agencies maintain their own Web sites that provide history, facts about elected officials, agendas and minutes of meetings, and other relevant data. For information on legislation, try THOMAS, a congressional online system; Congressional Record; congressional legislation digests; and directories of congressional members' e-mail addresses. Even the White House has its own Web site featuring news releases of the day, speech transcripts, and access to federal agencies.

Public Records

Routine government documents are considered public. The documents have been created by the government, which is supported by taxpayers' money. Researchers, writers, and anyone who wants the documents can request to see them or to have copies made. All states have laws that pertain to what is and what is not a public record. The general rule most journalists follow is that any document is considered a public record unless the agency or individual who has the document can cite the section of state or federal law that prevents its disclosure. If the agency cannot, it must relinquish the information.

Media writers should know the open records laws for their particular state. State press associations can provide the law and its exceptions. Publications such as *The News Media and the Law*, published by the Reporters Committee for Freedom of the Press, can be consulted. The Electronic Frontier Foundation is a valuable resource and can be accessed via the Internet.

Agencies can charge a reasonable fee for photocopying documents. Most states have regulations pertaining to computer storage of public documents and reasonable charges for making copies or providing access to electronic information.

Freedom of Information Act

In 1966, the U.S. Congress passed the federal Freedom of Information Act (FOIA). The act became law in 1967 and has been amended five times. The law is much like state laws regarding public records. Anyone is allowed to make a written request for information from any federal agency, but not all information is available. The act provides broad exemptions, such as information relating to national defense or foreign policy, internal personnel rules and practices of an agency, personnel and medical files that would constitute an invasion of privacy, information compiled for law enforcement purposes, and geophysical information such as that related to oil well locations.

In 1996 the Electronic Freedom of Information Act Amendments required federal agencies to release electronic files of certain types of records created after November 1, 1996. Because of the time needed to respond to requests for electronic data, the amendments extended the agencies' required response time from 10 to 20 days. In 2002 amendments to the FOIA affected requests from foreign governments or any requester acting on behalf of a foreign government to any agency considered part of the government's intelligence community. Changes under the "Open Government Act of 2007" further clarified government agencies' duties in regard to FOIA requests.

The media have worked continually to reduce the number of exemptions to FOIA. Michael Gartner, former president of the American Society of Newspaper Editors, once lamented in a speech on national Freedom of Information Day that the name "Freedom of Information" implies the government is holding information hostage. He objected to many of the restrictions, particularly those that prevent publication of what the United States broadcasts to developing countries over the Voice of America. Homeland security concerns have added to difficulties in accessing information in some settings. To help with access, George Washington University houses the National Security Archive, a repository of government documents and declassified material at www.nsarchive.org. Its Web site notes that it "is also a leading advocate and user of the Freedom of Information Act."

FOIA sets out the procedure for requesting information, the time required for an agency to respond, appeals procedures, and fees. Individuals must pay the cost of photocopying the information but can request a waiver of that cost if the release of the information is in the public interest. Writers or individuals seeking information under the act might be frustrated—delays can occur even when procedures are followed. The request must be specific and must be sent to the proper agency. When the information is uncovered, a reporter may receive a desired document, but with sections or entire pages inked out to protect exempted information. The reporter pays the cost of photocopying all pages—even the blackened ones.

FOIA searches can be time consuming and costly, but many journalists and researchers have used them to find information for fact-filled articles. For example, a student in an advanced reporting class filed an FOIA request with the Federal Communications Commission (FCC) to find out what kinds of complaints and how many had been lodged with the agency after singer Janet Jackson's breast was exposed during the Super Bowl 2004 halftime performance. The student's request was broad and asked for copies of the complaints. An FCC representative responded, asking for clarification and letting the student know that to provide copies of all the complaints—500,000 plus—would cost more than $125,000. Needless to say, the student amended the request and asked for a sampling of the complaints, a request that cost her $100.

Investigative Reporters and Editors presents awards each year to media that produce stories using public record searches and requests. Background on the award and award-winning stories are available at www.ire.org/foi/.

Online Research

Technology has changed the way writers collect, transmit, and share information. Distance from sources has become irrelevant. A public relations practitioner in Detroit can search online for background information on the success of drugs to treat acid reflux disease and e-mail it to a company official in Switzerland. Photographs and other color visuals can be e-mailed anywhere. Using a laptop, a reporter can write a breaking-news story and transmit it in a matter of seconds to the city desk 30 miles away.

A major change in recent years is how information is stored. People who began writing careers in the mid-1980s and earlier have seen phenomenal changes in the ways they seek information. In the "old days" before 1985, most searches for information centered on treks to libraries at a newspaper, city or county, university—wherever resource books were housed. People had to handle paper to get information.

Computers have allowed anyone who produces information to store it online so others can access it. When people get online, they search for information; download data, photos, or text to their computers; send e-mail, blog, or IM; or chat. Writers can call up information in a matter of seconds while sitting at computers in the office, at home, in the dorm, or in the library. Newspapers, books, magazines, library holdings, company profiles, and even job banks are online. Electronic indexes and databases offer citations, abstracts, and even full text records, and the number of databases available online grows daily in diversity and ease of access.

The ease of using the Internet and the breadth of information found there can lull novice reporters into a false sense of security in regard to accuracy. As much as students and professional writers have come to depend on the Internet, they must still have some skepticism about what they find there. All Web sites are not created alike. With the proliferation of information has come discussion of issues on privacy, legal uses, copyright, and ethics (discussed in detail in Chapter 12). A helpful publication is *Nora Paul's Computer Assisted Research*, published by the Poynter Institute in St. Petersburg, Florida. Updates are available online.

Pitfalls of Online Research

Convenience is one of the advantages of online research, but some important concerns persist. Online, identities may be cloaked, expertise exaggerated, and content tweaked in such a way that critical errors go undetected. Because blogging and social network tools have made it easy for anyone to publish, writers must realize that not everything they read online is true, just like not everything they hear on the street is true. Writers must take specific measures to establish the accuracy and credibility of sources and sites. In *Web Search Savvy: Strategies and Shortcuts for Online Research*, author Barbara Friedman suggests Web-based content be evaluated with the following five criteria:

- **Accuracy.** Impossible facts are a giveaway that a Web site is bogus, although some errors may simply be clerical. Yet if a site is riddled with spelling or grammar errors, it's a safe bet the author has been careless with overall content, and the researcher should be wary of using the material. The quickest way to spot inaccurate information is to check Web-based content against traditional or nondigital sources.

- **Authority.** What individual or organization claims responsibility for the site's content, and does it have the proper credentials to speak authoritatively on this particular subject? Use a site's contact information or a domain lookup, such as WHOIS or InterNic, to verify who's behind a site.

- **Currency.** Web sites may linger online long after their authors have stopped maintaining the content. Check the site for dates that indicate when the content was posted and last revised.

- **Audience.** Determining the intended audience for a Web site will help you evaluate the usefulness of the information. A site about political campaigns designed for an audience of elected officials may be too complicated if you are writing for elementary school students.

- **Agenda.** Whereas journalists are urged to remain impartial, in the online world everyone has an opinion. Bloggers, for example, publish views on a range of topics using personalized language that would be discouraged in traditional journalism. That bias is not intended to make you doubt a site, but rather understand its purpose. Knowing whether a Web site's author is motivated by a personal or professional agenda helps you find a context for the information.

Online research may be the first and most convenient choice for writers, but it is just one step in the research process. Taking the time to evaluate the integrity of Web-based content will go a long way in establishing your credibility as a researcher and writer.

Additional Online Search Strategies

Writers can find information quickly by typing key words into search engines, the very basis of an online search strategy. But search engines still miss a lot of information. A 2001 study estimated that 400 to 550 times the amount of information existed on the "hidden" Web compared to the amount found with search engines. Some of the information not easily found is on commercial or fee-based sites or is stored in data formats that Web search engines cannot easily crawl.

When searching online, reporters should remember that most search engines have advanced search functions. Google, for example, offers a step-by-step guide on how to look more precisely for information on a topic by typing in appropriate search requirements.

Writers should also be aware of the growing number of virtual library consortia, which offer a state's residents access to online library catalogues, reference materials, and commercial online databases. Librarian Barbara Semonche notes that the consortia "are a rich resource for freelance writers, reporters, students, and researchers who need free or very low cost access to extensive, sophisticated information and data."

For example, NCLIVE, the North Carolina Library link to the world at www.nclive.org, offers online access to complete articles from more than 4,000 newspapers, journals, and magazines, as well as indexing for more than 10,000 periodical titles. Galileo, Georgia's virtual library at http://www.galileo.usg.edu/welcome/, provides secured access to licensed products. Some states' virtual libraries are open only to educational institutions, including students, faculty, and staff, so writers need to find out the privileges for their particular states' digital libraries.

What You Can't Find Online

Writers today must remember that online information is a recent phenomenon. Most history is buried in letters, memos, newspapers, magazines, and other written material not catalogued in online databases. When writer

Nadine Cohodas began researching her book, *Spinning Blues into Gold: The Chess Brothers and the Legendary Chess Records*, she went hunting. Her research included visits to the Chicago neighborhoods where brothers Phil and Leonard Chess had offices and where the great blues singers performed.

Cohodas produced a book that brought information to readers they would not have gotten on their own. Finding the details required hours and hours of reading trade journals, such as *Billboard* and *Cash Box*, to understand the evolution of the record company; poring over Chicago newspapers; and scouring public records, such as old liquor licenses to trace the brothers' business beginnings, city phone books and directories to confirm relevant addresses, and the Federal Communications Commission archive for details about their radio stations. "You have to love the hunt," she said.

Every now and then, Cohodas had "eureka" moments when she found something that provided the telling detail for a piece of the story. For example, she needed information about the history of the Macomba Lounge, owned by the Chess brothers. She explains how she found it:

> To find out what the Macomba Lounge had been, I photocopied about 30 pages of the Chicago Yellow Pages in the tavern listings, then read them one by one to find the same address. Lo and behold, the Congress Buffet showed up at 3905 S. Cottage. I used that name to request the liquor license for that venue so I could trace the history further.
>
> Meanwhile, I found the only ad anyone knows of for the Macomba Lounge by going through the now defunct Chicago Bee week by week in the first or second year Leonard and Phil were in the club and that's when I saw the ad—a sweet moment.

The result of nearly three years' work was a fascinating account of two Polish immigrants who built a company promoting black singers, such as Muddy Waters, Chuck Berry, Bo Diddley, and Etta James. *The New York Times Book Review* named it one of the notable nonfiction books of 2000, and the book won the 2001 Blues Foundation "Keeping the Blues Alive" Award.

Observation

Observation—an old method of research—still is a key tool in gathering information. At the same time reporters note what speakers are saying, they should notice how speakers deliver their remarks, how they move their bodies, what they are wearing, and how the crowd reacts to their comments. Such details are part of the reporting process.

Many students and inexperienced writers, however, are reluctant to include too many details. They fear that audiences will doubt their descriptions. They believe using description borders on being subjective when, in fact, leaving out description might distort an event. For example, a story might reveal a speaker's eloquence and pointed remarks on U.S. trade with China, but the reporter might not mention that only 22 people were seated in an auditorium that holds 550 people. Although the speaker might have been eloquent, the speech's title failed to attract a sizable audience.

Seeing Isn't Enough

Many people notice their surroundings or the events happening around them in one dimension. They see. Rarely do people consciously smell, taste, hear, or touch their environment. Even using only sight, most people miss much of what goes on. So do writers. They have not trained themselves to observe events that happen simultaneously. At the state fair, a reporter might notice the lines in front of concessions but not see the child wailing for more cotton candy, the youth loaded with three bright green teddy bears, the overflowing garbage at a nearby trash can, and the cigarette hanging from the hawker's lips. The unobservant writer does not smell the odor of fried dough, taste the grease in the air near the ferris wheel, hear the ping-ping from the shooting gallery, or feel the slap of heat from the barbecue cookers.

To be skillful observers, writers must hone all their senses. To be complete and successful writers, they must describe scenes to absent audiences. Even when viewers see events on television, they still need the reporter's or news anchor's observations. When television covers the annual Thanksgiving Day parade in New York City, for example, reporters must identify floats and provide background on performers. Viewers need the information to understand what they are seeing.

General Observation

Many people exist on autopilot. They drive the same route to work, live in the same house or apartment for years, and work in the same office. They become less and less observant. What about you?

Any person or writer can sharpen observation skills. Try this experiment: Take a piece of paper. Describe what your roommate or friend wore to school or work today. Note colors and types of fabric, if possible. What did you eat for breakfast? Can you remember the smell as well as the taste? What about the color or feel? What sounds do you hear in this room? Can you name more than three?

Keep a notebook in your car, backpack, or pocket. Start recording what you see and hear in multidimensional ways. Use your cell phone to capture the visual and even audio. Although most people can note different sounds, it is harder to catch and record events happening simultaneously. The oft-told adage is that two people on a street corner would give two different accounts of an accident both witnessed. Think of ways to compare what you see with events or items that are common knowledge.

Remember the story on the burlesque queen? Writer Kathleen Hennessey uses simple language to describe Tempest Storm's physical attributes from the color of her hair to her fingernail polish. She notes her fingers "tremble with frustration. They are aged, knotted by arthritis and speckled with purple spots under paper-thin skin." Hennessey describes Storm's apartment, including her exercise bike and the photos that catalogue her relationships. Readers get a sense of Storm's physical surroundings as well as her philosophy of life.

How Observation Changes the Action.   The act of reporting, of being an observer, might have the unintended effect of changing the behavior of an individual you are observing. Think about a friend who would rush to pick up living room clutter when you pull out your cell phone and take a picture. Your presence can change the way events unfold.

The same tendency holds true when reporters attend a meeting or a rally or when they participate in an online discussion. Their presence affects how people behave. The town council members sit up straighter and look busy when the public access television channel is airing the meeting. Rally organizers look efficient and engaged when reporters approach. Store managers beam smiles of success on the first day of business.

The trick to accurate observing is to observe over time. Most people can maintain a facade for some time, but they cannot keep it up forever—even when they know a reporter is in the room. You might have to observe for more than a few minutes, taking notes or photographs unobtrusively. Two hours into a meeting, the mayor might forget the unobtrusive camera and rail against the accusations of an unhappy citizen.

With advanced technology, people can be observed and recorded when they don't know it. Those images can appear on video or photo-sharing Web sites, social networking sites, or other Internet venues—much to a person's surprise. As a reporter, you must be careful not to invade an individual's privacy, discussed in Chapter 12, as you record your observations. When people are involved in events considered public, such as a rally or a plane crash, they do lose their right to privacy. But if they are partying in the privacy of their apartment, then those actions cannot become visuals for a story taken surreptitiously with your cell phone.

Participant Observation

Social scientists have long used observation as a means of getting information about groups. They join a group as participants to observe individual behavior within a group and the individuals' interactions. Journalists also have adopted the practice, gaining admission and recording the interactions of the group. Such intrusion by journalists affects the way people interact. Over time, however, reporters become accepted, and other members might forget their role.

Because their presence does affect how members relate, some journalists have opted to become members of groups and not to identify themselves as reporters. In the 1890s, reporter Nellie Bly pretended to be a mental patient to get a true picture of how the insane were treated at Blackwell's Island, New York's asylum for the mentally ill. Some have joined cults, followed the Hell's Angels, or gotten jobs in nursing homes. One reporter in her mid-20s enrolled in a Philadelphia high school to observe it firsthand—and was invited to the senior prom. Before resorting to undercover work, reporters and their editors must determine that a change of identity is the only way to get the story.

In either case, problems can arise when it is time to write. Reporters might feel a kinship to the group and have difficulty setting themselves apart. Journalists who become group members put their impartiality at risk in writing a story. Writers might become too emotional or too attached to sources and not be able to distance themselves. They also run the risk of not knowing completely whether their presence altered the group in any way. They can double-check their reactions and observations, however, by interviewing a balanced mix of sources. Reporters might also get complaints from group members who feel betrayed when the article appears.

Nonverbal Communication

Although writers get the bulk of their information from sources and from interviewing, they can add details from nonverbal communication. Such cues come from the way people move or act when they say something. A politician might raise her eyebrows at a constituent's question. A child might shift his hands behind his back when leaving the kitchen. A teacher might frown while correcting student essays. Each action implies a thought or behavior to the observer. The politician might be surprised. The child might be guilty of swiping a cookie. The teacher might be unhappy about a good student's low grade.

When recording nonverbal cues either in note taking or with a camera, reporters must be careful. They must think beyond the obvious because the same cue could carry different meanings for different observers. Furrowed eyebrows might indicate puzzlement or anger. Waving hands can mean agitation or enthusiasm. A smile might be sincere or forced. Generally, one action alone is not sufficient to indicate how an individual is feeling. The gestures must be catalogued in addition to words and other body movements. A reporter might have to go so far as to ask an individual what a particular posture meant. For example, pacing during an interview may not be a result of nervousness; the interviewee may suffer from restless legs syndrome, but no reporter could tell that simply by observing.

In addition, nonverbal actions have different meanings across cultures. In some cultures or ethnic groups, individuals do not make eye contact while speaking. An ignorant or inexperienced reporter might be suspicious of such behavior, thereby including a cultural bias. When U.S. business leaders engage in negotiations with Japanese officials, they have to learn etiquette and protocol. For example, the Japanese consider it offensive to write on a business card, while in the United States, executives and others make notations or add home telephone numbers to business cards. The good reporter learns about cultural differences or asks questions to clarify behavior. Such sensitivity and awareness is essential to accurate reporting.

Dangers in Observation

John Salvi was charged with murdering two people and injuring five others in shootings at two abortion clinics in Boston. When Salvi was arraigned on weapons charges in conjunction with the shootings, Gary Tuchman of CNN gave a live report and description for audiences who were not in the courtroom.

Tuchman described Salvi as wearing a blue blazer, white shirt, white socks, loafers, and nice pants. The description implied that Salvi had dressed conservatively and neatly. A print news account reported that Salvi was wearing "an ill-fitting blazer." The implication here contradicted the neat appearance of Tuchman's report. Which account was right? Audiences who heard and read the two accounts might have noticed the discrepancy and been puzzled. Or maybe it just added to their belief that you cannot trust the media to be right.

Tuchman also took his reported observation one step further. He noted to viewers that if they had a stereotype of someone who would be charged with committing murder, Salvi did not look like that stereotype—that is, Salvi did not look like someone who would commit murder. Viewers may have wondered: "What does the stereotypical murderer look like? Why didn't Tuchman give us a description of that stereotype?"

Observation plays a major role in writing, but we must be circumspect about the descriptions we use. As will be discussed in Chapter 11, we as writers carry our prejudices and biases with us as we collect information and write. We must be careful. Think about Tuchman's reference to a stereotypical murderer. Can you describe one? Of course not. If murderers were readily identifiable, people who have been killed would have had some warning. But murderers vary in shape, size, age, gender, skin tone, hair color, and clothing preference. They do not all have greasy hair and shifty, beady eyes and act furtively or in a suspicious manner.

The Importance of Accuracy

As noted, Tuchman's observations might have been distorted by his experiences. He might have a stereotypical idea of what a murderer looks like. Writers can bring biases to observation, just as they can to any aspect of reporting.

Just as you double-check facts, you should be circumspect about your observations. Take emotions into account. If you covered an anti-abortion rally, you might have found your emotions surging if you are pro-choice. Despite your role as a journalist, your feelings might not be neutral. Your feelings could influence your description. Be aware.

To ensure accuracy, you should record impressions in your notebook or on your electronic equipment at the scene and then review to add context as soon as possible afterward. The longer you wait, the fewer details you will remember accurately. Memory fades over time.

Like other kinds of research, observation leads to a more complete message. Description that is simple, clear, fair, and complete also will aid accuracy. Writers should lay out description alongside other facts and allow audiences to judge for themselves. Audiences invariably will apply their own biases to the description and form their own opinions, but writers' choices of words should not be the deciding factor.

Exercises

1. Condoleezza Rice, former Secretary of State, is coming to campus to give a lecture. Before the lecture, she will have a news conference, which you will attend for the campus newspaper. First, you need to find out more information. Using three biographical sources, answer the following questions. Cite the reference used. One reference should be online.

   a. When and where was Rice born?
   b. Where did she go to college?
   c. What jobs did she hold before joining the Bush administration?
   d. What has she done since she left the State Department?
   e. Has she won any awards? If so, list them.

2. Identify a reporter in your college community or in your hometown by reading bylines and articles in the respective paper. Call the reporter and ask what sources he or she uses in researching stories. Note whether the reporter uses online sources to retrieve information. Find out how the reporter ensures accuracy in using sources. Share the information with your class.

3. You are the state desk researcher for the local newspaper. The state editor wants to do a story on parents charged with killing their children. Before making the assignment to a reporter, the editor asks you to do an online search of national newspapers and magazines to find accounts of such crimes. Your task is to prepare a memo to the state editor that lists six references to substantial articles on parents charged with killing their children. The references need to be annotated; that is, they should be accompanied by explanatory notes as well as enough information to enable the reporter to find the articles.

4. You discover that many adult day care facilities exist in your area, and you want to make a case to your editor that a feature story about these facilities would be a good one. Search online for information on these facilities and identify at least three in your area. Compare the completeness and the credibility—as well as the limitations—of the Web pages you use as you find information on adult day care.

5. Pick a place on campus or attend a town government meeting as an observer along with another student. Use your senses to take notes on what transpires outside the actions of passersby or officials. Write a description of the meeting, using aspects such as the room, the mood, the speakers' attitudes, the officials' attitudes, the tone of the meeting, and how many people attended. Then compare your account with the other student's accounts. See what each of you chose to include and chose to ignore. Compare the ways you described aspects of the meeting. Then discuss what made your observations different.

References

Nadine Cohodas, Using documents. Interview via e-mail, October 2001.

Barbara Friedman, *Web Search Savvy: Strategies and Shortcuts for Online Research.* Mahwah, NJ: Erlbaum, 2004.

Freedom of Information Act, 5 U.S.C. 552, 1966. Amended in 1974, 1976, 1986, 1996, 2002.

"FOIA Legislative History," National Security Archives, at http://www.gwu.edu/~nsarchiv/nsa/foialeghistory/legistfoia.htm.

Michael Gartner, Speech in honor of national Freedom of Information Day. Washington, DC, National Press Club, March 1989.

Mary McGuire, Linda Stilborne, Melinda McAdams, and Laurel Hyatt, *The Internet Handbook for Writers, Researchers, and Journalists.* New York: Guilford Press, 1997.

Nora Paul, *Computer Assisted Research: A Guide to Tapping Online Information,* 4th ed. St. Petersburg, FL: The Poynter Institute for Media Studies, 2001.

Barbara Semonche, Personal interview. Chapel Hill, NC, School of Journalism and Mass Communication, University of North Carolina at Chapel Hill, 1995, 2005.

CHAPTER 10

Interviewing, Quotes, and Attribution

Asking questions and collecting answers—interviewing—is an essential skill for all media writers. Becoming a skilled interviewer takes practice; it is not something someone does naturally.

Most of us interview in a casual way when introduced to someone new. We ask questions: Where are you from? Are you a student? What year are you in school? What is your major? We hope to get responses that help us learn more about the person.

But if you are going to write about that individual, your questions must be much more specific. You hardly have enough for a story if you know that Steve Monroe is a junior from Lake Geneva, New York, majoring in information and library science. You need more detailed information, perhaps his career objective and his views on information storage and retrieval.

So, good interviewing is more than just carrying on a casual conversation. It takes skill, and it takes practice. This chapter will start you on the road to becoming a good interviewer.

In this chapter, you will learn

- how to prepare for an interview,
- how to conduct an interview, including use of audio and video recorders,
- how to handle off-the-record information,
- how to use quotes, and
- the importance of accuracy, attribution, and punctuation in quotes.

240

Interviewing as a Challenge

Writers do interviews in different ways. The medium they work for, deadline pressures, the accessibility of sources, and people's willingness to talk affect how well a writer can plan and do interviews. More and more, reporters are mobile journalists, or mojos, capturing quotes and filing stories from cars or coffee shops. They need to plan whether a pad and pencil are adequate or if they need audio and video equipment to record sound and visuals for online postings. In today's media world, stories can be multidimensional, as noted in Chapter 7 on online content.

Writers face challenges as they work diligently to reach as many sources as possible before a deadline. They become detectives as they figure out just whom they should interview and how. Like anyone else, writers feel nervous and even excited when they have the chance to interview a well-known newsmaker or celebrity. And they feel great satisfaction and accomplishment when a source answers their questions and gives them something extra.

Reporters usually interview multiple sources to get the information they need for a story. See how many sources Mark Landler used to get the variety of opinions and description for the following story:

> HEILIGENKREUZ, Austria—As noon draws near, the monks glide into the church, their white cowls billowing behind them. They line up in silence, facing each other in long choir stalls. Wood carvings of saints peer down on them from the austere Romanesque nave.
>
> Bells peal and the chant begins—low at first, then swelling as all the monks join in. Their soft voices wash over the ancient stones, replacing the empty clatter of the day with something like the sound of eternity.
>
> Except, that is, for the clicks of a camera held by a photographer lurking behind a stone pillar.
>
> It has been like this since last spring, when word got out that the Cistercian monks of the Stift Heiligenkreuz, deep in the Vienna woods, had been signed by Universal Music to record an album of Gregorian chants.
>
> When the album, "Chant: Music for Paradise," was released in Europe in May—and shot to No. 7 in the British pop charts, at one point outselling releases from Amy Winehouse and Madonna—the trickle of press attention turned into a torrent. (The CD will be released in the United States on Tuesday.)

Now this monastery, where the daily rituals of prayer and work have guided life for 875 years, finds itself in a media whirligig at once exhilarating and unsettling for its 77 brothers.

"We're monks," said Johannes Paul Chavanne, 25, a Viennese who entered the monastery after studying law and is training to be a priest. "We're not pop stars, and we don't want to be pop stars."

Too late: the album has made the monks of Heiligenkreuz a crossover hit, the latest example of how Gregorian chant, a once-neglected 1,000-year-old part of the Roman Catholic liturgy, can be repackaged for a secular society that savors its soothing, otherworldly cadences.

Heiligenkreuz—the name means Holy Cross—has put one of its more worldly monks, Karl Wallner, in charge of public relations. When not in prayer, he spends his days fielding calls from reporters as far away as New Zealand. His cellphone, its ring tone set to chant, sings constantly.

"I'm like a shield around my community," said Father Wallner, who has been a monk for 26 years. "There was a lot of concern at first that this would destroy the serenity of the monastery."

Some monks also worried that putting chants, which are, after all, prayers, into a commercial product amounted to a kind of profanity—"like using Leonardo da Vinci as wallpaper," in the words of one. For most, those risks are outweighed by what they believe is the music's great potential: to stir feelings of faith in a society that has drifted far from religion.

Still, the making of these latest monastic stars may say more about the way the secular world, thanks to the power of the Internet, can penetrate even the most secluded of cloisters.

In 1994, the Benedictines of Santo Domingo de Silos in Spain prompted the last big revival of Gregorian chant with an album that became a phenomenon. More recently, the use of chant on the popular video game Halo has piqued interest.

Eager to get in on the trend, Universal's classical music label took out an advertisement in Catholic publications, inviting chant groups to submit their work. Finding another ensemble like the Benedictines was going to be a long shot, the label's executives figured.

"Not all monks want to enter into a commercial relationship because that's not what they spend their days doing," said Tom Lewis, the artist development manager in London for Universal Classics & Jazz.

But the advertisement was spotted by the grandson of a monk from here. He tipped off Father Wallner, who, in addition to his public-relations duties, runs the monastery's theological academy and its Web site.

"An Austrian monk would never know what Universal Music is," Father Wallner said. "We were chosen by divine providence to show that it is possible to have a healthy religious life today."

Divine providence may have less to do with it than one monk's resourcefulness. Father Wallner sent Mr. Lewis a short e-mail message with a link to a video of chants that the monks had uploaded to YouTube after Pope Benedict XVI visited the monastery last September.

While monks in many monasteries chant, Heiligenkreuz is particularly proud of its singing, which has been honed over years by one of the monks, who used to direct choirs in Germany.

Mr. Lewis was entranced, recalling that the video eclipsed the more than 100 other submissions. "There was a smoothness and softness to the voices that you associate with younger people," he said.

Universal negotiated a contract with the monks, who proved to be anything but naïve in the ways of business. It helped that the abbot, Gregor Henckel Donnersmark, has an M.B.A. and ran the Spanish outpost of a German shipping company before he entered the monastery in 1977.

Among the clauses he sought: Universal cannot use the chanting in video games or pop music. The monks will never tour or perform on stage. And Heiligenkreuz will earn a royalty based on the sales of the album, which the abbot said worked out to roughly 1 euro per CD sold.

The monastery's share, Father Henckel Donnersmark figures optimistically, could be between $1.5 million and $3.1 million, which it will use to help finance the theological studies of young men from developing countries. So far, Universal has sold nearly 200,000 copies.

"Money is not a source of fulfillment," the abbot said, though he pointed out that it would defray the monastery's expenses, which are high, partly because of its success in attracting novices.

Even before the album, these monks had encountered the world of show business. The abbot's nephew, Florian Henckel von Donnersmark, wrote the screenplay for "The Lives of Others," an Academy Award-winning film about East Germany, while holed up in a monk's cell at Heiligenkreuz. He brought his Oscar back to the monastery, where the monks took turns holding it.

"A place like that can recalibrate your moral compass," Mr. Henckel von Donnersmark said by telephone from Los Angeles. "These people do nothing but think about how to love and serve God."

For now, the monks seem sanguine that they can balance this solitary vocation with the glare of celebrity.

"If the problem becomes too big," the abbot said, "I'll take a plane down to Santo Domingo de Silos and ask the abbot there for advice."

Landler did not rely on just one monk or monastery representative or just one person on the outside world. In his own words, each told his perspective about why the monks would produce an album of Gregorian chants for public sale—and how they will benefit from the profits. Solid reporting requires multiple interviews and viewpoints. The space allotted to detailed interviews shows what print and online media can offer above broadcast media.

Research before Interviewing

The first step in interviewing, of course, is to know your topic, and that requires research. Before any interview, you should have knowledge of your topic and the people you will interview. The general rule is not to go into an interview cold. You will have more success if your source quickly sees you are prepared. Preparation shows that you are serious about the interview, and it flatters the source.

With deadline pressure, however, some journalists might find that they do not have time to do research before they have to be on site to cover an event. On some occasions, you might go into an interview unprepared. Experienced writers or reporters will tell you that such an experience is uncomfortable and often embarrassing. No one wants to walk up to the newest

Nobel Prize winner for medicine and ask, "Now just what was your work that caused you to win?"

With the advantages of technology today, a reporter can be on his or her way to an interview while a researcher searches files for background information. The reporter can get data from the researcher and arrive somewhat prepared. Or the reporter can stop and do some quick online research via his cell phone.

Writers—whether print or broadcast reporters, online journalists, freelancers, public relations practitioners, graphic designers, or advertising copywriters—look in their own files first for information, then move to the company's or community's library. They might find other articles or broadcasts about their topic, or they may consult research materials such as government sites. Specific sources are noted in Chapter 9.

Sometimes as part of research, media will do an informal survey of people's opinions; for example, reporters may ask for residents' views on changes in Social Security or on plans to widen Main Street. Those stories require meaningful questions to get good quotes and complete identification of respondents. Such stories are a way to get readers or viewers into the newspaper, on an online site, or on radio or television. Media, as well as public officials or professional pollsters, can uncover public sentiment.

Considering more formal poll results could also be part of your research before setting up an interview. Polling firms spend millions of dollars each year interviewing voters about their favorite candidates and consumers about their favorite products and services. Marketers use the results to promote everything from a specific politician to toothpaste. Their questions have to be worded carefully to avoid bias and to obtain relevant, pertinent, and accurate information. Such firms have professionals who draft questions, oversee interviews, and compile results.

Getting the Interview

Once you have sufficient knowledge, you must determine whom it is you want to interview. For a story on credit card fraud, a local bank president might be a primary interview. But you must also talk to experts in the financial services industry, consumers, and whoever is knowledgeable about the subject. Some names might appear during research, and some could come as referrals in other interviews.

Setting Up the Interview

When you know whom you want to interview, you need to determine the best method of interviewing and make an appointment, whether the interview is by telephone or in person. Some interviews can be conducted by e-mail. Online questions and answers are fast and convenient, but remember: They have serious limitations. The source might not be known to the writer. The writer who interviews only via e-mail loses the candid spontaneity that comes with live interviews, as well as any sense of the source's surroundings and personal characteristics. A low chuckle or a timely grin are impossible to detect in an e-mail.

In setting up any interview, you may have to go through a secretary or a public relations person who maintains the source's schedule, and that process can be time consuming. Or you may be able to call the person directly.

Make sure that a source has firsthand information. If you are working on a story that requires expert opinion, for example, be sure your source is an appropriate one. The primary surgeon for a lung transplant is a much better source than a hospital public information officer or a physician who assisted during the operation. People who have never been involved in a child abuse case and are just giving you secondhand or hearsay information are not good sources for a story on that subject. A few filter questions upfront can eliminate unnecessary interviews: "I am looking for people who tried to break into the country-western music market. Did you ever sing professionally? Or perhaps prepare a demonstration tape for an agent?"

In setting up an interview, be sure to specify the amount of time you will need. Don't underestimate, or you will lack time to ask all your questions. Some people may be willing to be interviewed on the spot when you call, so be ready with your questions. Others will want to set a specific time at a later date. Ask for more time than you will need.

Select a comfortable place for an interview. The source's terrain is best because he or she is usually more relaxed in a familiar environment. The reporter also has the opportunity to observe personal items, such as family photographs or collected memorabilia, that can add to the story.

Avoid doing interviews during meals. People have difficulty talking while eating, and a discussion over who should pay for food—source or writer—can be uncomfortable. If the individual is from out of town and staying at the local hotel, you may choose to do an interview over coffee—a fairly inexpensive way of meeting and talking.

Dress appropriately for the interview. If you are interviewing the chief executive officer of a Fortune 500 company, wear a suit. If you are meeting a peanut grower in his fields, shuck the cashmere coat. And, if you are meeting with teenagers at the local hangout, jeans are okay.

What to Work Out in Advance

Do not agree to pay for an interview. Only in very rare situations should you consider paying for information. A news organization may agree to pay because the source's information is newsworthy, but any payment should be worked out ahead of time and be consistent with company policy. If you are a freelancer, you should not agree to pay for information; publications might not buy your work if sources were lured by profit.

Work out arrangements if you plan to use an audio or video recorder. Do not just show up with the equipment. Sources might want to be prepared, particularly in regard to their physical appearance if they are to be filmed. A tape recorder is advisable if you are planning a long interview or one that might contain controversial or important information. You might want a tape as a backup if you suspect a source might question your quotes in the printed article. One good way to have a source agree to be taped is to stress your need for accuracy in getting quotes right. Few people will argue.

Of course, you will need audio equipment if you know you will be writing an online version of the story and sound will be part of the package an editor will prepare. The same applies if the online editor wants video clips. Be sure to reserve equipment in advance, make sure it is working and has batteries before you leave the office, and review any operations so you can use it comfortably.

If you are doing an interview by e-mail or telephone, establish a time period for questions and answers so you will get responses by your deadline. You also might want to agree on a code word that the source will include at the end of responses so you know the source answered the questions and not someone who had access—whether legally or illegally—to the e-mail account. Some writers use e-mail only as a follow-up to a telephone or face-to-face interview. Be sure to note in the story which quotes came from e-mail interviews, just as you would note "in a telephone interview."

Some people will want to see a list of questions before they agree to an interview. Such a request can be honored if sources need to collect specific information, such as statistics. People who are not used to being interviewed may want some time to formulate responses. Or, if you are getting an actuality to use in a broadcast, a source may want a few minutes to prepare a response so he or she will have a script to follow. In many cases, your deadline will determine whether you have the luxury of submitting questions and waiting for responses. In any case, don't give up the right to ask a question that is not on the list.

Some sources will ask if they can see the article before it is printed or listen to the tape before it is aired. Of course, if you are a public relations practitioner or an ad copywriter, your source—who may be your client—will have final approval. But in the news business, the answer is *no*. Deadline pressure generally precludes allowing time for a source to review the message. Sources can become editors, wanting to change more than what applies to them.

If a source insists on previewing the piece, check it out with an editor or producer. You might want to find someone else to interview. Be clear if the answer is no. One inexperienced reporter caused herself and her newspaper some unpleasantness because a source thought he would have the right to edit a story citing him before it was printed. The reporter did not flatly say no, and the source misunderstood, believing he could review the story in advance. When the story appeared, the source felt deceived.

Writing the Questions

Interviewers, no matter how skilled or practiced, should write a list of questions before an interview. The list can be typed and printed or scribbled on an envelope. The questions ensure that all important aspects are covered during an interview. A reporter can review the list before ending an interview to make sure all points were asked. Questions also serve to keep an interview on track. For example, a minister might divert an interview to a discussion of the writer's religious beliefs. The writer can refer to the list and remind the minister that she is there to interview him. The list can also fill in lags in the conversation.

Covering the Basics

Obviously, when you are planning questions, you want to ask the basics: *who, what, when, where, how,* and *why*. But you need to ask other questions to get more information and to make the message complete. One formula for interviewing is called *GOSS,* an acronym for *Goals–Obstacles–Solutions–Start,* devised by Professor LaRue Gilleland of the University of Nevada. It can be applied to many interviews and is based on the assumption that people have goals, obstacles loom before goals, and solutions can be found to obstacles. Talking about goals, obstacles, and solutions gives the source plenty to discuss. During the interview, you may discover that you need to "start"—to go back to the beginning of an event or topic to get a more complete understanding.

For example, you might interview a chemist who does research on polymers. Using GOSS, you would ask about the goals of the research, the obstacles to discovering new uses, and the solutions to overcome the obstacles. "Start" would lead you to ask more broadly about the field of polymer research and what is happening in this particular laboratory compared with others.

Ken Metzler, author of *Creative Interviewing*, has suggested two more letters to Gilleland's GOSS: *E* for *evaluation* and *Y* for *why*. Evaluation suggests a need for an overall assessment of the situation—seeking meaning beyond the facts. To get such information, the writer asks for the source's interpretation: What does all this (polymers and research) mean to you? The *Y* is a reminder not to forget to ask why a situation has occurred and why particular research is important.

Think about quantitative questions. How many times has the baseball star struck out? How many ounces of marijuana were confiscated, and what is its street value? How many tons of concrete are needed for the runway, and is that equal to filling the high school football stadium to the top row 15 times?

When formulating questions, think of the unusual aspects. Don't hesitate to include questions you and your audience would like answered. You might even ask friends or colleagues what questions they would include if given the chance to interview a particular source.

Conducting an Interview

Always be punctual for an interview. Making a source wait is rude and could cost you the interview. Call to let the individual know if you will be late.

If you are interviewing a celebrity or high-ranking official, avoid appearing to be a fan or worshiper, nervous or excited. Few people would be calm the first time they interviewed an Oscar winner or a country's head of state. Butterflies are to be expected, but you should show respect rather than adulation.

Getting Started

When you introduce yourself, always give your name and identify yourself as a reporter. Also state your employer or where you expect to have the story appear, and a summary of what you need from the interviewee. That introduction puts the interviewee on notice that anything he or she says is on the record or for publication in some format.

After you introduce yourself, start an interview with some questions that will set a relaxed mood. For example, if you are in the person's home, comment about trophies, collections, or decor. Show you are interested. Don't ask weighty questions right away.

Avoid starting an interview by asking people what they do or routine information. They will know you haven't done your homework, and they could be insulted. You might need to verify information, however. A student who interviewed author Barbara Victor discovered in a biographical source that she was born in 1944. A question revealed that Victor actually was born a year later, in 1945.

Before beginning an interview, ask yourself the questions in the checklist shown in Box 10.1.

Using Recording Equipment

Even if they don't edit the stories, reporters have to collect raw video that online editors can scan to find relevant images to the story being told. Most reporters can learn to use recording equipment in a few lessons and through trial and error.

BOX 10.1   Checklist for Interviews

- Have I researched thoroughly my subject and source?
- Have I selected the right people to interview?
- Have I set up the interview in a place conducive to the interviewee?
- Have I allotted adequate time?
- Have I worked out using a tape recorder? A video camera? Is the equipment in good working order?
- Have I written a thorough list of questions?
- Do I feel prepared and confident?

If you are using a voice recorder, hold the microphone about six inches below your interviewee's chin to get good audio free of distortions from your interviewee's breath.

Be sure you let sources know when the tape recorder is on. Most states require that you notify people if they are being recorded. If you are doing a telephone interview and plan to record it, you must ask the individual's permission before you turn the recorder on. Rarely, if ever, will you need to hide a tape recorder in your briefcase or under your clothing.

If you are using video equipment and doing the recording yourself, get cover or overall shots first so that you can then focus on the interview. If a videographer is doing the shooting, use the time he or she is setting up the equipment to ask questions to put the person at ease and distract them away from the equipment. Many recorded interviews are done in offices where the lighting can be enhanced and little outside noise detracts or interferes with the sound.

Remember, when recording outside, any noises can interfere with the quality of the recorded interview. Stay away from streets, try to avoid wind, and watch the person's head position so he or she doesn't turn away from the recorder. Visually, what's going on in the background might distract viewers from the interview subject as they watch the action behind.

Remember to think of your microphone as if it were a camera lens. If you want the sounds of an event, move back to capture the jumble of noises as well as the panorama. Then move in close for the more specific.

Asking the Questions

Ask the easy questions first. This technique allows the person to relax and feel comfortable when responding. How to ask the tough questions is covered in the next section.

Be straightforward and specific in questioning. "So, Mr. Rich, you have investments and your construction business. And you have inherited money from your uncle and aunt. I imagine there are lots of people out there who are wondering how much you are worth." Of course, you can preface a question with a statement, but don't talk around a question—ask it. "Mr. Rich, you have investments and inheritance that have many people asking the question: Just how much are you worth?"

As you take notes, be sure to read back any confusing quotes to ensure you have complete and accurate statements. Sometimes a person will talk quickly or start a sentence, stop midway, and begin again. You might need to repeat part of a quote and ask the speaker to confirm or clarify what he or she said.

Maintain control. Don't let the person lead you. Keeping an interview on track might be difficult for a student writer or inexperienced reporter. Someone accustomed to being interviewed could have an agenda or might have what seem like canned responses. A politician, for example, might ignore a question about changes in tax laws and answer instead about his or her plan for economic development. If the person digresses, wait for a suitable pause, then steer the person back to the subject. Use your list of questions as a reference. If you interrupt, you could be cutting off some valuable comments.

Try to keep yourself out of an interview. Often a person will throw questions at the interviewer. Be polite and firm, and remember that you are there to do an interview, not to be interviewed.

Watch your body language. Avoid any behavior, such as nodding your head, that could subtly indicate you agree with comments. If the source believes you are sympathetic and empathetic, he or she might expect a positive story.

Maintain a friendly but professional distance. Do not become the source's friend. Writers who get too chummy with their sources can create tension when the article is published. The source might believe the writer betrayed confidences.

Leave all preconceptions and misconceptions at home. You might be a single working journalist with no children, and your interview is with a stay-at-home mother with five children. Mask any feelings of envy of her domestic life or notions that her job is not as fulfilling as yours. Do not be antagonistic if you disagree with a person's philosophy. Some people will open up, however, if they sense that you do not agree with them.

Listen to the source. Be aware of inconsistencies. Be willing to divert the conversation from the prescribed list of questions if you hear a tidbit that should be developed through another line of questioning. If you do not understand a response, ask for clarification. Remember: If you aren't clear about information, you'll never convey it clearly to audiences.

The Tough Questions

Save all embarrassing and controversial questions for the end of the interview, such as those dealing with a person's gambling debts or reports that a presidential candidate has had an extramarital affair. Of course, if a suitable occasion to ask such a question occurs during an interview, ask it. Be aware that you run the risk of having an interview terminated if you ask a particularly sensitive question. When asking these questions, be straightforward. If you act embarrassed, you will transmit that feeling and possibly not get a response.

The fact that a person does not answer a tough question is often noteworthy in a story. A former foreign service diplomat who settled in a small town was arrested on charges of shoplifting. When he refused to answer reporters' questions after his trial, one reporter noted his refusal in the story. His silence supported statements that he was close-mouthed about his current life. But don't fail to ask a question in the expectation a person might not answer it. You might get a response.

Many times writers must interview people who have suffered trauma or witnessed a traumatic event. An individual might have endured years of repeated physical abuse, survived a plane crash, been a hostage in a domestic dispute, or been wounded. A person might have witnessed a friend's drowning, seen a fiery truck crash, or found a house full of diseased and starving animals.

Writers must understand that people who have suffered trauma or an atrocity recover from those events in different ways and at different times, depending on the particular trauma and their personalities. Judith Lewis Herman notes in her book, *Trauma and Recovery*, that part of the healing process is remembering and telling the event. People seeking quotes and information might find individuals quite willing to talk and others who refuse to be interviewed. Herman writes:

> *People who have survived atrocities often tell their stories in a highly emotional, contradictory, and fragmented manner, which undermines their credibility.... It is difficult for an observer to remain clearheaded and calm, to see more than a few fragments of the picture at one time, to retain all the pieces, and to fit them together. It is even more difficult to find a language that conveys fully and persuasively what one has seen. Those who attempt to describe the atrocities that they have witnessed also risk their own credibility.*

Reporters must be aware of the psychological state of people who have just experienced a tragedy or atrocity, such as a subway bombing. Interviewers should ask the questions but understand when they do not get complete or even accurate responses. Interviewing more than one source might be required to get a full picture of what actually happened. Reporters might have to come back for follow-up interviews well after a traumatic event occurs.

Just as it is difficult to approach victims and witnesses, it is hard to interview victims' families. The media, particularly the electronic media, have drawn criticism for asking family members of victims "How do you feel?" only minutes or hours after a relative's death. Although some view such questioning as aggressive, others regard it as heartless. In some instances, reporters might find that a family member is willing to talk and is helped by remembering the individual. Reporters must use judgment and good taste in how far they should go in trying to get information. Reporters must try to ask the questions, but they must respect a person's right not to answer.

Interviewing during traumatic situations takes special care. The Dart Center for Journalism & Trauma at the University of Washington has an informative Web site—www.dartcenter.org—that defines trauma, gives specific advice on interviewing trauma victims or witnesses, and outlines what clues reporters should recognize if they are adding to the stress through interviewing.

Off-the-Record Information

In the middle of an interview, a public official says, "The following information needs to be off the record." Stop the official. Don't let him or her talk any longer. Off the record means you cannot use the information. As a writer you don't want information you cannot use. Politely refuse the information. Then you can proceed to clarify what the official means. People have different definitions of what off the record means: Don't use the information at all; use it but don't attribute it to me; or use it to ask questions of others, but I never said it.

A source might want to go off the record because he fears retribution if certain comments can be attributed to him. Sources also might have an ulterior motive in sharing what they imply is a secret, so reporters must be sure the information is valid and can't be learned any other way.

If you refuse to accept off-the-record information, the source might open up. People who have juicy information usually feel important and want to show they know something you don't. Think about it. Has a friend told you some gossip about someone else and sworn you to secrecy? Within 24 hours, had you shared it with someone else, despite your promise? Few secrets exist that are known only by one person.

As an interviewer, you must remember that many people who have information want to share it but may not want to take responsibility for making it public. They will let you as the writer do it anonymously, or let you find someone else to confirm it and become the public source. Be careful. Audiences do not necessarily believe information attributed to "a source close to the president" or "a high-level State Department official."

Some people will want to do interviews for background or just to educate you about a situation or to give you context. That means they are giving you information not to be attributed to them. For example, a bank executive might give you background on lenders and home mortgages. The information helps you in explaining the process to your readers or in asking questions of executives at other banks.

A final warning: Make sure you and the source are clear on how the information can be used before you accept it. If you agree to use the information but not the individual's name, you can use the information but not for attribution. If you agree the tidbit is confidential, you must not publish it. You might want that person as a source again. If you act unethically and violate the agreement, you can write that person off your source list, and you might attract unflattering attention to yourself and your employer.

Note-Taking Tips for Interviews

Most people talk faster than an interviewer can write. If you are not using a tape recorder and if you have trouble keeping up, politely stop the source and ask for a moment to catch up on notes. You could preface it by saying, "I want to make sure I record this correctly, so I need a moment to complete your last comment." Few sources would respond: "I don't care if you get it right. I want to keep talking."

Be sure when you are writing comments that you get them completely rather than in bits and pieces that might not fit together when you write the article. Complete notes help you avoid taking quotes out of context or misinterpreting quotes later.

If you have a quote that is complete, put it within quotation marks in your notebook. Then you will know you have the speaker's exact words when you review your notes and are ready to write. If you are using a tape recorder and hear a quote that you know you want to use, you can quickly check the counter on the recorder and write the time next to the quote in your notebook.

You might find it handy to flag your notes as you take them. Put a word or two in the margin to indicate where certain information occurs. For example, you may have a wide-ranging interview with the incoming Democratic speaker of the state legislature. "Welfare," "tax cuts," "power," and "education" would remind you where each topic was discussed. If you're using a tape recorder, it might also be useful to write down the "timestamp"—the number of minutes and seconds after the start of the recording—of each interesting statement by the source. That can help you write not only the correct words in a text report, but it will also reduce the amount of time you spend on editing audio if you are doing a multimedia report.

At the end of an interview, take a few moments to ensure you have asked all your questions. Most sources won't mind waiting while you double-check. If a quote is not clear, ask the source to repeat it. "You said earlier, Mr. Speaker, that changing the rules will help the House pass legislation faster. Could you clarify the parliamentary procedure a little more?" You also might want to ask if you can telephone or e-mail if any clarification is needed when you are producing the story.

After an Interview

Take time soon after you leave an interview to review your notes. Fill in any blanks that might appear confusing later. Note your feelings, the qualities of the source, any additional description, and other details while they are fresh in your mind. You should transcribe your notes as soon as possible to retain important details or impressions. If you store your notes on your computer, you can call them up easily when it is time to create the piece.

After an interview, you might want to write the person a thank-you note.

Selecting and Using Quotes

You have pages of notes from your interview. How do you determine which quotes to use? The same rules for using quotes from interviews apply to selecting quotes from speeches, presentations, or even published works. Selected quotes should be vivid, show opinion, reflect the speaker's personality, support the speaker's thesis, and unify a piece of writing.

When to Use Quotes

In organizing material, writers have to decide whether to quote an individual, then whether to use that information in an indirect or direct quote.

Direct quotes give the exact words of the speaker. The quotation marks signify to readers "here's exactly what was said." Direct quotes are used for colorful statements, opinion, and emotions. Direct quotes can convey an individual's personality and manner of speaking. Here's one rule to follow: Use a direct quote if it is better than any paraphrase.

Direct quotes can be either complete quotes or partial quotes. Here is a complete direct quote:

> "Russia needs to honor the agreement and withdraw its forces and, of course, end military operations," the president said.

Or:

> "If Speaker Pelosi and her Democratic colleagues were truly serious about increasing production of American energy and lowering the price of gasoline, they would call Congress back into session immediately to vote on our 'all of the above' energy plan," said Rep. John A. Boehner of Ohio, the Republican leader.

A partial direct quote would be written as:

> House Speaker Nancy Pelosi said legislation being assembled by Democrats "will consider opening portions of the Outer Continental Shelf for drilling, with appropriate safeguards and without taxpayer subsidies to big oil."

Or:

> A 27-year-old Egyptian woman gave birth to septuplets in what one of her doctors called "a very rare pregnancy—something I have never witnessed over my past 33 years in this profession."

Be careful not to switch person even in a partial quote—for example, switching from third person ("the senator") to the first person ("my influence"), as in the following sentence:

> The senator vowed to "use every last little bit of my influence" to block the bill increasing military spending.

A grammatical sentence would use the words "his influence," but then the quote would be inaccurate. In such cases, as in this example, rewrite as:

> The senator vowed "to use every last little bit" of his influence to block the bill increasing military spending.

As a note, most writers avoid using what are called orphan quotes—that is, quotation marks used for emphasis on a single word.

> The special envoy said the cease-fire represented a "monumental" effort.

Why use quotations? "Monumental" is hardly an inflammatory phrase or an unusual adjective.

To Paraphrase or Not

Indirect quotes are used to summarize or paraphrase what individuals say, particularly if they have rambled about an issue or topic. They do not use a speaker's exact words and are not set off with quotation marks. Writers use indirect quotes to keep quotes relevant and precise.

Many writers find indirect quotes particularly valuable when speakers have digressed from the main topic or when they inject jokes or anecdotal material that cannot be used. After deciding that Connecticut was unfairly burdened by the No Child Left Behind education act, Attorney General Richard Blumenthal announced that the state would sue the federal government. Part of his comments needed to be paraphrased. Here is an excerpt from his comments:

> *Give up your unfunded mandates or give us the money…if I believed that the $8 million cost of adding additional tests in grades, three, five and seven was educationally beneficial to Connecticut's students, I'd be the first one in line advocating for the expense. The cost, however, is not worth the questionable educational benefit. After multiple failed attempts to attain a mutually agreeable resolution to our reasonable, research-based requests, it is time to see resolution in another forum—the courts.*

Good media writing summed up Blumenthal's position in this lead from *The New York Times:*

> The State of Connecticut will sue the federal government over President Bush's signature education law, arguing that it forces Connecticut to spend millions on new tests without providing sufficient additional aid, the state attorney general announced yesterday.

Correcting Speakers' Grammar and Other Slips

Reporters who covered a high-level state official quickly learned that the man was not a good speaker. He had a vernacular accent for that region of the state, used incorrect grammar, and stated goals that seemed out of reach. How to quote him?

Early in the official's tenure, some print journalists chose to paraphrase his remarks so they could clean up the grammar errors. But others chose to clean up the grammar in direct quotes, making the official sound well schooled. But they soon discovered that cleaning up the official's language was not good practice. Audiences who also watched local television broadcasts saw and heard the official as he really was. The image they read in the newspaper did not match.

Journalists are faced continually with deciding how to use quotes. If a speaker uses improper subject–verb agreement, should the writer correct it in a direct quote? How far should writers go in cleaning up quotes? In the case of the state official, print journalists figured out they had to be true to the quotes or else paraphrase. They could not dramatically clean up the quotes, put them in direct quotations, and tell audiences, "Here's exactly what the man said." He didn't.

The Associated Press Stylebook advises writers:

> *Never alter quotations even to correct minor grammatical errors or word usage. Casual minor tongue slips may be removed by using ellipses but even that should be done with extreme caution. If there is a question about a quote, either don't use it or ask the speaker to clarify.*

Are Profanities and Obscenities Acceptable?

The Associated Press Stylebook also advises writers not to use profanity, obscenities, or vulgarities unless they are part of direct quotations and there is a compelling reason for them. Writers are cautioned to warn editors of writing that contains such language. The language should be confined to a single paragraph so that it can be easily deleted. Writers should not modify profanity, such as changing "damn" to "darn." Editors may change the word to "d—" to indicate that profanity was used by the speaker if no compelling reason exists to spell it out in the story.

Writers need to check with their publications and media organizations to determine their particular rules on profanity, obscenities, and vulgarities. Some specialized publications, listservs, blogs, or television shows allow such language. Audiences who subscribe to or view such programs are familiar with the language and either do not find it offensive or overlook it.

Sometimes a reporter will not include profanity in the news story on which the interview is based, but they will when it is part of an associated full transcript of the interview. Writers who link to the transcript from the online news story may want to consider ways to warn the reader that the transcript contains language that some readers may consider vulgar.

General Rules about Quotes

- Never make up a quote. Quotes must be accurate.
- Don't take a question answered "yes" or "no" and turn it into a direct quote. For example, if an interviewer asks a high school basketball coach if he believed many students bet on the outcome of games and the coach answered, "No," the quotation in the newspaper should not read:

    Coach Lyman Jones said, "I don't think many students bet on the outcome of our basketball games."

  All you can really say is this: When asked whether he thought many students bet on the outcomes of games, Coach Lyman Jones replied, "No."
- Watch out for redundancies when setting up quotes. Use the direct quotes to expand or add to the information in the indirect quote.

  Avoid:

    She said she was surprised at being chosen the school's outstanding senior. "I was so surprised when they called my name," Gonzalez said.

Prefer:

Melissa said she was surprised when the principal called her name. "I couldn't move or react," she added. "I felt glued to my chair in shock."

■ **Set up situations before using the quote so readers will have a context for quotes, as in the following Associated Press story:**

An exercise program supported by the federal government and the trucking industry is aimed at eliminating spare tires on the truckers.

The goal is to make interstate drivers slimmer, healthier—and safer.

The Rolling Strong Gym has opened at a truck stop in North Little Rock, Ark., and others are planned elsewhere along Interstate 40. The president of the Richardson, Texas, health club company, as well as government and industry officials, are watching to see if the truckers will work out.

"It's been long overdue," said Paul Todorovich of Myrtle Beach, S.C., an independent driver. "I'm hoping it catches on and they flourish."

Transportation Department officials also hope so. "Research shows that drivers who are physically fit are safe drivers and that exercise is key to getting people into healthier lifestyles," said Transportation Secretary Rodney E. Slater in a statement endorsing the concept.

■ **Use "according to" only with printed or factual information. Do not use it as an attribution to a person.**

Avoid:

The state's prison system is 3,456 inmates above the legally allowed level, according to the secretary of correction.

Prefer:

The state's prison system is 3,456 inmates above the legally allowed level, said the secretary of correction. According to prison documents, the level has exceeded capacity for the past seven years.

- Use attribution in the middle of a sentence only if it occurs at a natural break. Otherwise, put it at the beginning or the end so that you don't interrupt the flow of the person's statement.

Avoid:

"We can always," he said, "commission a new statue for the college commons."

Prefer:

"We can always commission a new statue for the college commons," he said.

Acceptable:

"The marine sciences lab is vital to the state's economy," he said, "and we must persuade the legislature to allocate more funds this year."

- Always use attribution for statements that use "hope," "feel," or "believes." You as a writer are not inside another person's head; you know how he or she feels, thinks, or believes because you were told.

The district attorney said she believes the verdict fell short of what she expected the jury to do. She said she believes the community will be angered that Ammons was not found guilty of first-degree murder.

More on Attribution

Quotes, whether direct or indirect, must be attributed completely and adequately. Readers or listeners must know who is talking and who is making each statement. They need to know the proper sources of information. The general rule is that attribution should go at the beginning of each new quote or at the end of the first sentence, whether the quote is one sentence or more than one sentence.

If the quote goes on for several paragraphs, attribution usually is placed at least once in every paragraph, and most writers follow the rule of attribution somewhere in the first sentence. Some writers will omit attribution in a middle paragraph if they have several short paragraphs of quotes by the same speaker. The key is to ensure that readers know who is talking.

If paragraphs contain strong statements of opinion, however, the writer must use attribution for every sentence.

For many writers, particularly news writers, "said" is the attribution word of choice. "Said" carries no underlying connotation as to a speaker's emphasis or meaning; it is neutral. "Added" and "told" are also fairly neutral. Attribution words that contain subtle meanings include "emphasized," "stressed," "declared," "demanded," "ordered," "stated," "criticized," and "contended." Writers avoid many of these words.

Do not use words such as "smiled," "laughed," "grimaced," "chuckled," and so on as attribution words. They are descriptive words that tell how a person was behaving when she or he said something. Rather than writing "'Hello,' he smiled," use "he said with a smile." Phrases such as "she said, and frowned," "he said, and grimaced," and "she said, then laughed" are preferred.

When using attribution that includes a person's title, do not place the title between the person's name and the attribution verb.

Avoid:

The University will accept 3,475 freshmen for the incoming class, Polly Wilson, director of undergraduate admissions, said.

Prefer:

The University will accept 3,475 freshmen for the incoming class, said Polly Wilson, director of undergraduate admissions.

Punctuating Quotes

General punctuation rules are discussed in Chapter 2. Here are the basic rules for punctuating quotes:

- Attribution at the end of a quote—whether direct or indirect—must be set off with punctuation. In most cases, the punctuation will be a comma.

  Fifteen barrels of sardines will be delivered Wednesday, he said.

  "Fifteen stinking, dripping barrels of sardines will be delivered Wednesday," he said.

  "Will you deliver the barrels of sardines before noon?" he asked.

■ Attribution at the beginning of an indirect quote is not set off with punctuation.

He said 15 barrels of sardines will be delivered Wednesday.

■ Attribution at the beginning of a direct quote requires punctuation. If the quote is only one sentence long, use a comma. If the quote is two or more sentences long, use a colon.

Johnson said, "We have spent three days examining the department's accounts and have found no evidence of impropriety."

Johnson said: "We have spent three days examining the department's accounts and have found no evidence of impropriety. We will recommend that no further action be taken."

■ Quotes within a direct quote are set off with single quotation marks.

"He said, 'Go ahead and throw it away, just like you have done every game,' and he walked out and slammed the door," Smithers said.

"I think 'War of the Worlds' was a frightening movie," she said.

■ Commas and periods go inside quotation marks in direct quotes.

"Fifteen stinking, dripping barrels of sardines will be delivered Wednesday," he said.

Matthews said, "This race should be the test of every man's and every woman's physical and mental stamina."

■ When placing the attribution at the end of the first sentence in a direct quote, the attribution is closed with a period. It marks the end of a sentence.

Wrong:

"The new gymnasium is fantastic and humungous," said basketball player Brad Jones, "We're proud to play there. We really feel important playing our games now."

Right:

"The new gymnasium is fantastic and humungous," said basketball player Brad Jones. "We're proud to play there. We really feel important playing our games now."

■ Question marks go inside or outside quotation marks depending on whether they are part of the quote.

Mark said, "Are you asking me whether I cheated on the exam?"

One of Dionne Warwick's popular renditions included "Do You Know the Way to San Jose?"

■ Consider what may be slightly confusing but correct punctuation here:

Sara asked Kate, "Have you ever seen the movie 'Gone With the Wind'?"

Here, the writer has a movie title that must be set off with quotation marks within a direct quote plus a question mark that is not part of the title.

■ If the attribution breaks up a direct quote, it must be set off with commas and the quotation marks continued.

"Go ahead and throw it away," said Smithers, "just like you have done every game."

- If a speaker is quoted for several continuing paragraphs, the quotation marks are closed only at the final paragraph. Each paragraph must open with quotation marks to indicate the person is still speaking.

> Resident John Loftis of Hollowell Road said, "We have been waiting two years for the southeast area to be annexed, and we are getting annoyed that the town council has further delayed a decision.
>
> "I have written and my neighbors have written all the council members to say we want town services and are willing to pay for them.
>
> "We just don't understand what the holdup is," Loftis said. "If a decision doesn't come after the next public hearing, I plan to picket city hall."

Not closing the quotation marks at the end of the first and second paragraphs tells the reader that Loftis has not finished talking. The quotation marks at the beginning of graphs 2 and 3 reopen the continuous quote from Loftis.

Writers must ensure that readers know who is speaking and when a person stops speaking. Attributing a quote to the wrong person because punctuation is incorrect could cause problems, ranging from jeopardizing a writer's relationships with sources to more serious issues of damaging credibility or even leading to defamation lawsuits. Careful writers pay attention to detail and accuracy, down to every quotation mark.

Remember:

- Be circumspect in your use of quotations. Just because you have a quote doesn't mean you have to use it.
- Look for variety in quotes when writing, and use a mix of indirect and direct quotes.
- Check *The Associated Press Stylebook* rule about correcting quotes.
- If you are not sure about a quote, follow this rule: When in doubt, leave it out. Don't try to reconstruct it as a direct quote. And be sure you have the gist of the remarks if you convert the comments to an indirect quote.
- Develop recording skills so you can use electronic equipment to add visuals and sound or to assist in long or complicated interviews.

Exercises

1. Interview a friend or classmate about political life on your campus. Consider using a tape recorder to practice taking notes and listening to the tape again to double-check accuracy. Take careful notes. Then list five quotes, with correct attribution, that you might use in a finished story about political life at your school. Focus on correct attribution and use of both indirect and direct quotes.

2. Identify a campus leader who has been in the news recently. Select a specific topic related to the leader's expertise. Set up an interview and prepare questions as outlined in the chapter. If possible, take a video camera to record the interview. While interviewing, take notes on the surroundings to add description. When the interview is over, compare your notes to the tape. Write a story that focuses on the campus leader's view. Use a mix of direct and indirect quotes. Select 30 seconds of video to use as well.

3. You are a reporter for the campus newspaper. Your editor has asked you to come up with a story based on money, specific to the campus. Ideas might be the cost of tuition or books, lack of enough financial aid, lack of funds to maintain classrooms, cost of getting settled in a job after graduation, increased student fees. Think of a story that would interest your audience: students. Stick to the campus for interviews. You must use more than one source. If the story relates to campus funding, you will need to talk to an administrator. You would also want to talk with a student who is affected. Be sure to have enough sources. After the interviews, write a story showing all sides of the issue.

4. Many publications reveal how average citizens feel about or react to an event. Editors will select a current topic and assign a reporter to get public reactions. Scan today's daily newspaper and select a current topic, such as an ongoing international conflict, national legislation, a campus issue, or another major event that students and staff would have read or heard about. Interview 10 people. Ask each one the same question. If you have to ask a question that is answered yes or no, you will need the follow-up question—"Why?"—or your responses will be skimpy. Get each individual's name (check the spelling) and two other identifying labels: year in school, academic major, hometown, age, and residence. Your attribution would look like this: Jane Smith, a senior chemistry major; or Alex Jones, 19, of Whiteville.

Write the story. The first paragraph should have a summary lead, giving the results of your informal poll, such as "Five of 10 university students interviewed Thursday at the student union said they believed the presidency is a tough job that receives little credit, and not one student would want the job." The second paragraph gives the question: "The students were asked, 'What is your assessment of the job of president, and would you want the job?'" Then you can proceed with each person's response.

5. Find a story in your local newspaper and the same story on the newspaper's Web site but with audio and video components added. Listen and view the recorded pieces. How do audio and visual elements add to the story? What can they tell that print alone cannot? E-mail or call the reporter and find out whether he or she was trained to use broadcast equipment and how such skills were learned. What advice does the reporter offer in extending interviewing beyond just pad and pencil?

References

John Brady, *The Craft of Interviewing*. Cincinnati: Writer's Digest, 1976.

Rene J. Cappon, *The Word: An Associated Press Guide to Good News Writing*. New York: Associated Press, 1991.

Norm Goldstein, ed. *The Associated Press Stylebook 2005 and Briefing on Media Law*. New York: Associated Press, 2005.

Mark Landler, "Heiligenkreuz Journal: Sacred Songs Sell, Drawing Attention to Their Source," *The New York Times*, June 26, 2008, accessed at http://www.nytimes.com/2008/06/26/world/europe/26monk.html?_r=1&oref=slogin&ref=world&pagewanted=print, accessed July 1, 2008.

Judith Lewis Herman, *Trauma and Recovery*. New York: Basic Books, 1992.

Ken Metzler, *Creative Interviewing, 2nd ed.* Englewood Cliffs, NJ: Prentice-Hall, 1989.

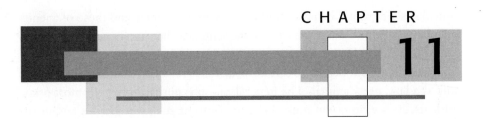

Recognizing Bias and Stereotypes

Understanding bias means considering your own background as well as the backgrounds of others. Many people believe they can write about other people without allowing any personal bias to creep into their stories, news spots, or news releases. But few people can step outside personal bias because most people are unaware of how ingrained their beliefs and attitudes can be. All of us have biases or preconceived notions about others. Bias is not just overt, as racial prejudice or political beliefs are. It is subtle—and it comes from who you are.

Consider your background. Did you come from a suburban middle-class home where you attended a school with little ethnic diversity? Did you speak a language other than English at home? What is your family's ethnic or racial background? Did you grow up in an urban ethnic neighborhood—Italian, African American, or Laotian?

Did you live in a subsidized housing project, in an inner city, or in a small town of 5,000 people or fewer? Maybe you grew up on a farm or ranch, and your nearest neighbor was a half mile away. Did your grandparents or another relative live near you? Did you attend private or public schools?

What is your gender? Do you or does someone in your family have a physical or mental disability? What is your religion? What political party do you claim?

All these aspects of your background and many others helped to build your attitudes and beliefs. As a communicator, you must become aware of your attitudes and beliefs to curb the bias still evident in many stories produced by the media today—and the bias that keeps many stories from appearing.

Bias often surfaces in stereotypes that show up in adjectives or nouns used to describe certain groups. People form stereotypes from their perceptions of individuals' or groups' behavior and from their experiences and those of friends and relatives. Think about the label in the sentence "Jane is a typical college student who wants to have a good time and study as little as possible." As a student, you would not want people to ignore your full array of attributes and view you only as a lazy, party animal. The generalization is not fair to you or most other students. As a writer, you must learn to confront such stereotypes and avoid perpetuating negative overgeneralizations about groups.

In this chapter, you will learn

- how writers can begin to recognize bias,
- how bias in writing affects specific individuals and groups, and
- specific tips on how to avoid bias in writing about individuals and groups.

The Bias Habit

Journalists' cultural values can affect their ability to be truly fair. Because of the way the brain processes information, people must categorize and label people and events. Walter Lippmann referred to this phenomenon in 1922:

> *The real environment is altogether too big, too complex and too fleeting for direct acquaintance. We are not equipped to deal with so much subtlety, so much variety, so many permutations and combinations. And although we have to act in that environment, we have to reconstruct it on a simpler model before we can manage it.*

The *adaptive process* means people do not consider as many perspectives as possible, or they develop a view that does not accurately reflect reality. Most important, in this adaptive process, people often will select the information that confirms their existing attitudes and beliefs, say journalism researchers Holly Stocking and Paget Gross, who add that people may not even be aware they process information with a cognitive bias. They do not have to make a conscious effort to be biased; in fact, they may be trying to be unbiased, as journalists do in attempting objectivity.

It is important to remember that bias surfaces in many arenas. Adjectives and nouns are ascribed to people because of where they live, their political beliefs, their sexual orientation, and their religion. Bias attributes certain characteristics to women, men, people with disabilities, children, older people, and members of ethnic and racial groups. Labels are dangerous. They often are offensive and usually imply inferiority. They can exclude or oppress. Labels do not accurately describe individuals nor do they accurately apply to groups. Writers who do not think beyond labels perpetuate negative stereotypes and myths.

Not all stereotypes necessarily appear negative, however. For example, a majority-culture stereotype has been exhibited in several kinds of traditionally American stories such as cowboy stories, soap operas, or musicals where the heroes usually are depicted as tall, broad-shouldered, white, and handsome and where women most frequently play minor roles.

Another example of a positive stereotype is the "model minority" in the Asian American community, where people are depicted as geniuses in music, math, and science. That generalization, although it seems complimentary, is not true and affects the majority of Asian Americans who might not have aptitudes in these particular fields.

Usage also changes as perception and bias changes. Writers who rely on *The Associated Press Stylebook* for guidance on word choice notice the changes in each annual edition. For example, the 2008 edition notes "mentally disabled" as the preferred term, replacing "mentally retarded."

Bias in Writing

Groups such as journalists can construct a shared view of "reality" because of the similarities in the way they view the world. Timothy Crouse in his book, *The Boys on the Bus*, explained the close working relationship among political reporters on the campaign trail:

> *It was just these womblike conditions that gave rise to the notorious phenomenon called "pack journalism" (also known as "herd journalism" and "fuselage journalism"). A group of reporters were assigned to follow a single candidate for weeks or months at a time, like a pack of hounds sicked on a fox. Trapped on the same bus or plane, they ate, drank, gambled, and compared notes with the same bunch of colleagues week after week.*

As early as 1950, one famous study showed how wire editors relied on their own values to select the news. David Manning White reported that "as 'gatekeeper' the newspaper editor sees to it (even though he may never be consciously aware of it) that the community shall hear as a fact only those events which the newsman, as representative of his culture, believes to be true."

Almost half a century after the Civil Rights Movement became a force in the United States, inequities based on race and ethnic background persist. Mass media have both helped and hindered the effort for equal rights in this country. On the one hand, they give voice to various social movements and allow the message of equality to reach a mass audience. On the other hand, they perpetuate misinformation and ignore a myriad of other ethnic groups.

Although the complexion of management is changing, most people who run the media are of Western European descent, and a large majority are male. They have little context, therefore, to help them know what it is like to be an African American, Native American, Asian American, Hispanic American, or other person of color in the United States. (Only about 13 percent of journalists nationwide are from these groups. Journalists as a group are educated, and few grew up in poverty.) Too often, stories about those communities are reported with an outsider's perspective, resulting in misinformation or stereotypes. In other cases, the stories might not be reported; the group might be invisible to the journalist.

The issue of race and the media—both how the media cover race and the racial makeup of newsrooms—surfaced in the 1968 Kerner Commission Report. The report was commissioned by President Lyndon Johnson's administration after the race riots in Los Angeles in August 1965. As part of the report, the committee looked at media and race. Ten years later, another study, *Window Dressing on the Set: Women and Minorities in Television: A Report of the United States Commission on Civil Rights*, noted the token roles played by women and minorities in TV news and sitcoms. The two are considered classic cases that started media managers looking at racial issues and prompted news organizations, such as the American Society of Newspaper Editors, to launch diversity committees.

Consider some of these other overt problems of bias in coverage:

■ *The New Yorker* cover that depicted then-presidential candidate Barack Obama in a turban fist-bumping his wife, Michelle, who had a rifle slung over her shoulder.

■ The rush to believe that even Muslims who were U.S. citizens were affiliated with the radical fringe accused of the World Trade Center and Pentagon attacks in 2001.

■ The belief that teens with dyed, spiky hair and black leather jackets are drug users.

- The use of black or Hispanic women as the subject of photos about welfare when the majority of welfare recipients are white, not black or Hispanic.
- The use of photographs of gay men in ballet tutus to illustrate a story about gay civil rights.

Breaking the Bias Habit

Today, writers and reporters are trying, through better awareness, to overcome their own biases in addition to cultural bias implanted in the news. But old habits die hard. A first step is for writers to be aware of their own biases and how easily biases can slip into communication. Take religion as an example. Our religious beliefs may contain opinions about others that we should not include in our writing, even though we firmly believe them. Some writers may have Biblical or "sacred text" attitudes and opinions about homosexuals, Jews, gentiles, African Americans, and women. In other words, religion may teach us things about those who don't believe as we do.

Another important way to break the bias habit is to know your own biases. You can check yourself by taking the Implicit Association Test, a University of Washington and Yale University test that measures biases regarding race, age, gender, and ethnicity. You can find it online at https://implicit.harvard.edu/implicit/. What's important in the real world is that communicators do not convey these preconceived notions in their communication, even if they believe them.

Writers also must not fall into the habit of ascribing tired adjectives to certain groups, as noted earlier in the chapter. Writers unconsciously tend to write on traditional stereotyped templates, such as "rural–urban or inner city," "black–white," "rich–poor/tale of two cities," "old–young," or "rags to riches/Cinderella." Writers need original and accurate language to describe individuals.

Society itself helps writers. Today a multicultural approach is being integrated into numerous aspects of society, from school textbooks to television advertisements. All types of cultures in the United States are gaining a voice. Coverage of the 2008 Olympics in Beijing gave many reporters and people around the world a look into a communist country that is emerging as a world economic force. As someone disseminating information, you can learn to tap into these cultures for stories and diverse insights.

Media can have an impact in breaking the bias habit. As newsrooms become more diverse, the types of stories aired or printed will continue to become diverse.

Reporters can describe people as individuals, not cast them in broad terms ascribed to a group. Reporters can also become circumspect when using language and learn which terminology individuals and groups prefer. Diverse groups should be covered year-round, not just on holidays or in certain months.

Many organizations have developed guidelines on language use. Professional journalism organizations have Web sites that often include examples of stereotyping or negative portrayals. For example, the National Association of Black Journalists has posted on its Web site "NABJ Style" under its "Newsroom" link. The committee that spent three years compiling the entries notes that the style guide is "a first draft, an evolving document." Anyone, from journalists to students, can find definition and preferred usage for terms listed alphabetically at http://www.nabj.org/newsroom/stylebook/index.php.

Students can become more familiar with groups, their goals, their membership, and current issues by accessing Web sites for organizations that support those groups, such as the American Association of Retired Persons at www.aarp.org. Professional media organizations are also good sources. The Asian American Journalists Association can be found at www.aaja.org; National Association of Black Journalists at www.nabj.org; Native American Journalists Association at www.naja.org; National Association of Hispanic Journalists at www.nahj.org; and the National Lesbian & Gay Journalists Association at NLGJA.org. Most sites have links to related organizations. Other helpful Web sites are listed in Box 11.1.

BOX 11.1   Helpful Web Sites with Cross-Links to Other Informative Sites

www.ciij.org—Center for Integration and Improvement of Journalism's comprehensive site with links to major associations of minority journalists and the National Lesbian and Gay Journalists Association, among others. It includes diversity news and media sites.

www.unityjournalists.org—The UNITY Web Site, self-described as "a strategic alliance advocating news coverage about people of color." It includes a link to the National Association of Black Journalists' style guide.

www.mosaicweb.com/index2.htm—A multicultural site that is constantly updated. It includes links to "Filipino-American," "Caribbean," "women," and "multicultural."

www.spj.org/diversity.asp—The Society of Professional Journalists' guide to diversity with links to other articles as well as to its "Guidelines for Countering Racial, Ethnic and Religious Profiling."

Considering Specific Groups

John Mitrano, executive director of the National Organization of Italian Students and Educators, noted the following in a survey:

> *While there is usually a grain of truth to stereotypes, over time, these become no longer salient. With the twilight of ethnicity upon us in third and fourth generation families, new portrayals must be used to depict groups accurately. Television shows, movies, and advertisements must emphasize the qualities that we see ourselves as having. We must also become vocal and mobilized when we do not like the way we are portrayed.*

Many words and images applied to specific groups have historically negative and derogatory connotations. Writers must be aware of them and avoid them.

Race or ethnicity often has relevance for stories and should be used only when pertinent. Writers should avoid racial identifiers that imprecisely identify someone as black, Latino, or Asian American, particularly in crime stories. Keith Woods, dean at the Poynter Institute, in using the example of describing a man solely as Hispanic, writes:

> *Think about it this way: In order for everyone reading, watching, or listening to the story to conjure up the same image in their mind's eye, they must all share a common understanding of what a Latino person looks like. In other words, people who are Latino would have to look alike.*
>
> *What does a Hispanic man look like? Is his skin dark brown? Reddish brown? Pale? Is his hair straight? Curly? Coarse? Fine? Does he have a flat, curved nose or is it narrow and straight?*

Woods advises journalists to "challenge the presence of racial identifiers" and to "demand more from the people who give vague, meaningless descriptions, just as you do whenever a politician gives you vague or meaningless information."

Writers should also avoid descriptive words that strengthen stereotypes, such as "oil-rich" and "nomadic" to characterize Arab Americans, says former newspaper editor Fernando Dovalina. He notes the problems surrounding the terms "illegal alien" and "illegal immigrant," which for many have become synonymous with Hispanic, particularly Mexican Americans. Dovalina writes:

> *"Illegal aliens" and "illegal immigrants" were created because of the need to have short and handy phrases to describe people who cross the border illegally....We have no perfect alternative, but the other choices, "undocumented immigrants" or "undocumented workers" are slightly better, even though they are awkward and unwieldy and smack of political correctness.*

Racial and Ethnic Groups

Writers must avoid terminology perpetuating beliefs that all members of any group look alike, talk alike, think alike, or belong to the same political party. Having the first black candidate for U.S. president in 2008 brought attention to race, culture, and language. Some discussions proved positive and others negative, as evidenced in the fallout from the Rev. Jeremiah Wright's comments and Barack Obama distancing himself from his former pastor.

Some language, although it may seem biased, can be appropriate when used in a historical context or with cultural sensitivity, noted Pale Moon Rose, president of the American Indian Heritage Foundation. Terms such as "redskin" and "brave" are acceptable if used appropriately and in a historical context.

The use of Native American names as sports team mascots, such as the Florida State Seminoles and the Washington Redskins, has generated criticism. In another article, Poynter's Keith Woods writes,

> *The harm here is not that all Native American nicknames are insults on the order of Washington's Redskins. It's that nearly all of them freeze Native Americans in an all-encompassing, one-dimensional pose: the raging, spear-wielding, bareback-riding, cowboy-killing, woo-woo-wooing warriors this country has caricatured, demonized, and tried mightily to exterminate.*

Dovalina, retired assistant managing editor for international coverage of *The Houston Chronicle*, developed a list of diversity questions for a national copy editors' workshop. The questions came from his 37-year career and the experiences of other journalist colleagues. The following were among Dovalina's questions:

■ Do you absolutely have to say that a black person or Hispanic or Asian or Native American is the first of his or her race to have attained the distinction in question?...Sometimes the news is that it took so long for a black female or a Hispanic male to be named the first head of a city or college department.

■ Do you assume that all blacks are African Americans or Africans? Remember that culturally some blacks are Jamaicans and Haitians and Brazilians....Some Latin Americans are more German and Italian than Spanish....To people south of the Rio Grande, the term "America" does not refer to the United States alone. It refers to the hemisphere, and they too are Americans.

Use of the term "minority" is problematic in an international sense because people of color make up the majority of the world's population, and population changes in the United States mean that some ethnic groups are the majority in certain locations. Remember also that "minority" always refers to a group rather than to certain individuals; it is best to use the term "members of minority groups" rather than "minorities." Always look for a diversity of sources when writing. A Native American might be interviewed about political struggles instead of the meaning of a ceremonial dance. Dovalina reminds us, "Just as there are no Anglo leaders who speak for all Anglos, there are no black leaders or Hispanic leaders who speak for all blacks or all Hispanics." Keith Woods of Poynter has guidelines for racial identification in the form of five questions (Box 11.2). He notes that delicate material can be handled better "if we flag every racial reference and ask these questions." His questions should be considered when writing about any underrepresented group in society; just substitute the name of the group for "race."

Sexism

Women have risen to powerful jobs in both the public and private sectors, but they have not gained enough power to transform their image fully in the media. Many writers thoughtlessly use language that treats women as inferior or that is demeaning or insulting. They are sometimes referred to as girls or mothers and are described by their physical attributes such as "attractive" or "brunette" or "shapely."

Writers should use description when it is complete and adds to the understanding of an individual's personality. Feature writers must be especially careful when creating a mood. Often what looks like interesting detail might come

> ### BOX 11.2   Guidelines for Racial Identification
>
> 1. **Is it relevant?** Race is relevant when the story is about race. Just because people in conflict are of different races does not mean that race is the source of their dispute. A story about interracial dating, however, is a story about race.
>
> 2. **Have I explained the relevance?** Journalists too frequently assume that readers will know the significance of race in stories. The result is often radically different interpretations. This is imprecise journalism, and its harm may be magnified by the lens of race.
>
> 3. **Is it free of codes?** Be careful not to use "welfare," "inner-city," "underprivileged," "blue collar," "conservative," "suburban," "exotic," "middle-class" "Uptown," "South Side" or "wealthy" as euphemisms for racial groups. By definition, the White House is in the inner-city. Say what you mean.
>
> 4. **Are racial identifiers used evenly?** If the race of a person charging discrimination is important, then so is the race of the person being charged.
>
> 5. **Should I consult someone of another race/ethnicity?** Consider another question: Do I have expertise on other races/cultures? If not, broaden your perspective by asking someone who knows something more about your subject. Why should we treat reporting on racial issues any differently from reporting on an area of science or religion that we do not know well?
>
> Reprinted with permission of the Poynter Institute.

across as sexism in disguise. Writers should guard against describing women in terms of their physical appearance and men in terms of wealth and power.

Issues of sexism in coverage came to the fore in Sen. Hillary Clinton's bid for the Democratic presidential nomination in 2008. An example was the hundreds of column inches and hours of air time spent on Clinton's laugh, which became labeled as the "Clinton Cackle." One *New York Times* writer wrote an entire column on her laugh. Clinton defenders charged that coverage of male candidates didn't characterize their laughs in such a demeaning way and that it was irrelevant to presidential coverage. Dee Dee Myers, a former presidential press secretary, noted: "Have we had more male candidates with funny laughs? Almost certainly. Have they gotten as much attention? Certainly not. But it just reflects a sexist strain in society that certain things are not acceptable in women."

The laugh characterization proved fairly mild compared to other pundits' use of language to describe Clinton, ranging from the debate over whether the word "bitch" applied to *Washington Post* columnist Maureen Dowd's note that Clinton had moved from "nag to wag." Having the first woman presidential candidate offered new fodder for political writers and plowed new ground in coverage. Clinton supporter Susan Estrich, who had been involved in other presidential campaigns, noted in a National Public Radio report that the role of a woman as the nation's leader had not been defined when Clinton ran for office. "I think that's why there's been so much attention to Hillary's clothes and to Hillary's cleavage and to Hillary's husband and to Hillary's marriage and her motherhood and her own daughter," Estrich says.

On the other political side, many stories on Cindy McCain, wife of Republican candidate John McCain, mentioned the size of her jeans. She was also described as a "blond, blue-eyed former rodeo queen and cheerleader" as opposed to her philanthropy and work in third-world countries. During the campaign, both she and Michelle Obama, a Harvard-educated lawyer, received praise for their fashion style more than for their accomplishments. After McCain announced Alaska Gov. Sarah Palin as his vice presidential running mate, debate erupted on blogs and elsewhere about media characterizations that were deemed sexist. Among them, discussions of whether Palin, a mother of five and former beauty queen, would have time or talents to be vice president. Such questions are not asked of male candidates, they said.

Words such as "chairman" have a male bias. *The Associated Press Stylebook* says to avoid "chairperson" unless an organization uses it as a formal title. When possible, use "firefighter," "flight attendant," "postal service worker," or "letter carrier." Writers should also know their publication's policy about courtesy titles. Many organizations have eliminated courtesy titles, such as Mrs., Miss, and Ms., before women's names. Only the last name is used on second reference.

Sexual Orientation

Writers should also avoid perpetuating negative images based on sexual orientation. Gay and lesbian rights movements since the mid-1950s have worked diligently to recast gay and lesbian portrayals in society. Until the mid-1970s, most news stories that referred to gays and lesbians did so only in the context of police reports or mental illness. Gay and lesbian issues have been addressed in the schools, in the workplace, and in the military. Despite increased coverage, some editors and reporters still produce stories that present homosexuality as deviant, and negative stereotypes continue.

Writers and broadcasters must be careful not to make value judgments when a source is gay or lesbian or when the subject deals with homosexuality. Saying, for example, that a source "confessed" to being gay communicates negative, secretive feelings about homosexuality that your openly gay source will resent.

A person's gender or sexual orientation should be ignored in a message unless it is relevant. People's sexual orientation might be part of the fabric of the message but should be woven in as part of who they are, not presented as their complete identity.

Associated Press writer Kristen Gelineau wrote a piece about openly gay Southern legislators, focusing on Adam Ebbin, a Democrat from Alexandria, Virginia. The story primarily examined how Ebbin and others handled and felt about anti-gay legislation and the resulting debates as state legislators. Such stories must be written accurately and without bias. Gelineau let her sources tell the story, as evidenced in this quote from Rep. Ebbin: "I know that any time that people are gonna tell lies about gays and lesbians on the House floor, that I can grab my mike and speak—and that's really empowering...." Or in this statement from New York Assemblywoman Deborah Glick: "... It is rare that my colleagues who are straight get to hear directly some of the incredibly mean-spirited attitudes so clearly enunciated."

Writers should never make assumptions about people's sexual orientation or people's sentiments toward gay and lesbian issues. Some people favor equality for all people. Remember that many people who are not gay or lesbian support gay and lesbian rights, just as many white people support civil rights for people of color. Writers should also not feel the need to balance every story that initiates from a gay rights source or event. In covering any group, sometimes balance is not appropriate, adds a shallow reporting element, or reduces the impact of the event.

Disabilities

Unless you or someone in your family has a physical or mental disability, as a writer you may tend to forget people with disabilities exist. Among the derogatory labels applied to disabled people are "crippled," "deformed," and "invalid."

The Disabilities Committee of the American Society of Newspaper Editors noted a list of terms to avoid, including "special," which is considered as patronizing; "stricken with or suffers from" instead of "a person who has" a specific disability; "victim of" rather than "a person who has" AIDS or cerebral palsy.

Unlike other groups that are discriminated against because of social norms, people with disabilities face discrimination from attitudes and actual barriers created by society's architectural and communication designs. Maybe you have never seen a person who uses a wheelchair in your local grocery store because there is no curb cut in the sidewalk in front of the store or no ramp at the door of the store. Maybe you have had little interaction with a profoundly deaf person because you do not know where to find a Telecommunications Device for the Deaf (TDD), which would allow you to call the person on the phone.

Many people, including writers, forget that people with disabilities constitute a vital, and numerous, part of our society. Under the New Freedom Initiative for Persons with Disabilities, the federal government has taken steps to remove barriers that people with disabilities still face. DisabilityInfo.gov is a Web portal that provides information about federal programs.

According to the American Community Survey, about 15 percent of the U.S. population not living in an institution reports some type of disability. That's more than 41 million people. Therefore, a significant number of today's audiences either has a disability or knows someone who does. Civil rights violations, new technology, legislation, and changes in business practices are possible story topics that are of interest to these audiences.

The late John Clogston, a journalism professor at Northern Illinois University, said that writers often portray people with disabilities in one of three demeaning ways: They imply that people who have a disability are somehow less human than other people; they present them as medically defective or somehow deviant or different in society; or they go overboard in trying to portray them positively, thus making them superhuman or "supercrips," as Clogston called them. Writers have a tendency to focus stories on the individual rather than the issues surrounding a disability, and they tend to wrap people with disabilities in pity and sympathy.

The Associated Press Stylebook cautions writers not to describe a person as disabled or handicapped "unless it is clearly pertinent to a story....Avoid such euphemisms as mentally challenged and descriptions that connote pity, such as afflicted with or suffers from multiple sclerosis. Rather, has multiple sclerosis."

Such language carries negative connotations and can exclude people with disabilities. The focus should be on the person, not on the physical impairment.

Be careful about writing that someone succeeded "in spite of" a disability—a phrase often viewed by people with disabilities as extremely patronizing. Some writers may contend that a disability implies that individuals are not able, and if they succeed, then the news value of emotional impact and conflict is there to attract readers. Never assume an accomplishment by a person with a disability is unusual.

At one time, leaders' disabilities often were not a visible part of reporting. When the late Sen. John East ran for election in North Carolina, all photographs showed him sitting. Few voters realized he used a wheelchair. President Franklin D. Roosevelt conducted business from a wheelchair, and controversy arose when one panel in the FDR Memorial in Washington, D.C., showed him seated in a wheelchair. A Kennedy family book and documentary film footage released several decades after his death showed President John F. Kennedy unable to lift his children or to bend deeply.

In general, people specializing in coverage of disability issues recommend two easy rules in writing about people with disabilities. First, avoid clichés and clichéd constructions. Use value-neutral terms—that is, words that do not stereotype. Avoid saying someone is confined. The person gets out of the wheelchair to sleep and to bathe. To that individual, the wheelchair is liberating. It is more accurate to say the individual uses a wheelchair. Second, never inject pity or a condescending tone into copy.

Ageism

Older people may also face stigmatization by society, and the mass media play a role in that process. In some instances, older people are labeled as forgetful, senile, rigid, meddlesome, childlike, feeble, fragile, frail, gray, inactive, withered, or doddering. Such adjectives might describe older people at some point in their lives or may be medically appropriate. But if such words are used indiscriminately, they demean older people and perpetuate inaccurate stereotypes. With the repeal of mandatory retirement, older people continue to work into their 70s and even 80s if they choose. They do most things that younger people do.

The Associated Press Stylebook cautions to use terms such as "elderly" and "senior citizen" sparingly and carefully. "If the intent is to show that an individual's faculties have deteriorated, cite a graphic example and give attribution for it," the stylebook notes.

The older population is growing in the United States; the latest census predicts the 65- to 74-year-old age group to grow 16 percent by 2010. The numbers will be even greater after that date as baby boomers turn 65. Many journalists and others focused on Republican John McCain's age during the 2008 presidential campaign and his ability to lead as a septagenarian.

Syndicated columnist Lucille deView, who writes on aging, suggests that writers avoid these myths about older people:

- Older people can participate in a variety of activities, so do not adopt a "gee whiz" attitude toward their abilities. Most people over the age of 50 continue the physical activities they enjoyed when younger, whether swimming, hiking, or playing tennis.
- People are continuing to work well into their 60s, 70s, and even 80s. The American Association of Retired Persons produces a list of the Best Employers for Workers over 50.
- Older people should be seen as individuals, not as members of a senior age group in which people are believed to have the same interests and abilities. Older people's interests are just as varied as those of individuals in other groups.
- Older people are not stereotyped in appearance. They dress in numerous fashions, and not all older people have physical problems or even gray hair.
- Age does not mean loneliness or loss of sexual interest. According to a 2005 AARP study, two-thirds of the individuals polled said they lived with a spouse or a partner or that they had a regular sexual partner.

DeView says writers should focus on realistic presentations of older people. Some older people have no financial problems, whereas others struggle financially in later life. Not all older people have ill health or are unable to cope with poor health. Serious medical conditions may not severely limit their participation in society. Only about 5 percent of older people live in nursing homes.

Children also should not be portrayed in an unpleasant light. Not all children are immature, naive, whining, sneaky, dishonest, or lazy. Children mature and develop at different paces. Some are responsible, creative, athletically gifted, loving, aggravating, and mean. Each must be considered individually and be allowed to ascribe traits to himself or herself, as did one 5-foot teenager, who described herself as being "vertically challenged."

Poverty

One societal group cuts across all racial, ethnic, and other groups: the people who live at or below the poverty level. In 2005, that level was defined as a family of four earning less than $20,000.

Although the United States is a leading world power, the number of Americans who live in poverty is 36.5 million, according to the U.S. Census. Household income has not increased in recent years. Even though people living in poverty may be limited media consumers, they still are part of U.S. society. Poverty, often not breaking news, affects every city in the United States. How the less-fortunate subsist should be part of regular, ongoing coverage—not just at holiday times when their plight stirs a need to give or during recessionary times when more people suffer economically.

Poverty overlaps many areas of coverage: health, religion, social services, local government, nonprofit sector, and education. Many school systems provide poor children with free or reduced-cost breakfasts and lunches. Lack of health insurance forces many people to use emergency rooms for medical care. Almost any story touches poorer segments of society. Reporters can find sources among nonprofit organizations, such as poverty assistance programs; community resources, including government officials; and churches that operate shelters and kitchens. When stories of less-fortunate residents appear, they help agencies and the needy get a boost.

When reporters write about lower-income people, they must watch their language. The word "poor" implies "disadvantaged" and often is ascribed to people of color, as are "welfare recipient" and "public housing resident." Editor Dovalina points out that a larger percentage of blacks and Hispanics are poor compared with whites, but most poor people are white.

Religion

Religion news, which has grown in importance and visibility since the terrorist attacks on September 11, 2001, showed U.S. audiences and media how little was known about different forms of Islam. The intricacies and differences among religions can lead to writers unknowingly conveying biased and misleading information.

Maha ElGenaidi, executive director of the Islamic Networks Group, an educational outreach organization, was quoted in *The San Jose Mercury News*:

> *In all religious traditions, people tend to blame the religion for what a few people have done in misapplying the religion or using it for political ends.*

Her quote could apply to Islam and to U.S. politicians who have invoked religion as a basis for their positions or votes on public policy or law.

In writing about religion, reporters must be aware that religion stories often involve other issues, such as politics, medicine, or community services. While some might see cloning as a medical or scientific story, the topic generates strong opinions from religious organizations. Same-sex marriage stories include politics, religion, and sexual orientation issues and cause people to consider "What is marriage?" Even the Harry Potter children's book series stirred discussions of witchcraft and whether the stories were anti-Christian.

Anyone who covers religion must also examine his or her own religious beliefs before developing questions and interviewing sources. Because the United States is dominated by Judeo-Christian traditions, many writers might be unaware of non-Christian faiths. While most of us grew up with some exposure to religion, whether within our families or our communities, that does not automatically make us tolerant of other people's views and beliefs.

Writers can do research to increase their knowledge and understanding of religions and denominations. Web sites provide information on denominations, beliefs, and practices and even positions on social, political, and ethical issues. One such site—www.beliefnet.com—has information on different religions.

Overcoming Bias in Writing

Even after a discussion of bias such as the one in this chapter, traces of insensitivity can still creep into writing. You need to be constantly aware of your own background and attitudes to understand when and how bias might surface in writing, to recognize it, and to exorcise it.

Writers, reporters, and broadcasters today must be trained to avoid the flaws of their predecessors in the mass media. They must learn to question their own beliefs and assumptions to understand better the diverse ethnic groups within society.

Today's writers, through greater awareness, are trying to overcome cultural bias by sifting through information and presenting the least stereotypical and

biased picture possible. Messages—from school textbooks to television advertisements—use a multicultural approach that presents all kinds of people. But
despite education, old biases die hard for many; every time a bias is confirmed by
a writer, it is strengthened for readers.

Beginning and even experienced writers sometimes pass along stereotypes,
such as the ditzy blonde or dishonest politician, because they think people like
and understand such shorthand portrayals, just as they like cartoons. Therein lies
the danger. Because mass media professionals present distinctive images of people and groups, they can determine how consumers view people and groups who
are not like themselves. Thus, writers must work responsibly in disseminating
information rather than misinformation.

Stereotypes communicate inaccurate information and can undermine the
quality of your work. Make sure what you write or broadcast does not perpetuate stereotypes. Use anecdotes rather than adjectives to show people's attitudes
and behaviors. Sensing stereotypes and avoiding them is a critical step on the
path to better writing.

Exercises

1. Describe yourself culturally and ethnically. List any physical disabilities
    or other pertinent differences. Make a list of words or phrases, both neg-
    ative and positive, that you have seen used in reference to your special
    traits. Compare your list with those of others in your class, and compile a
    directory of words you should avoid when writing—and why. Explain the
    connotation of each word. Make a list of acceptable words or phrases.

2. What is the ethnic makeup of your college or university? The town or
    city where your school is located? Do a five-day content analysis of your
    local or student newspaper. Count the number of stories each day in the
    news, sports, and features sections. Count the number that focuses on an
    ethnic group or an issue related to an ethnic group. At the end of the five
    days, calculate the percentage of newspaper stories related to ethnic
    groups. Do the percentages match the groups' makeup in the university's
    or town's population? Was coverage positive, negative, or neutral? What
    types of stories do you believe are missing?

3. Do a similar content analysis of the evening news broadcast, locally and
    for a national network. Count the total stories and the number concerning

ethnic groups. Give your impressions about whether the general coverage was positive, negative, or neutral.

4. You have the opportunity to interview the incoming student government president, a son of two Uzbek refugees. List five objective questions you could use to begin the interview, then list two effective questions you could ask to determine his experiences with cultural differences in the United States.

5. Examine your local or student newspaper. Find examples of stories about various ethnic communities or societal groups that do a good job of unbiased writing. Bring examples to class to share and indicate why the stories could be models for writing.

References

Caren Bohan, "Michelle Obama, Cindy McCain are study in contrast." *Reuter News*, at http://www.reuters.com/article/idUSN2937505020080610, accessed June 10, 2008.

Matthew Brault, "Disability Status and the Characteristics of People in Group Quarters: A Brief Analysis of Disability Prevalence Among the Civilian Noninstitutionalized and Total Populations in the American Community Survey." February 2008. Accessed at http://www.census.gov/hhes/www/disability/disability.html on August 12, 2008.

Timothy Crouse, *The Boys on the Bus*. New York: Random House, 1993.

Ashleigh Crowther, "Sexist Language in Media Coverage of Hillary Clinton," on Media Crit, posted December 12, 2007 at http://mediacrit.wetpaint.com/page/Sexist+Language+in+Media+Coverage+of+Hillary+Clinton, accessed June 10, 2008.

Lucille deView, "Regardless of age: Toward communication sensitive to older people and children," in *Without Bias: A Guidebook for Nondiscriminatory Communication*. New York: John Wiley & Sons, 1982.

Fernando Dovalina, Presentation for the Institute for Midcareer Copy Editors, Chapel Hill, North Carolina, Summer 2005, accessed at www.ibiblio.org/copyed/diversity.html.

David Folkenflik, "Clinton Coverage Reflects Tensions of Historic Bid," National Public Radio, "Morning Edition," May 28, 2008 at http://www.npr.org/templates/story/story.php?storyId=90880203, accessed June 10, 2008.

Walter Lippmann, *Public Opinion*. New York: Harcourt, Brace and Co., 1922.

Julie Patel, "Countering Stereotypes," *San Jose Mercury News*, May 30, 2005.

J. Pickens, ed., *Without Bias*. New York: John Wiley & Sons, 1982.

Taylor Marsh, "We Have Not Come a Long Way, Baby," accessed at www.huffingtonpost.com/taylor-marsh/we-have-not-come-a-long-w_b_123242.html, on Sept. 4, 2008.

Pale Moon Rose and John Mitrano, Comments, in Surveys of Ethnic and Racial Groups, by Jan Johnson Elliott, associate professor, University of North Carolina at Chapel Hill, Fall 1993.

Poverty 2006 Highlights. U.S. Census Bureau at http://www.census.gov/hhes/www/poverty/poverty06/pov06hi.html, accessed August 12, 2008.

Holly Stocking and Paget Gross, *How Do Journalists Think? A Proposal for the Study of Cognitive Bias in Newsmaking.* Bloomington, IN: Eric Clearinghouse on Reading and Communication Skills, 1989.

The Associated Press 2008 Stylebook and Briefing on Media Law. New York: The Associated Press, 2008.

"The News Media and the Disorders," Chapter 15 of Report of the National Advisory Commission on Civil Disorders, Kerner Commission Report, 1968.

David Manning White, "The 'gatekeeper,'" *Journalism Quarterly*, Vol. 27, No. 3, Fall 1950, p. 383.

Window Dressing on the Set: Women and Minorities in Television: A Report of the United States Commission on Civil Rights, 1977.

Keith M. Woods, "The Language of Race," Poynter Online at www.poynter.org/special/tipsheets2/diversity.htm, accessed September 28, 2005.

Keith M. Woods, "Nicknames & Mascots: Complicity in Bigotry," Poynter Institute at www.poynter.org/column.asp?id558&aid587263, accessed September 4, 2005.

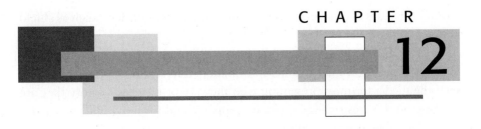

CHAPTER

12

Legal and Ethical Issues

A newspaper intern is fired after editors discover that he has plagiarized parts of several stories from other publications.

A major broadcast network is sued after it airs a story criticizing a grocery store chain's meat packaging. One problem is that two reporters who worked in a meat department didn't state on their job applications that they were members of the news media.

An actor sues a tabloid for libel after it reports she was drunk and disorderly in a Washington, D.C., restaurant. The magazine had not a single reliable source for the story.

A reporter writes a story about a company's alleged bad business practices, using information from executives' voice mails he accessed without their permission. The newspaper renounced the articles and removed them from its Web site, paid a huge out-of-court settlement, and fired its reporter.

These scenarios may sound improbable, but each is true. Each story and the newsgathering methods used to produce it had consequences for the reporter and the media outlet that printed or aired the story. In gathering and using information, writers often face a mix of legal and ethical issues. Decisions are not always easy because laws and ethics constantly change.

In many cases, state and federal laws aid reporters in their quest for information. For example, shield laws protect reporters from revealing their sources in court. Libel laws outline the conditions under which individuals can sue when they feel falsely defamed. Although state laws protect citizens and public figures in regard to privacy, implied consent may protect a reporter who goes on private property to get a story. Many laws have been

289

around for years and have evolved through the courts. Others, such as shield laws, are more recent.

Over the last decade, the media law battlefront has moved from libel cases to disputes over how media gather information. Subjects of news coverage have sued the media for misrepresenting who they are or the type of story they are working on, for trespassing on private property, and for using hidden cameras or hidden tape recorders. Some media observers say the methods represent unethical behavior by reporters, and some courts have begun to rule that such actions violate the law.

Other issues for writers in the information age have been plagiarism and copyright violations. Information gathering today via the Internet makes it easy to commandeer information and claim it as the writer's own work—whether unintentionally or purposefully. Sometimes the writer stores information and later inadvertently uses it without attributing the original source. In other cases, the material is stolen outright. In any case, the writer may have plagiarized and possibly infringed on another's copyright.

Copyright violations occur when writers use another's work and don't get permission. It is not sufficient simply to credit the original author, unless the material falls under a category known as fair use, explained later in the chapter.

In this chapter, you will learn

- what libel is,
- the issues of privacy and the relationship between sources and writers,
- the dangers of plagiarism and what constitutes copyrighted material,
- how ethics policies guide writers, and
- when writers cross the line in gathering information.

Libel

Writers can unknowingly or carelessly damage an individual's reputation by publishing false and defamatory statements about that individual. Even if a slip is unintentional, if the libel is in print or is aired, the writer can be sued, as can a newspaper, a television station, a church administration, or a non-profit group.

Libel can occur in any written form: a news article, a news release, a public service announcement, annual reports, corporate financial statements, a television talk show, a student's Web site, or a church bulletin. If a news release that has a false and defamatory statement about a person is mailed but not printed by any of the newspapers that receive it, the writer of the news release might still be sued successfully. Mailing the release to others who read it can be considered "publication" under defamation law. A radio or television station that broadcasts slander (oral defamation) or libelous statements can be sued under the state's libel laws.

Libel often occurs when people write about topics they do not really understand. Inexperienced reporters, student writers, and occasional writers are most at risk. They need to evaluate critically information they uncover. They can be held legally liable for accurately republishing a false and defamatory statement that someone else made. Good data collection, complete identification, and good writing techniques can prevent many libel problems, however. Mass communication professors advise their students to be accurate, thorough, and scrupulously fair in what they write. The legal system generally will protect writers who do a good job of investigating and who use many sources. Innocent mistakes that are not negligent or malicious are not usually actionable in a defamation lawsuit.

A huge body of law exists on libel. Thousands of libel cases have been filed. Although most editors, writers, and copy editors do not need to be lawyers, they do need to know the basics of libel law. A writer may be the only member of a nonprofit organization's communication staff; he or she needs to know what might cause trouble. Libel laws differ from state to state. For example, the statute of limitations—the time within which a person can file a libel suit—varies; it is usually from one to two years. Writers should be familiar with the libel laws in their states or in the states in which the material will be disseminated. Writers can stay current on freedom of the press issues through the First Amendment Center at Vanderbilt University. Information can be accessed online at www.firstamendmentcenter.org.

Elements of Libel

Writers who know about libel law do not have to be afraid to write negative information. If they know the essential elements of libel, they won't be chilled into self-censorship.

An individual—the person written about—has to prove six essential elements to win a libel case:

1. **Defamatory content.** The individual has to show the information was defamatory or bad enough to cause him or her to be held up to hatred, ridicule, or contempt.

2. **Identification.**   The story clearly identifies the individual by name, in a recognizable photo, or through description from which others can reasonably identify the individual. In rare cases, courts have allowed individuals to recover when a false and defamatory statement has been made about a group to which they belong even though the statement does not single out anyone by name.

3. **Publication.**   The memo was circulated, the story printed, the news release received, the report aired, or the message communicated to at least one person other than the person defamed.

4. **Falsity.**   The information published was not true. In a few cases, the burden of proof falls on the media, which attempt to prove the information was true.

5. **Harm or injury.**   The individual has to show harm to his or her reputation or emotional well-being. Proof of monetary loss can increase the amount of money the media will have to pay if they lose.

6. **Fault.**   The individual has to prove that the newspaper, radio station, or other party was at fault in presenting the libel.

To win a case, most plaintiffs have to prove all six elements. On the sixth item, court decisions have set different criteria for private citizens and public figures. In most cases, ordinary folks usually have to prove a standard of fault, called *negligence*, to win a libel suit. They must show that the writer failed to follow professional standards or acted unreasonably in carrying out his or her research and in writing.

Public officials including politicians, public figures including many celebrities and prominent business executives, and otherwise private individuals who prominently involve themselves in public controversies often must prove more than negligence in establishing fault when suing for libel. In most cases, they must prove the writer knew the information was false or showed reckless disregard as to whether the information was true or false. That is called *actual malice*. That element came about through the 1964 *New York Times v. Sullivan* case, in which the U.S. Supreme Court ruled that a public official cannot recover damages for a defamatory falsehood relating to his or her official conduct unless he or she proves the statement was made with actual malice. Actual malice is extremely difficult to prove and is the major hurdle for most plaintiffs.

Let's say you are writing a story about your town's mayor. During interviews, an unreliable source tells you the mayor leaves town twice a year to meet his childhood sweetheart—not his wife—at a mountain cabin. If you were to write that bit of information without further investigation, you would be setting yourself up for a libel suit. Your reliance on a single, unreliable source would be reckless disregard for whether the information was true.

People are defamed, perhaps falsely, every day. Just think about the hundreds of police reports naming people who have been arrested. They can prove many of the six elements, such as publication, identification, and defamation. But would they win a libel suit? Rarely.

A Writer's Defenses in a Libel Suit

Nothing can prevent someone from filing a libel claim. But, within the legal system are defenses and privileges writers can use to avoid liability or to reduce damages. The major defenses are these:

1. **Truth.** The writer can prove the information was substantially true through reliable witnesses and documentary evidence.

2. **Qualified privilege.** Writers are protected when they report fairly and accurately matters of public concern from official government proceedings or reports, such as meetings, trials, or a sheriff's news conference. This defense is one reason why news media rely so heavily on government meetings and sessions. A witness in court can falsely accuse someone of committing murder, and you as a reporter can print the accusation. Your reporting must be accurate, fair, and complete; attributed to the government meeting or record; and not motivated by spite or ill will.

3. **Wire service defense.** Some states have adopted what is known as the wire service defense. Newspapers and other media organizations are protected if they get and reprint a story from the wire services or other reputable news agencies, such as the Associated Press. They would not be protected if they knew or had reason to know the story contained falsities or if they altered the story substantially. It would be impossible for writers to verify every fact in a wire service story. Wire service clients have to trust that the information sent to them is true.

4. **Statute of limitations.**   Individuals cannot sue after a specific number of years has passed from the date of publication. The statute of limitations in libel cases varies from state to state, and in some rare instances, a plaintiff might be entitled to extend the statute of limitations in his or her case, depending on the circumstances.

5. **Opinion defense.**   The opinion defense protects two kinds of statements. Writers are protected if they are critiquing a performance or service as long as they give a general assessment that cannot be proved true or false. For example, a restaurant critic could probably write that the restaurant food did not taste good to her without much fear of being convicted of defamation. The critic could not say that the chef stole the high-quality meats for his family, leaving lesser meats for the restaurant dishes—unless that were true, of course.

In addition, many courts consider humor, satire, parody, and rhetorical hyperbole to be privileged under defamation law if the statements are so exaggerated and outlandish that reasonable people would not believe they are true. For example, the Supreme Court ruled *Hustler* magazine had a First Amendment right to publish an outrageous insult directed at television evangelist Jerry Falwell who sued the magazine after it published a cartoon parody of Campari liqueur's "first time" advertising campaign. The cartoon depicted the Rev. Falwell as having his "first time"—his first sexual encounter—while drunk with his mother in an outhouse. The jury at trial ruled against Falwell on his libel claim and found that the ad parody could not be reasonably believed as "describing actual events…or facts." Although the case proceeded to the U.S. Supreme Court on other issues, the jury's verdict on the libel claim was not overturned on appeal.

In a case in 2004, the Texas Supreme Court concluded that a satirical and humorous—but totally false—column about a local district attorney and judge could not be the subject of a defamation lawsuit because the content was not reasonably believable.

Writers should know they cannot be sued successfully for libel by the government—state, local, or federal. Writers can say the federal government or some part of it is an overgrown, bumbling bureaucratic mess without fear of being sued. But, they cannot falsely accuse the director of a government agency of misspending public funds without risking a lawsuit by the director individually.

Minimizing the Risk of Being Sued

Writers do not want to be sued for libel—even if they win. Libel suits are costly, time consuming, and emotionally draining. They can go on for years, then be dismissed. People do win libel cases against media. For example, CapCities Communications lost $11.5 million in a libel suit when one of its New York television stations incorrectly identified a restaurant owner as having ties with organized crime. In 1994, an attorney won a $24 million judgment against *The Philadelphia Inquirer*, which had reported he quashed a homicide investigation when he was an assistant district attorney because it involved the son of a police officer. The case took more than 10 years to conclude.

Ninety percent of libel cases filed never make it to court. Some are dropped, and some end up in out-of-court settlements, which cost media actual payouts and attorneys' fees. Libel suits are to be avoided. The following are some recommendations:

- Don't write lies and publish them.
- Use credible, reliable, multiple sources.
- Recognize the importance of fairness.
- Be accurate.
- Be complete.

Also, be polite if someone complains about inaccuracy. One study showed that most people who sued decided to do so after they were treated rudely when they pointed out the mistake.

Corrections

Most publications have a policy on writing corrections when errors have been made and run corrections because they believe they should correct their mistakes and not lie. Lawyers might caution against widespread use of corrections because they could be used as an admission of guilt: The correction states that the media outlet made a mistake. In most cases, the correction includes the correct title, statistic, address, or whatever was wrong and does not repeat the erroneous information. Many states have retraction or correction statutes that specify ways individuals or media can reduce or avoid damages.

Some editors say that any correction should be as prominently displayed as the error; that is, if the error is in a front-page headline, then the correction needs to be large and on the front page, not buried on page 22. Policies might require requests to be referred to editors and even lawyers. Ignoring a request could have legal consequences.

When to Publish or Not

Media often take criticism when they publish too much information. For example, critics charge that the public doesn't have a right to know the name of a crime victim, such as a rape victim. They contend that the public needs to know when and where such crimes occur, but not the victim's name or address.

Most newspapers do not publish names of rape victims. Some states have laws that allow police to withhold the names of any crime victim if they believe publication will put the person in danger or cause him or her more harm. Some media will publish or broadcast victims' names only with their permission. Others note that the names are part of public record and if a person is charged, the name of the victim or accuser should also be included.

Media can get into trouble if they republish defamatory information not protected under the wire service defense. They must ensure that any story used is accurate. Media also can get into trouble when they publish quotes they believe are relevant but in reality are libelous. For example, a newspaper reporter is covering the trial of a woman charged with involuntary manslaughter in the death of her 6-month-old daughter. The reporter walks a litigious tightrope if he or she includes a family member's quote that implies the woman's guilt and that was said outside the courtroom. If the family member makes the comment as part of court testimony, the reporter generally is protected against a libel suit. But if the remark is said in a parking lot while the trial is underway, the reporter and the editor must be careful not to republish any of the libelous statements. If they do, they can be sued for libel.

Most newspapers follow the policy of publishing private information if it relates to or affects public officials' or public figures' civic duties. For example, when Washington, D.C., intern Chandra Levy disappeared, attention eventually focused on the private life of Congressman Gary Condit. His relationship with Levy emerged, as did his relationships with other women outside his marriage. Many voters questioned Condit's judgment and even called for his resignation after learning more about his personal life. The media believed they had a responsibility to publish the personal information.

Privacy

Reporters frequently face privacy dilemmas in their quest to gather and report the news. These dilemmas are both legal and ethical and provoke loud protests when the public believes the media are trampling the privacy rights of individuals in the news.

Right of Privacy

The doctrine of the right to privacy has evolved to protect individuals and to give them the right to be left alone, particularly from unwarranted publicity. Decisions from lower courts up to the U.S. Supreme Court have involved individuals' right to privacy.

Privacy law varies considerably from state to state, and writers should know what constitutes invasion of privacy in their states or in the state where articles will be published or stories aired, and whether certain torts or injuries are recognized. Generally, however, writers sometimes invade individuals' privacy in four ways while gathering and writing information.

First, a journalist might go on private property without permission to get a story. The writer then could be sued for intruding on the property owner's privacy. But people could still sue for *intrusion* in a public place, even though people in public places have less expectation of privacy than when they are in private places. For example, some news-gathering techniques, such as secretly recording someone with high-powered audio or video equipment, could be considered highly offensive to reasonable people—even if it occurred in a public venue. A reporter, for example, could be cited for intruding either physically or with electronic equipment. In such cases, the journalist is sued for his or her means of gathering information, not for the content of what he or she wrote. The writer could be sued successfully even if no story resulted.

Second, a writer might disclose private and embarrassing but true facts about an individual, who could claim the facts should not have been published. Winning such suits could be difficult, however, because of the qualified First Amendment privilege to publicize lawfully obtained information that is truthful and involves a legitimate matter of public concern. Also, courts have recognized a common law defense in such cases when information published is considered newsworthy. Also, express or implied consent from an individual allows media to publish *embarrassing or private facts* about him or her and is a defense. But that protection might not extend to people giving their consent for media to publish embarrassing facts about others or, depending on the circumstances, when minors reveal private facts about themselves to reporters.

Third, *The Associated Press Stylebook* notes that the news media "may be liable for invasion of privacy if the facts of a story are changed deliberately or recklessly, or 'fictionalized.'" An individual can sue in such *false-light* privacy cases even if the publicity seems to be positive. The bottom line is that the publicity is considered false and objectionable, even if it is not defamatory. Plaintiffs in false privacy cases have to prove that the language would be highly offensive to a reasonable person and that the writer acted in reckless disregard to the falsity and the image it would create. These privacy cases closely resemble defamation cases, and just as with libel considerations, writers must be careful to be accurate and thorough.

Media can be sued for a fourth privacy injury or tort: *appropriation*. Most of these types of cases involve the unauthorized use of a person's image or likeness for commercial purposes, such as advertising a product or service to consumers. Appropriation cases can also arise when the content is news-editorial and not commercial, although in such non-commercial cases, courts have required plaintiffs to prove actual malice. Actor Dustin Hoffman sued *The Los Angeles Times* for a digitized photograph of himself that appeared in *The Los Angeles Times* magazine: a head shot from his role in the movie *Tootsie* superimposed on the body of a model. Hoffman won $1.5 million in damages, but the verdict was overturned on appeal. In that case, the image was used in editorial—not commercial—content, and the evidence was insufficient for Hoffman to prove actual malice.

In some states, privacy law is so protective of the media that privacy is more of an ethical problem than a legal one. In dealing with the ethics of privacy, many media outlets have categories of individuals and treat them differently. For example, compared with private citizens, politicians and public officials are held to a higher standard of behavior in what journalists will or will not pursue.

Media also hold to a high standard public figures who trade on their public image or who are briefly prominent in the news. Reporters may assume a higher standard means such figures have less privacy. Other people, like you and me, garner more privacy from the media.

Public versus Private Property

Some privacy disputes hinge on whether the news took place on public or private property. For example, a Christmas parade on city streets is considered a public event in a public place, and reporters—whether print or broadcast—would have access to people viewing or participating in the parade. Furthermore, people in public places should expect their actions to be public—and those actions can be reported in the media legally. In other venues, individuals have a reasonable expectation of privacy. A grandmother who attends the parade and whose photo is printed in the local newspaper probably cannot sue successfully for invasion of privacy. However, if a reporter used a microphone to record secretly the conversation of the woman and her daughter at the parade, that action would probably exceed a reasonable expectation of privacy.

Courts consider people's homes to be the most private places, so reporters need to be especially cautious when they gather news in people's homes. Places between private homes and the Christmas parade sometimes are more difficult to locate on the public/private property continuum. Shopping centers and restaurants are quasi-public places. Working reporters asked to leave shopping centers must do so, no matter what the news event, or face a trespassing charge.

In all court cases concerning privacy violations, consent might be a useful media defense. The best consent defense results when a reporter is invited onto private property or told explicitly that she or he has permission to be there. Next best is implied consent, which occurs when media are on the property and are not asked to leave. The media might not be protected if a property owner says okay but the tenant feels his zone of privacy was invaded, or they might not be protected if a police officer gives the okay for media to be on private property. The Supreme Court has ruled that police violate the Fourth Amendment rights of homeowners when they give permission.

At the same time, reporters must heed a police officer's order to leave property and can be charged with trespassing if they don't. Consider the Reporters Committee on Freedom of the Press's guidelines on access:

> *Regardless of whether news occurs on public or private property, if you ignore police orders regarding access, you risk arrest and prosecution. Case law makes clear that police can limit media access when they believe such restrictions are needed for public safety or to prevent interference with an investigation, and that the First Amendment does not provide immunity from criminal sanctions for disobeying police orders.*

Copyright and Plagiarism

Copyright and plagiarism become concerns when writers take original work they did not create and use it without permission. A copyright is a right granted to the creator of an original work to control copies and reproductions of his or her work, derivatives of his or her work, and the rights to perform and display his or her work. Others who want to use the creator's work—such as reproducing copyrighted photos on a personal Web site—must either receive permission in writing (and usually pay for that use) or agree to a license that specifies terms of the use, such as using a computer program.

Plagiarism is an ethical issue; it occurs when a writer takes original material and claims it as his or her own. A writer can violate copyright law without plagiarizing, and a writer can plagiarize without violating laws. In both instances, however, the penalties can be severe.

Copyright: A Definition

Copyright is the legal ownership of a story, publication, book, song, online article—anything produced as original work and fixed in any tangible medium, such as a newspaper or CD-ROM. When a work is copyrighted, the owner has exclusive legal rights to its use for a limited time. Anyone can copyright material by applying to the Copyright Office in the Library of Congress. Anyone can claim a working copyright as soon as a piece is created. But without registration, an individual is limited from seeking certain damages under the federal copyright statute. Generally, an individual has ownership of the work for his or her lifetime plus 70 years for work produced after January 1, 1978. For corporations, the time is longer: 95 years from publication or 120 years from creation, whichever is shorter.

People, such as authors or songwriters, copyright their work so they can benefit solely from royalties or the money it earns. Newspaper companies copyright each issue of the newspaper, a series, or longer articles. Online sites are also copyrighted. Copyright is designed to encourage the creation of more works and to benefit the public. If authors are given exclusive rights to their works for a period of time, the assumption is that they will create more.

In most cases, anyone who wants to use any portion of copyrighted material has to get permission—and often must pay a fee to use the material. For example, a writer who is doing a book on authors of horror stories cannot quote extensively from author Stephen King's work without permission. An advertising copywriter who wants to use the music from an Andrew Lloyd Webber song must get permission. In both cases, the writers would probably pay a fee based on how much is used and in what context.

Some material can be used without permission or payment of fees. Anything produced by the federal government is considered public domain and can be used. If a private organization does a report for the government, however, that material might be copyrighted.

Generally, copyright law does not protect facts, ideas, procedures, processes, or methods of operation that might be protected under patent law. That means the fact that the United States was a British colony or the text of Einstein's theory of relativity can be used. But a historian's analysis of the British impact on the colonies or a researcher's interpretation of Einstein's work may be copyright protected.

The Copyright Act of 1976, Section 107, allows *fair use* of copyrighted material for "criticism, comment, news reporting, teaching, scholarship, or research." Fair use of material is not an infringement of copyright and does not require the permission of the copyright holder. For example, a book reviewer who wants to quote from Stephen King's novel in his review would not have to get permission to use the excerpt so long as the amount excerpted is reasonable. Because a fair or reasonable amount is debatable, a judge or jury might ultimately resolve a specific use. The factors to consider for fair use are:

1. purpose and character of the use, including whether such use is of a commercial nature or is for nonprofit educational purposes;
2. nature of the copyrighted work;
3. amount and substantiality of the portion used in relation to the copyrighted work as a whole; and
4. effect of the use on the potential market for or value of the copyrighted work.

Translated, a writer cannot use a major portion of the material without permission, particularly if its use could violate the copyright owner's rights. The individual also cannot use a major portion of the material. Some people follow a 5 percent rule; that is, no more than 5 percent of the copyrighted work can be used without permission. Some follow a 50-word rule. To avoid any question over how much is acceptable use, get permission or check out a copyright holder's stipulations. For example, some newspapers do not require permission to use 30 words or less of a story. You can find out through their permissions offices.

Getting into Trouble

With the development of the Internet and the proliferation of computers, more and more material, including software, is illegally copied. Copyright holders sue for copyright infringement and hope to collect monetary damages, including an amount for lost royalties.

Writers get into trouble with copyrights when they believe the material they are using is fair use. Sometimes they believe they are not using a substantial part or that their use is somehow exempt for educational reasons. Or they believe the work has been quoted so much that it has become part of the public domain and can be used. Some also erroneously assume that citing the author or source and giving credit protects against copyright suits.

If writers have questions about copyright infringement, they should consult an attorney familiar with copyright law. The discussion here is not to frighten students or media writers away from using material; however, all writers must be aware of laws and penalties for using others' work without proper credit or authorization.

Recent Copyright Conflicts

A major issue in copyright in recent years has been the unauthorized copying of songs and movies. Artists who made money, or royalties, from the sale and use of their CDs, DVDs, or videos began suing to keep from losing income. One issue in this conflict is who owns the rights to a piece: the artist, the company that distributed the work, or the individual who bought a copy. Ownership is important in any litigation and in determining lost revenue.

To address copyright infringement of digital media, Congress passed the Digital Millennium Copyright Act, signed into law in 1998. Among other items, the act amended copyright law to provide limits on the liability of service providers, or sites that stored information online, from the conduct of their users who might violate copyrights. If service providers are aware of violations and do nothing, they, too, can be liable.

In one case, a group of freelancers sued several publishers because they contended that the distribution of their work to online databases like LexisNexis was not part of the rights they transferred and sold to these publications. The freelancers won. However, after the case, many publishing companies altered their freelance contracts to include these rights specifically.

Copyright will always be an issue for people who want to ensure they receive credit for and earn income from the work they produce. You as a writer must be aware of copyright laws and ensure that whatever material you use falls under fair use. If you are not sure, consult a lawyer—or find out who owns the copyright, secure permission, and pay any requested fees.

If the fee is expensive, then you will have to determine whether the material justifies the cost. Don't try to get around copyright law by paraphrasing—it will not protect you. If the paraphrase can be readily identifiable as the author's words or if the work is substantially similar, you can get into trouble.

Plagiarism: A Definition

Plagiarism occurs when people take information, copyrighted or not, and use it as their own without crediting the original source. With the growth of the Internet, plagiarism occurs more often, intentionally and unintentionally. Attribution of sources can help mitigate plagiarism, but it is not always a protection against charges of plagiarism.

An intern at *The San Jose Mercury News* was fired after editors found he had plagiarized articles from *The Washington Post* and other publications. A reporter for *The San Francisco Chronicle* saw similarities between articles the intern wrote and stories that appeared in *The Post*. When editors investigated, they found that information had been copied from other publications, too.

The Indianapolis Star and *The Indianapolis News* suspended their television columnist when editors discovered he had plagiarized a column by a TV writer at another newspaper. The columnist admitted he had lifted the column, which editors discovered before it was published.

A sports columnist for a college newspaper was fired after the editor learned that sections of his column were taken from a *Sports Illustrated* columnist's work. The editor wrote an open letter to the newspaper's readers to explain how the plagiarism occurred and the resulting action.

Student and novice reporters often get themselves in trouble by using information and not properly crediting the source. Sometimes the error occurs out of ignorance rather than deliberately stealing material and using it as their own. In other cases, reporters may take material because of pressures of meeting deadlines, the lack of ideas, or inadequate information through their own research.

Whatever the reason, the consequences are dire. The owners of copyrighted material can sue for copyright infringement. In most cases of plagiarism, however, writers who steal will be suspended or fired—and their credibility will be severely impaired.

How to Avoid Plagiarism

The easiest way to avoid plagiarism is to be honest. Honesty covers how reporters gather information, store it, and use it. When reporters gather material, they need to be meticulous in their note taking and in citations. If they download a story from the Internet, they must ensure they have included the source and date. If they copy information from a book, newspaper, or magazine, they must include a citation. Noting sources completely is necessary for proper attribution, that is, giving the original source credit. (Attribution is discussed in Chapter 10.)

If writers are working on a project that takes days or even months of investigation, they must be exceedingly careful when they return to notes they have not viewed in a while. When fashioning the story, they must be aware of which notes were their own and which ones came from another source. Remember from the discussion earlier in the chapter that even material that is condensed, summarized, and rewritten from another source should be attributed, as should any material used verbatim.

Of course, you should never take another person's work and claim it as your own, regardless of deadline pressure. A professor in a reporting class became suspicious when a student turned in a final project story that was much better than her other work throughout the semester. A quick check on the Internet pulled up dozens of stories on the student's topic— and blocks of copy pulled from three or four articles. The student had submitted the work as her own and violated the university's honor code, punishable by suspension. The outcome proved more severe than the penalty of not writing the story at all.

Ethics in Gathering Information

What is ethical in writing? Just as in any profession, ethics in journalism is a set of moral guidelines regarding what writers should and should not do when gathering and disseminating information. Journalists' ethical decisions determine their behavior.

Communicators must behave ethically. In most cases, you can't be sued for ethical violations. States don't have ethics laws, like libel laws. You can't go to jail for revealing the source of your story even after you promised you wouldn't, but you could be sued for breach of contract.

You might not be sued for libel, but you could be sued for the method you used in getting information. You won't get disbarred like a lawyer or lose your license like a physician, but if you violate your code of ethics or that of your publication, you lose your credibility or your source—and possibly your job. The bottom line is your professional reputation.

When it comes to ethics, mass communicators often are criticized for publishing certain information and for violating individuals' privacy, as discussed earlier in the chapter. They are criticized for failing to remain objective and for stepping over the line from reporting to commenting. They are criticized for violent or sexual content. They are also criticized for the way they collect information, from stealing to deceiving to harassing unwilling sources.

Former newspaper editor and ABC News president Michael Gartner notes that communicators have an ethical responsibility in the age of technology. "Readers don't know what is fact or fiction, what is an enhanced photo, what is slanted or straight, or what is the docu in docudrama," he cautions. "What comes out of a computer can be just as biased as what comes from a pulpit."

Communicators must be just as careful with their language and how it is interpreted as they are with their news-gathering techniques. In some situations, writers have ethics policies to guide them; in other instances, they have to use gut instinct.

Ethics Policies

Most news organizations, advertising agencies, public relations firms, online sites, and other mass communication businesses have ethics guidelines. Some policies come from parent companies, such as Gannett, which rewrote its ethics policy in 1999 and then conducted in-house training at its more than

80 newspapers and media outlets. Other media rely on professional organizations for guidance, such as the American Advertising Federation.

Most ethics policies establish an environment in which employees are to work. Some companies use ethics contracts, and employees agree to them when they are hired. Policies outline areas where ethical considerations arise, such as conflict of interest, confidentiality of sources, impartiality of reporting, accuracy, acceptance of gifts or honoraria, and community or political involvement. Policies may be extensive, such as Gannett's policy (accessed at www.gannett.org), or they can be as short as one page.

In addition to written ethics policies as guides, journalists should have their own ethical standards. In some cases, reporters have to use what their gut says, rather than refer to the company policy. For example, an editor learns that the son of a popular, local minister has become an out-of-wedlock father. The editor wants you—the reporter—to write a story because the minister has attracted a large following because of his views on teen abstinence. What does your ethical compass say about pursuing this story?

Deception.   In recent years, the media have been criticized more and more for using deception to get their information. Deception occurs in everything from posing as other people to giving false promises of confidentiality to using hidden cameras or tape recorders to gather news. When is deception acceptable? Most editors would agree to deception if the information cannot be obtained any other way. The information would have to be of such importance that knowingly deceiving sources is acceptable. And editors and lawyers would have to be part of the decision to resort to such news-gathering techniques.

Deceptive news gathering is not new. One of the most well-known cases occurred in the late 1970s when *The Chicago Sun Times* set up a bar called the Mirage. Reporters posed as bartenders and waiters and used hidden cameras and tape recorders to secure evidence that building inspectors, police officers, and other city officials were soliciting bribes to allow the bar to operate. The series won several awards and was nominated for a Pulitzer Prize, the highest award in journalism. The Pulitzer Prize board rejected the series, however, because it felt that the *Sun Times'* methods were deceptive and unethical.

Students in an advanced reporting class were investigating whether citizens treated homeless people differently from others on downtown streets. As part of the story, students approached residents and asked for directions. Some students were well dressed and neat in appearance; others wore disheveled clothes and had not shaved or combed their hair. The students found significant differences in residents' demeanor and interaction toward students who were neat and those who were not. They incorporated the reactions into their stories.

Such investigation, sometimes called participant observation, can produce information that adds to a story. However, reporters should not inject themselves into a situation in a way that could change the outcome of the story.

Deception was at the heart of the highly visible ABC/Food Lion case in 1992 in which ABC reporters applied for jobs at a Food Lion store to check out complaints about how Food Lion repackaged meats for sale. The reporters used false résumés that omitted the fact that they were journalists. They used hidden cameras to film their work that subsequently was aired on ABC's "Prime Time Live."

The reports alleged that Food Lion workers repackaged outdated meats, bleached meats, and committed other offenses. Food Lion executives sued, not for libel or falsity in the reports themselves, but for fraud, trespassing, and breach of loyalty. Initially, a North Carolina jury awarded Food Lion $5.5 million, but on appeal, the amount was cut to only $2. Despite the ultimate reduction in a monetary settlement, reporters' credibility had been damaged and their behavior hanged in the public eye.

Reporters should always consult their editors when they plan to use deception or any other method to get information. They should determine that they have exhausted all other means and that the benefit of going under-cover outweighs any negative impact. When the stories are published, editors should be forthcoming in letting audiences know how the information was gathered and why such methods were used.

The San Jose Mercury News fired a reporter who used his status as a graduate student at the University of Iowa to obtain information from the university archives and use it in a story. The article revealed that university researchers had used children from an orphanage in a project on stuttering—actually turning the children into stutterers. The archives are open only to students, staff, and faculty members, and anyone using the archives must sign a form that the use is for research only. The reporter got the information a month before he began his internship at the newspaper—and wrote on the form that he was a graduate student in psychology when he really was a student in journalism.

Such cases show that the legal battlefield for media is shifting from individuals or companies suing for libel to acting on their concerns with methods used to gather information.

Fabrication.   The bottom line: Reporters do not make up information or people or attribute made-up quotes to individuals. Some journalism teachers boil that even more simply: Don't lie. But in some cases, a tiny alteration in a quote or description that makes it through the editing process can lead writers of any experience level to even greater fabrication.

Trying to save time required to do a weekly poll that posed a single question to a local resident cost two young reporters at *The Reidsville* (N.C.) *Review* their jobs. The reporters shared the responsibility for asking a citizen each day a single-topic question, such as name your favorite singer and why. But rather than actually asking the question, the reporters used mug shots of college friends posted on Facebook. Then they made up quotes.

The fabrication surfaced when a sister publication owned by the same media group reported the story. The *Review* editor wrote a letter to the paper's readers to explain how the fabrication occurred and why it went unnoticed. The two reporters were fired, and the editor resigned.

The Associated Press fired a reporter after it reviewed several of his stories and could not find the people quoted. Although the reporter claimed the people were real, editors could not. He also cited an organization in Chicago that editors could not locate.

Any journalist can cite the cases of Jayson Blair of *The New York Times* and Jack Kelley of *USA Today*—and the outcome—after editors discovered parts of their stories had been fabricated. In another case, the U.S. Supreme Court upheld a false light invasion of privacy verdict against a newspaper whose reporter made up portions of a story about a woman whose husband had been killed in a bridge collapse. The court concluded that the evidence was sufficient to establish actual malice in the case.

Confidential Sources.   When gathering information, sometimes reporters are asked to protect the identity of a source. Some media do not allow unnamed sources to be quoted in stories; others require editors to know the source's name. The Associated Press and the Associated Press Managing Editors Association jointly surveyed U.S. newspapers about their policies on anonymous sources and learned that one in four of the 419 newspapers that responded never allowed reporters to quote anonymous sources. Others had specific policies.

Journalists know that if they promise confidentiality to a source and then break it, they damage their reputation. In one case, the U.S. Supreme Court concluded that the First Amendment did not prevent a source from recovering damages from newspapers that had breached promises of confidentiality to the source. The source had lost his job after the newspapers published articles identifying him as having notified the newspapers about negative court documents regarding a political candidate. This type of action might not be available to confidential sources when reporters are compelled by a court to identify their sources in a criminal or civil proceeding, even though many journalists refuse to testify under such circumstances and instead face possible contempt sanctions, including fines and even jail time.

The most visible case in recent years of a journalist going to jail to protect a source occurred when *New York Times* reporter Judith Miller refused to name who revealed to her the identity of a CIA agent. Miller never wrote a story, but she still refused to identify her source. After months of legal sparring, a judge sentenced her to four months in prison. After spending 85 days in jail, Miller was released when her source, I. Lewis "Scooter" Libby, former chief of staff for then Vice President Dick Cheney, signed a waiver of confidentiality. Miller then testified before a grand jury investigating who leaked the identity of the undercover CIA operative, Valerie Plame.

While judges invoke the Sixth Amendment as the reason journalists must comply with their orders to testify or to turn over notes and other materials, journalists contend that the free flow of information will be jeopardized if they cannot offer sources anonymity. Thirty states have shield laws that protect journalists from naming sources in a criminal case or judicial proceeding. Laws also establish who is defined as a journalist, what kinds of information the privilege protects, and when the privilege is waived. Reporters should always know their state laws as well as the policy of their publications or employers. No federal shield law exists, although bills have been introduced before Congress.

More recently, journalists have been concerned about how to protect sources' confidentiality when the reporters have kept their notes on their computers. The computer notes can be subpoenaed and the computers confiscated. Even if the notes are deleted, they could be recoverable. Even a reporter's phone records could be subpoenaed and checked to determine whom the reporter had called, as were Judith Miller's phone records. The advantages of technology can also affect a reporter's ability to get information from confidential sources, who might not feel so protected.

Other Dilemmas. Other ethical issues arise in information gathering, particularly in reporters' and editors' discussions about whether a story warrants media attention. You suspect a public official is having extramarital relations, so you stake out his house and discover he spent the night in an apartment of a woman, not his wife. Do you write the story? You learn an anti-abortion rights activist had an abortion as a 15-year-old. Do you include that information in a story when she leads an anti-abortion protest?

Public officials' behavior has been the focus of many news stories since *The Miami Herald* staked out the apartment of Democratic presidential contender Gary Hart in Washington, D.C. The news media published photos of Hart with a woman, not his wife. Although Hart never admitted his relationship with model Donna Rice was sexual, he withdrew from the race. Former President Bill Clinton went through an impeachment trial on charges that he committed perjury and obstructed justice in denying a relationship with intern Monica Lewinsky.

Is reporting such behavior unethical? Journalists would cry no; they are reporting the news. The public outcry comes when the stories report and re-report lurid and seemingly minor details of such relationships. Audiences become saturated. The answers to such publication issues have to be reached case by case, medium by medium. What one publication decides to print, another may refuse to air.

In addition, reporters must use their judgment when gathering information. Their behavior might prove illegal and could generate ethical questions. Such questioning occurred when *The Miami Herald* fired long-time metro columnist Jim DeFede for tape-recording a conversation with Arthur E. Teele Jr., a former city commissioner, shortly before he committed suicide. The local state's attorney charged DeFede with violating the state law making it illegal to tape record individuals without their knowledge. The case was later dismissed.

DeFede lost his job for breaking the law and because the paper's editors felt the reporter had acted unethically by not telling Teele he was being recorded. Editors said the taping could damage sources' trust in reporters. Despite management's position, DeFede's firing became the topic of other media articles and generated criticism and unhappiness among *Herald* staff. Some might question whether DeFede should have intervened upon hearing the emotion in Teele's voice, which he later said was unusual in a man he had covered for 14 years. Reporters generally are observers rather than participants in events. They should choose not to become part of the story.

In the days following Hurricane Katrina's assault on the Gulf Coast, many reporters showed their sadness at the plight of those who could not evacuate and their anger and frustration at the response of government officials. In some instances, reporters controlled their feelings while others did not. Reporters are human beings and must be aware that their emotions could influence readers and viewers.

A good policy is to gather news in a manner that allows the public focus to go where it should—to the wrongdoing you are reporting, advises Associate Professor Cathy Packer at the University of North Carolina at Chapel Hill. Unethical and illegal news-gathering techniques shift the public focus to the media, and the bad guys walk away looking like victims, she notes.

Without circumspect decision making and honesty with audiences, any medium—and the reporter—will lose credibility. When credibility is lost, so are audiences.

Aspiring journalists should be honest, ethical, and legal in information gathering. Methods should be unquestionable. Information should be accurate. Editors should always know a reporter's source and serve as backup in the event someone has doubts about a source's or the reporter's credibility.

Exercises

1. Can you lawfully use the following information in a story? Explain your reasoning and any defenses you could use if you were sued for libel.

    a. You are doing a story on drug use in the county. A police source tells you that a certain spot on Main Street, a bench outside Walton's restaurant, is a known place for drug deals.

    b. You are covering a case about a man charged with involuntary manslaughter in a car accident that killed two teenagers. You do a search using public records of prior convictions and find he has two for careless and reckless driving in another state.

    c. A state senator running for re-election tells you that her opponent is a tax evader who has not paid any state income taxes in the last five years.

    d. You are covering the performance of Alice Batar, a local resident who has begun a successful acting career. You have been assigned to write a review of her performance in the community theater's production of "Who's Afraid of Virginia Woolf?" Prior to the performance, you overhear two people next to you talking about Batar's latest divorce and what one called "a really pathetic settlement on her part."

e. You are to write a story about the chancellor of your university. You interview a faculty member who says the chancellor "runs off at the mouth and doesn't pay enough attention to faculty members' needs."

2. Write a two-page report on plagiarism, using at least three sources. Include a fellow classmate's views on plagiarism. Include at least one example other than what is in this chapter. Include your views on plagiarism as an ethical issue and what the consequences should be for a reporter who plagiarizes.

3. Go online and find the site for your hometown newspaper. See if you can find on the site the newspaper's code of ethics. If not, e-mail the editor and find out if the newspaper has a written code or how ethical behavior is conveyed to the staff. Bring in the code or information to share with class members.

4. Look at codes of ethics from professional organizations such as the American Society of Newspaper Editors, the American Advertising Federation, Public Relations Society of America, and others. Compare the issues that each covers as ethical considerations.

5. Consider the following scenarios. Discuss in class how you would behave in each situation and whether you would use the information gathered.

   a. You are a state legislative reporter. A number of legislators meet every Thursday night for dinner at a local restaurant. One of the legislators whom you cover on a regular basis invites you to come along one night. Do you go?

   b. You are interviewing the director of the local community theater for a story on the upcoming season. You are having lunch together at a local restaurant. At the end of the meal and interview, the director picks up the tab and goes to pay for both of you. Your portion of the bill is $6.50. What do you do?

   c. You suspect a local real estate company is discriminating against Hispanic tenants when it comes to rental housing. Your editor suggests that you and another reporter, who is Hispanic, pose as a couple and try to rent a house from the company. What should you do?

d. You cover the financial industry as a business reporter. At the end of an interview on mortgage rates, the banker says to contact him whenever you are ready to buy a house and he'll make sure you get a really good interest rate. Do you call him when you are mortgage hunting?

References

"AP Fires Reporter after Source Query," Yahoo! News, accessed September 17, 2002, at http://story.news.yahoo.com/news?tmpl5story2&cid1519&u5ap2002916/ap_on_re_us/reporter_dismis.

"Appeals Court Sides with ABC in Food Lion Lawsuit," ABCNews.com, October 20, 1999, at http://abcnews.go.com/sections/us/DailyNews/foodlion 991020.html.

"California Paper Fires Intern for Plagiarism," *Publishers' Auxiliary*, January 22, 2001, Vol. 147, No. 2, p. 20.

Cantrell v. Forest City Publishing Co., 419 U.S. 245 (1974).

Chuck Strouse, "The Agony of DeFede," Newtimes.com, accessed September 18, 2005, at www.newtimesbpb.com/Issues/2005-09-15/ news/news2.html.

Cohen v. Cowles Media Co., 501 U.S. 693 (1991).

Copyright Act of 1976, Section 107, at http://www.loc.gov/copyright/title17/.

"Ex-commissioner kills self in newspaper lobby," CNN.com, accessed July 28, 2005, at www.cnn.com/2005/US/07/28/miami.teele.ap/index.html.

Don Fost, "Mercury News Case Stirs Debate over Ethics of Deception," *San Francisco Chronicle*, August 8, 2001.

Michael Gartner, keynote address, Association for Education in Journalism and Mass Communication, Washington, DC, August 5, 2001.

Hustler Magazine, Inc. v. Falwell, 485 U.S. 46 (1988).

New Times, Inc. v. Isaaks, 146. W. 3d 144 (Texas 2004).

New York Times Co. v. Tasini, 535 U.S. 483 (2001).

Cathy Packer, interview, School of Journalism and Mass Communication, September 4, 2008.

"Poll finds many newspapers bar anonymous sourcing," The Associated Press, as reported on the Web site of The First Amendment Center, at www.firstamendmentcenter.org/news.aspx?id515417, accessed September 23, 2005.

Reporters Committee for Freedom of the Press, at www.rcfp.org.

Joe Strupp, "TV Columnist Canned," *Editor and Publisher*, September 11, 1999, at www.archives.editorandpublisher.com.

The Associated Press 2008 Stylebook and Briefing on Media Law. New York: The Associated Press, 2008.

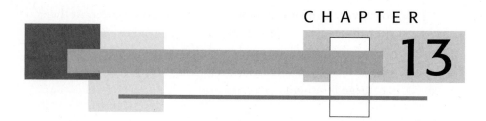

Broadcast Media

WHEN YOU WRITE FOR BROADCAST
MEDIA, YOUR COPY WILL LOOK
LIKE THIS: A SCRIPT FORMAT THAT
OCCUPIES HALF THE WIDTH OF
THE PAGE. BUT THE CONTENT WILL
REMAIN ACCURATE, CONCISE, AND
COMPLETE, JUST AS IN ANY WRITING
YOU DO.

Writing for radio and television requires the basic writing skills discussed in earlier chapters. Broadcast messages must be concise, clear, and simple so that audiences can understand the information.

Broadcast news writing differs in some respects from writing news for print. First, it differs in what it requires of the audience. Tuning in to radio, for example, audiences have to rely on careful listening. Radio writing has to be simple and specific. Fashioned after radio, television news also captures attention quickly, as TV messages breeze by passive audiences who cannot rewind or re-read items of interest. That has changed for more and more Americans who are watching video online, or with DVR devices, such as TiVo. Watching the saved broadcasts later, viewers of on-demand video can bypass ads or replay news. But typically, broadcast writers, whether for radio or television, have only one chance to get audience attention.

While broadcast reporters must use good writing skills, they must also look beyond the written word. They must find audio and video content that will attract audiences and enhance the message.

In this chapter, you will learn

- how print, broadcast, and online writing are alike and how they differ,
- the essential qualities of effective broadcast writing, and
- basic writing techniques for radio and television.

The Medium Changes the Style

Print journalists think in terms of a story or article because these items fit best in the pages of print media, such as newspapers, magazines, and newsletters. But broadcast journalists learned early that just reading news over the airways was dull. They realized that newer media required sound, voices, and visuals. As a result, formats for producing radio and television programming have become distinct from other media in several important ways.

While print media use photographs to enhance their stories, broadcast messages are best when voices accompany sounds and images from real life. For example, a radio reporter on the campaign trail can use actual comments from politicians along with the sounds of a cheering crowd. The sounds serve two purposes: They attract audience attention, and they add depth to the report. Audio and visual content complement writing and make any report come alive by appealing to the audience's senses.

Behind every newspaper reporter are editors and production staff to get the story from the computer to the printed page. In broadcast, the supporting cast is more visible. For a newscast, a central anchorperson or people serve as moderators for the newscast. They introduce the work of individual reporters. A producer determines the story order, edits the writing, and puts the show together.

Also, rather than typing stories in news article formats, broadcast reporters create a story with a careful mix of recordings: interviews with experts or bystanders, background or scenic information (usually with a "voiceover" of the reporter relating information), and a reporter standing and relaying information. The reporter's identity and location close out the piece. For TV reporters, their story might be a package; in radio, a wrap, short for "wraparound."

Print versus Broadcast Copy

A well-written broadcast story has much in common with any good print or online story. In all three types, writers work to focus the audience's attention on news values. All insist on accuracy and clarity; however, differences in technologies and audiences result in different formats and approaches.

Similarities

The Writing Process. The skills learned in the writing process discussed in Chapter 1 apply to broadcast writers. Broadcast reporters start with an idea for a news package, then work with a producer. They do research and interviews, then produce copy that is well written and relevant to their audiences. Outlining is critical for broadcast writers, who must write and shoot or record package materials before they leave the scene of an event. They must collect a variety of sounds or images to illustrate the news, as well as quotes. Once in editing, they usually don't have time to go back and catch additional sources or visuals before deadline.

News Values. All mass communication writing must include some news values from among those discussed in Chapter 5: prominence, timeliness, proximity, impact, magnitude, conflict, oddity, and emotional impact. Broadcast writing is no exception. Timeliness is the most defining news value for broadcast media, which makes broadcast more similar to online than print in this regard. Radio and television, because of their ability to broadcast live, can get information out to audiences in real time, as news events actually occur. Online news coverage can also be done live and in real time. Immediacy is a key factor in the success of broadcast news. In radio and television, news that happened in the morning may be revised, refreshed, or even replaced in the afternoon. Consider how immediate and up-to-date information, such as the approach of a hurricane, can be updated by the minute on broadcast media, while print outlets are limited to overall summaries of the previous day's events. In weather disasters, both print and broadcast would focus on the news values of impact, magnitude, and emotion.

Clear, Concise Writing. Particularly critical in broadcast writing are the rules of using short sentences, active voice, and short words; avoiding jargon and technical language; cutting wordiness; and getting to the point quickly. Broadcast stories generally are shorter than those in print. A print news story may use 250 to 500 words to tell about an event. A broadcast report might have

15 to 30 seconds or 30 to 75 words. Every word takes time away from other reports. In addition, listeners and viewers who don't understand jargon or complicated language usually don't have the chance to go back and hear the word again. Broadcast stories must be clear to the entire audience on the first pass.

Research.   Like print reporters, broadcast reporters develop sources and do research and interviews. Research can be difficult when time is limited. Broadcast reporters must be generalists and cover a variety of topics even within a single day. Many reporters have multiple beats. They might attend the governor's news conference in the morning and cover a hotel fire that same afternoon. In trying to stay informed, broadcast reporters use the same library and online resources as their print colleagues. Some broadcast reporters have the opportunity for in-depth research when they specialize in a particular area or beat, such as medicine or business.

Differences

Deadlines.   Broadcast reporters often work under multiple, tight deadlines. Print reporters generally have one or two deadlines each day, usually in the evening for the next morning's newspaper. For broadcasts, deadlines come early and often. Newscasts appear at morning, noon, evening, and late night, with updates in between. A single reporter may be developing several stories for any single broadcast. Once a story is aired, it may need to be reviewed and refreshed prior to the next news show. Deadlines might be more frequent for both print and broadcast reporters if they are also writing news for the company's online site or for a 24-hour television news service.

Writing Structure.   Because radio and television reports are shorter than print versions, they must be understood immediately. Broadcast messages have only one chance to be heard, so they must make it through clutter. Effective communicators know that radio and television audiences are doing other things: driving, working, caring for kids, cooking, cleaning, and commuting.

To meet their special challenges with active audiences, broadcast writers use a slight variation of the inverted pyramid style. They typically begin any news item with a hook or headline that will grab listeners or viewers. Then they give the actual lead to the story, setting up some context and giving essential information. Next comes a more detailed explanation, followed by a wrap-up that may mention impact or future possibilities.

Broadcast writers also use a *diamond structure*, in which they start with a specific person or example, then broaden the story to explore the bigger picture. Then they return to the original person or example to close out the story. The example is similar to the use of anecdotal leads discussed in Chapter 5.

Style.   Broadcast writers, like many online writers, use a more conversational style. Often the style is narrative, focusing on people and events—more like telling a story to a friend. Words and phrases are less formal and more colloquial, similar to the style found in many blogs. A reporter might use contractions or colloquialisms in sentences or follow specific style, such as writing out numbers smaller than two digits or larger than three, explained later in this chapter.

Format.   Because broadcast media require sounds and images, they use a specific format that differs from how print reporters type their stories. All journalists, both print and broadcast, double-space their copy, but broadcast reporters must leave space for cues and instructions indicating when audio and visual elements are to be added.

Radio reports are typed across the page, just as print journalism stories are, but they include notes on what pre-recorded elements are to be inserted between blocks of copy that will be read aloud. In television reports, copy that will be heard fills the right-hand side of the page; cues for the technical members of the crew appear in the left-hand column. Some broadcast journalists type their copy all in capital letters, but others prefer upper and lower case. In broadcast writing, paragraphs are not split between pages, and each new story begins on a new page. Specific broadcast style rules on how to use abbreviations, numbers, and attributions are explained later in this chapter.

The Differences in Practice

A radio reporter and a print journalist are rewriting wire service copy for their respective media. How would their leads look, based on the differences between broadcast and print writing? Let's see. The print journalist writes:

> NEW ORLEANS—Mayor Ray Nagin has plans to begin moving New Orleans' residents back into the city, although federal officials want to hold off on citizens' return to the hurricane-ravaged city.

The broadcast journalist writes:

> IF THE NEW ORLEANS MAYOR HAS HIS WAY, RESIDENTS MAY RETURN TO THE
> CITY AS EARLY AS NEXT WEEK.

The broadcast writer does not use a dateline, uses the present tense, avoids a proper name, and establishes the location—New Orleans—as context for listeners and viewers. Consider two other examples:

> A SURVEY REPORTS THAT ALL WOMEN HAVE SIMILAR CONCERNS.

> WOMEN ARE MOST CONCERNED ABOUT BALANCING HOME AND JOB, HEALTH
> INSURANCE, AND STRESS, ACCORDING TO A SURVEY RELEASED TODAY.

Which is the broadcast lead? The first one is. It is short and uses attribution at the beginning to establish the source immediately. It also establishes a context for the story to follow.

Leads and Structure

No matter where an electronic journalist works, the need for clear, concise writing is essential. Sabrina Smith Davis began her career as a radio reporter and then made the transition from radio to television as a reporter for KOAT-TV in Albuquerque, New Mexico, the ABC affiliate. She summarized the need for good writing:

> *You have to be able to write. In radio, all audiences have is your voice and what they hear. As a reporter, you have to write the story colorfully and to visualize for audiences what they only can hear. If you can do that, you are ahead of the game. In television, good writing is also essential. So many people in television write in a boring way because they rely on visuals. Do this test: To see if the video matches, turn down the volume and just watch the video to see if you know what the story is about. As a viewer, you should have some idea. If you can write well and integrate visuals well, then you will do well as an electronic media journalist.*

Writing for radio and television means writing for the ear by using short sentences, conversational speech, subject–verb–object sentence order, clear and understandable copy, and smooth, clear transitions between thoughts. Let's look at producing broadcast copy, following these guidelines.

Broadcast Leads

A broadcast lead is short and gives basic information. It should be written in present or future tense to set the tone of breaking news. The lead may be catchy and even entertaining. It causes the audience to stop and listen to the story. As noted earlier, the lead generally establishes a context for the story. Such leads ensure specific information will follow:

THIRTEEN PEOPLE GET RICH IN INDIANA.

TOMORROW THE MAYOR WILL ANNOUNCE THAT NEW JOBS ARE COMING TO THE AREA.

The context is clear in each example. The first story will be about Powerball lottery winners. The second lead sets up audiences for a story on economics, with information about how many and what kinds of jobs and the name of the company. In both instances, the leads are much shorter than in print.

Broadcast writers who cover continuing or recurring stories try to find leads that will pique audience attention and interest in just a few words:

RIGHT NOW UNION WORKERS ARE WALKING A PICKET LINE AT BALTIMORE HARBOR.

A SURPRISE WITNESS MAY TESTIFY BEFORE CONGRESS TODAY IN THE ENRON INVESTIGATION.

WHAT'S UP IN THE STOCK MARKET TODAY?

Broadcast Structure in the Message

Again, the structure of any electronic message must appeal to the audience's ear. The message must be clear and direct. Sentences are short and written primarily in subject–verb–object order. Language must be simple. The writer develops the story using the three-part format: context, explanation, and effect. It sets out the context or the reason why the story is being written. It may focus on a particular news value or the latest information—that is, timeliness. The second part is explanation, in which listeners or viewers get more information, whether it is background, a historical perspective, or more details of the current situation. Then the writer wraps up with the effect, generally with a look to the future or the impact of the event. Look at this story:

> IN ESPANOLA STUDENTS WILL RETURN TO FAIRVIEW ELEMENTARY SCHOOL TOMORROW AFTER ALMOST TWO WEEKS OF NO SCHOOL.
>
> THE SCHOOL CLOSED MONDAY OF LAST WEEK AFTER A PLUMBER DOING ROUTINE MAINTENANCE WORK DISCOVERED A GAS LEAK. THE SCHOOL WAS BUILT IN 1966, AND ADMINISTRATORS SAY EXTENSIVE REPAIRS WERE NEEDED.
>
> SCHOOL OFFICIALS PRICED THE REPAIRS AT MORE THAN 40 THOUSAND DOLLARS. THEY SAY THE SYSTEM'S OTHER SCHOOLS WILL BE CHECKED FOR LEAKS, TOO.

The message clearly lets parents in the audience know that children will go back to school, and it gives other general-interest members an update on a story that has been in the news. The writer follows the lead with context by giving background on why the school was closed. The next sentence explains why the school was closed for so long. Listeners then learn the repairs were expensive. The effect, or impact, is an investigation of other schools' plumbing.

As for language, all words are simple. According to the readability formula discussed in Chapter 4, this story is easy for viewers to understand. The most complicated words are "maintenance" and "extensive."

Writing Guidelines

Basic writing principles apply for broadcast stories. Because timeliness is crucial to electronic media, writers should open their stories in the present tense, explaining the latest developments. Even if they have to shift to past tense later in the story, present tense is preferable in the lead.

Avoid:

A CONVICTED RAPIST WAS EXECUTED TODAY AFTER MONTHS OF APPEALS FAILED.

Prefer:

A CONVICTED RAPIST DIES AFTER MONTHS OF APPEALS.

Avoid:

SIXTEEN WINNERS WERE DECLARED IN THE LONG-AWAITED STATE LOTTERY.

Prefer:

SIXTEEN PEOPLE ARE WINNERS IN THE LONG-AWAITED STATE LOTTERY.

Some other writing rules to follow:

- Introduce unfamiliar people before using their names. Describe people in terms of employment, life's work, or relevance to the story. Then name them, as in "sprinter John Jones" or "angry ticketholder Billy Cupp." Only the instantly recognizable names of widely known people should be used without prior explanation.

  A ROCKLAND SECOND-GRADE TEACHER IS THE NATION'S TEACHER OF THE YEAR.

  RONNIE MILLER,...

  Or

  ROCKLAND MAYOR JOAN TILLIS IS IN GOOD CONDITION AFTER BACK SURGERY.

- Avoid tongue twisters that can cause problems when reports are read on air. Always read copy aloud before it is broadcast. "The clandestine clan committed continual crimes" or "the player's black plastic pants" may look clever on paper, but it may be difficult for an announcer to enunciate.
- Use action verbs. Remember that verbs can paint pictures, an especially important aspect of radio reports. "Race car driver Rusty Wallace roared to victory" has more life than "Race car driver Rusty Wallace won."
- Use quotes sparingly. Paraphrased statements are more easily understood. If a quote is particularly good, use it live from the source. Make sure the writing does not imply the statement is from the reporter or newscaster. Direct quotes that use "I" or "we" can cause such confusion. Consider this quote: "Chamber of Commerce president David Fall says, 'I have doubts about the town's development practices.'" Listeners who miss the attribution may infer the reporter is doubtful. Instead, write: "Chamber of Commerce President David Fall says he has doubts about the town's development practices."

- Put attribution at the beginning of a quotation: "Medical experts say the new treatment may cause cancer cells to die." If you must use a direct quote, try "Johnson said in his own words, 'The new treatment may cause cancer cells to die.'"

- Avoid writing that uses a lot of punctuation. Punctuation—even a question mark—cannot be heard. Listeners may miss the inflection.

- Avoid long introductory clauses with participles, like this one: "While doing a routine maintenance check at the school, a plumber found...." The story example used earlier puts that information at the end of the sentence.

- Avoid separating subjects and verbs, particularly with phrases in apposition. "Marian Johnson, a director for the Rockland Little Theater, will leave her job in two weeks" becomes "Rockland's Little Theater director will leave her job within two weeks. Marian Johnson...." Don't leave verbs at the end of the sentence. Follow subject–verb–object order as much as possible.

- Break up lengthy series of modifiers and adjectives, such as this one: "Police described the man as blond, long-haired, blue-eyed, and five-feet, six-inches tall." Rather, write: "Police say the suspect has long blond hair and blue eyes. They also say he is about five feet, six inches tall."

- Avoid negatives. A listener may miss the negative words "no" and "not" in a broadcast and thereby be misinformed. Use alternatives: "Police could find no motive for the shootings" can be translated "Police say the motive for the shootings is unknown."

- If your report runs long, say more than 30 seconds, look for ways to unify the story. Repetition of key words is one way to help listeners and viewers follow along.

Style in Copy

In Chapter 3, we looked at copyediting style for print. Broadcast writers also follow style rules for preparing copy:

- In the case of a word that might be mispronounced, spell it phonetically, just as you would with complicated names. For example, if you are reporting about lead content in paint, write it "led." Even though it is misspelled for the usage, you don't have to worry about an anchor reading "lead" as "leed" paint.

■ If a name is difficult, write it out phonetically. Anchors and reporters can stumble in stating people's names. Sound it out. For example, names with "ei" or "ie" can be confusing, such as Janice Weinberger. Write out "Wine Burger" so the anchor will use a long "i" pronunciation. For former Iraqi leader Saddam Hussein, the pronunciation spelling is "Who Sayn."

■ Put titles before names and keep them short. Use "former Florida Governor Jeb Bush" rather than "Jeb Bush, the former governor of Florida." A university vice chancellor for institutional research services becomes "a university administrator." You can use a descriptive title if audiences easily identify a person that way, such as "evangelist Billy Graham" or "singer Sheryl Crow."

■ Use people's names the way they are commonly cited. Former President Clinton is known as Bill Clinton, not William Clinton. Former Vice President Al Gore is rarely called Albert Gore, Jr.

■ Write out single-digit numbers. Use numerals for two- and three-digit numbers. Return to words for thousand, million, etc; write out numbers between zero and nine. Use numerals for 10 through 999. Above 999, you can combine numerals and words. For example, write "nine thousand 45," "10 thousand 200," and "22 billion."

■ Round off numbers. Say "more than 10 thousand" rather than "10 thousand 232 subscribers."

■ Write out amounts for dollars and cents, percent, and fractions:

GASOLINE PRICES ARE THREE TO FOUR CENTS A GALLON HIGHER.

THREE-FOURTHS OF TOWN RESIDENTS SAY THEY ARE PLEASED WITH THE MAYOR'S PERFORMANCE.

ABOUT FIFTY-FIVE PERCENT OF WHAT YOU READ, YOU REMEMBER.

■ Use numerals for phone numbers and years: 919-555-1212, 1999, or 1865.

■ Keep statistics to a minimum. Put them in a format people will understand. If a poll says 67 percent of the state's residents support NASA's plan for a lunar space station, report that "two out of three state residents say they favor NASA's plan for a lunar station."

- Write out Roman numerals. Write out "Harry Holland the third" rather than "Harry Holland III," or "Queen Elizabeth the second," not "Queen Elizabeth II."
- Avoid acronyms on first reference unless an organization is better known by its initials than by its full name, such as E-S-P-N, F-B-I, and N-C-A-A. Insert hyphens between letters if they are to be read individually. Omit hyphens if the acronym is to be read as a word, such as in FEMA. For local or state law enforcement, it is better just to say police or law officials on subsequent references.

Broadcast Formats

A major difference between print and broadcast media is the format for the final message, as noted earlier. Broadcast media use a script format that indicates the text along with the sound bites or visuals. Time is critical in broadcast writing. Scripts indicate how long the total story runs plus the length of specific segments within the story. Radio reports are typed across the page, much like a print story, with audio cues. Following is an example of a radio news script:

7/30 MK Road Construction

SPEEDING ALONG HIGHWAY 86 IN NORTH CHAPEL HILL COULD COST YOU AS MUCH AS 165 DOLLARS. THAT'S THE WARNING FROM THE CHAPEL HILL POLICE TRAFFIC UNIT. OFFICER CHUCK QUINLAN SAYS A CONSTRUCTION WORK ZONE WILL STRETCH FROM ASHLEY FOREST TO INTERSTATE 40 FOR THE NEXT YEAR-AND-A HALF. QUINLAN SAYS THE WORK ZONE WILL HAVE A UNIFORM 35-MILE-PER-HOUR SPEED LIMIT WITHIN WEEKS. THAT MEANS DRIVERS NEED TO PAY ATTENTION.[*]

#145 QUINLAN:21 A:....ROAD, ETC.

QUINLAN SAYS HE AND HIS COLLEAGUES HAVE BEEN DEALING WITH REAR END COLLISIONS IN THE WORK AREA. AND HE SAYS THE SITUATION COULD GET WORSE, AS CREWS CONTINUE MOVING DIRT NEAR THE ROADWAY.[*]

[*]Reprinted with permission from Mitch Kokai, WCHL-AM radio, Chapel Hill, NC.

In television reports, the cues on the left-hand side of the page give such information as the title or slug of the story, what newscast it will appear on, the tape number, the length of the story, the name of the anchor, and any graphics to be used, as shown earlier in the chapter. After the story text begins, cues will tell whether the story has a voiceover that is read by the anchor along with the visuals. Cues also indicate who is speaking—for example, a source interviewed for the story, the reporter, or the anchor.

When the story text is typed, sometimes all capital letters are used. That helps clarify writing where a lowercase "l" might resemble a capital "I" and create problems for announcers. Capital letters are also easier to read from a distance. But some writers are moving to using upper- and lower-case letters, as in print journalism.

When students study broadcast journalism, they learn the codes and copy preparation style early on. A complete radio story, such as the script shown earlier, may seem longer than a story typed for print because cues take up space on the left-hand side of the page. The goal is to make the copy legible for the anchor and the reporter who read from the copy.

Trends in Broadcast Media

Television is a regulated and competitive medium that depends heavily on technology. And in the past decade, it has been on a rollercoaster of change. Audiences use television primarily as an entertainment medium but also for news. Almost every household in the United States has a television set, and about three out of four homes have more than one.

In the last quarter of the 20th century, the television industry went from a handful of networks and few cable or satellite services to almost a dozen major networks and to cable and satellite distribution companies that increased the U.S. media buffet to hundreds of channels. The broad reach of television is extended now by connections to Internet sites and other media. This coming together of powerful media formats is known as convergence.

As one of the latest trends evolving, particularly in broadcast media, convergence can take several forms, such as shared information or shared staffs. In shared information, a news reporter for a television station might give information about an event to a reporter from a sister newspaper with which it has a sharing agreement. A television station might do a promotion for a story in a sister newspaper. With shared staffs, a television reporter may write a story and then rewrite it for the station's Web site. Or a newspaper reporter may write versions of a story for the newspaper and for the online site.

Some see convergence as a permanent fixture in U.S. media; others see it as just an experiment. Some media observers say newspapers and their sister online sites and TV and radio stations already represent convergence, which is getting support from publishers and media owners who see shared staffs as a way to reduce newsroom expenses. A plus for the business side is the ability to sell advertising packages that include ads for all media in a certain market: newspaper, radio, television, and online. Advertisers get a reduced rate to advertise in more than one medium. Supporters say each medium—newspaper, radio, television, online—can maintain its values and basic structure but have the benefit of broader resources and expanded reach among audiences.

The trend toward convergence has prompted some schools of journalism and mass communication to teach students to write across platforms or different media styles. At the very least, those hiring students want them to know how writing styles differ and how to be comfortable with different media. Phil Currie, vice president of news for Gannett, commented at a journalism educators' meeting that he wanted newspaper reporters to be comfortable being interviewed on television even if they were not trained specifically to write television copy.

The television industry is also moving to HDTV, or high-definition television, that changes the way television signals are transmitted. The picture viewers see on HDTV screens is much crisper and more detailed, giving the feeling of seeing images in a three-dimensional form. All full-power television stations nationwide were expected to move to DTV transmission in February 2009, ending analog broadcasts. Television viewers had several options to allow their television sets to receive the HDTV broadcasts if they could not afford to buy a new television set.

While the federally mandated changes affect the visual aspect of television programming, they do not affect how writers produce content. Writing styles and structures remain the same, and news videographers have learned that their pictures air on a wider format with greater clarity.

Mobile digital television, which uses a Mobile Pedestrian Handheld (MPH) system, is in early development and allows broadcasters to deliver DTV to mobile devices, including cellular phones, laptops, and personal media players.

Exercises _____

1. Write a broadcast lead for each of the following stories:

   ■ Sam Snyder, president of the Chamber of Commerce, has been elected to the board of directors of the National Chamber of Commerce.

   ■ The Federal Reserve Board raised interest rates one-quarter percent, which means consumers will be paying higher rates on their adjustable-rate home mortgages if they are seeking mortgages.

   ■ David Parkinson of Waverly County won first place at the county fair yesterday for the largest squash. It weighed 6 and 1/2 pounds. David is 6 years old.

   ■ Competition begins Thursday for the National Collegiate Athletic Association title. The tough competition in basketball has been dubbed March Madness.

2. Using the formula that a 60-space typed line equals 4 seconds of air time, write a 20-second radio script for the following information:

   > A masked man robbed the university dining hall of $3,000 and escaped after locking the dining hall manager in a closet.
   >
   > Tony Jones, the manager, escaped unharmed. Police are looking for a heavy-set white man about 5-feet, 5 inches, and weighing about 175 pounds. He has a round face and broad shoulders. Jones could give no description of the man's facial features because he had a stocking pulled over his face.
   >
   > Jones was preparing the payroll when he heard a noise in the kitchen. When he went to investigate, he said, the man came charging at him. The man ordered him to open the safe and put money in a blue sack. Jones complied, and the robber locked him in a closet before leaving.

3. Write a 20-second radio script for the following information and indicate an audio you could use to illustrate the spot:

   > The legal age for minors to buy cigarettes in most states is 18. Studies show that underage youth or minors still buy up to 500 million packs of cigarettes a year, despite the states' laws. About 25 states have agreed

there should be stricter laws on tobacco products, and even tobacco industry officials claim their advertising is not geared to teenagers.

4. Write a 30-second television script for the following information. Type the copy in the right-hand column and indicate on the left what visuals you would use.

> A coalition of child-care advocates marched on the state legislature today. They distributed flyers encouraging legislators to approve monies during the current session that would subsidize the cost of day care for families earning below $16,000 a year. They claim that day-care costs in the state have skyrocketed, and even working families are finding it hard to pay for quality day care out of their salaries. The coalition estimated 15 percent of the state's population fell below the federal poverty level guidelines last year. The coalition officials said that last year it had to turn away almost 400 families who needed financial assistance because funds just were not available.

5. Watch the local evening news. Do a tally that covers the number of stories, story topics, whether they were local or based on a national event, the length of each, and numbers and types of sources used. Write several paragraphs on whether you felt adequately informed about news items from the television account.

6. Based on the information collected in Exercise 5, look at the local or regional newspaper the following day. See how many stories from your evening television newscast were covered in the newspaper. Look at the length of those stories and what new information you learned.

References

Felicity Barringer, "Growing Audience Is Turning to Established News Media Online," *The New York Times*, August 27, 2001.

Phil Currie, panel on convergence, Association for Education in Journalism and Mass Communication, Washington, DC, August 6, 2001.

Seth Finn, *Broadcast Writing as a Liberal Art*. Englewood Cliffs, NJ: Prentice-Hall, 1991.

Cecilia Friend, Don Challenger, and Katherine C. McAdams, *Contemporary Editing*. Chicago: NTC/Contemporary Publishing Group, 2000.

Radio-Television News Directors Association Web site. Available at: www.rtnda.org.

C. A. Tuggle, Forrest Carr, and Suzanne Hoffman, *Broadcast News Handbook: Writing, Reporting, and Producing in a Converged Media World*. New York: McGraw-Hill, 2006.

Leslie Walker, "Web-Page Collection Preserves the Online Response to Horror," *The Washington Post*, September 26, 2001.

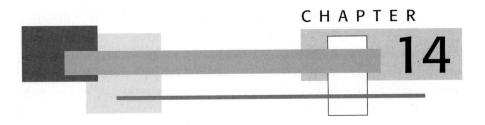

Strategic Communication

The president of a national company that operates health clubs and sells exercise equipment wants to improve its corporate image. In addition, he wants to increase the company's name recognition in the fitness market. He needs to develop a plan for advertising in a variety of media, including online, with public relations efforts in the community around each health club. But he doesn't know how.

That's when he seeks the talents of professionals who can develop a strategic plan to target specific audiences and develop the communications tools to reach them. The plan will use public relations and advertising in an integrated marketing program that might include news releases, pop-up Internet ads, sponsorship in a community bike race, and local appearances of well-known athletes at company gyms.

This book has focused on producing factual, non-opinionated content for audiences. Many writers, editors, multimedia producers, and others in advertising and public relations jobs perform the same tasks. But in addition to factual information, they usually have a specific, persuasive message to share. The goal is to influence people to buy their products and services or to take some other sort of action.

Most journalism and mass communication programs separate public relations and advertising as courses of study, but many students take one or two courses in the other subject. Some jobs specifically require PR skills, others just advertising, and others knowledge of both. Public relations practitioners who work for nonprofit organizations, for example, might write news releases, the annual report, and all advertising copy. As the PR director for your town's historical society, you might write the advertising copy to promote the society's annual Christmas tour of homes, then possibly solicit a local company to underwrite the cost and give the company credit within the ad.

Many advertising and PR professionals are joined in what the industry is calling integrated marketing communications—and what we will refer to in this chapter as strategic communication. This type of communication requires strategy developed from input and planning for all aspects of message delivery from advertising to direct marketing to news releases—whatever is necessary to get a client's message to the audience.

This chapter looks at the importance of

- good writing in strategic communication,
- the practice of public relations,
- public relations communications tools,
- advertising strategies, including branding and product placement,
- guidelines for effective ad writing, and
- strategic communication in an online world.

The Importance of Good Writing

Within strategic communication, good writing is at the heart of every successful and effective campaign and event. Strategic communicators must send news releases and buy ad space so audiences, including media, know their organizations or businesses exist and what they do. The reporter must receive the media advisory before writing a story. The mother must read the brochure on a community's child-care offerings before calling for more details. The college student must peruse the company's home page to learn about its internship program.

Practitioners of strategic communication must identify audiences to determine the best methods to reach them, then conduct research, plan and carry out communication strategy, develop specific tools, and evaluate plans. Writing is crucial at each stage, but particularly in crafting the messages to important audiences.

As writers, strategic communicators must be able to adopt different styles and tones because they have many more audiences than the writer for a newspaper or specialized publication. In the morning, they might write a general-interest news release and in the afternoon a speech in the language style of the company president. Or they might write an article for the employee newsletter, proofread ads in a statewide magazine, and later consult with a production company on a video script for an upcoming stockholders meeting.

PR and advertising students often take media-writing courses to learn the inverted pyramid and other formats. The courses also teach the fundamentals of grammar, punctuation, and style, and they stress the need for clear, concise, and accurate writing that interests and attracts targeted audiences. Students are also trained in building and maintaining Web sites for specific audiences.

Strategic communicators generally divide writing into two categories: informational and persuasive. The organization's or company's objective will determine the type and tone of the writing.

Informational writing is just what it says: It presents materials in a straightforward, factual manner—just as in journalistic writing. A brochure can be informational, simply listing an organization's history, services, address, and telephone number. A brochure might give specifics about an upcoming program or new service.

A brochure can also be persuasive. Persuasive writing clearly pitches a particular point of view and reflects a specific attitude and behavior. Some types of communication are deliberately persuasive. A direct mail letter to university alumni will try to persuade them to donate to endowed professorships. A public service announcement on radio will encourage listeners to donate canned goods to the local food bank.

Persuasive writing follows the tenets of good writing: accuracy, clarity, and conciseness. A brochure can be persuasive and still be informational, using facts and graphics to portray positively the company's position.

Such writing adheres to journalistic standards of fairness and impartiality. Experienced practitioners know that arguments explained factually will have more impact than those that are biased and long-winded.

Public Relations in Practice

Professor James Grunig at the University of Maryland defines public relations as the management of communication between an organization and its publics, or audiences: employees, clients, customers, investors, or alumni. Grunig emphasizes the importance of strategy and analysis in approaching those relationships.

Successful public relations builds and maintains good relationships between an organization and its publics through balanced, open communication. Public relations may be as simple as an announcement by the local literacy council about its success rate for the past year. Or it may be a complicated integrated marketing program that incorporates public relations with advertising, investor relations, and market research.

Diverse organizations use public relations: local, state, and national nonprofit organizations, such as the American Heart Association; schools and universities; small companies; multinational corporations; and local, state, and federal government, including the president and the armed services. Public relations practitioners share information with the public to help the organization achieve its objectives. The objective of PR efforts may be to announce new products or to show how a company works as a good corporate citizen or as a leader in its field. The objective may be public service, as in broadcast messages to reduce teenage pregnancy or to warn smokers about the risks of heart attacks.

Some people erroneously think of public relations as free publicity, believing there is no cost. But real public relations—ongoing programs of communication with various publics—is expensive. Organizations must pay salaries and production costs, buy supplies and equipment, and cover additional overhead expenses, such as office space, computer support, and utilities. Most are hidden costs the public does not see or consider.

Public Relations Stages

In the late 1960s, Scott Cutlip and Allen Center identified four stages of a PR campaign: research, planning, communication, and evaluation. Public relations practitioners still follow those stages today.

For example, a bank plans to change its checking account service in three months. The PR department is charged with informing the bank's publics of the change. Look at how the PR practitioner would use each stage.

Research.   Research is essential to enable the bank to state public relations goals, identify relevant publics, describe the service, and identify its strengths and weaknesses. For example, the bank's reputation would be a strength; competition from other banks' services would be a weakness. Research could use focus groups or surveys to determine what the bank's customers would like in a checking account.

Planning.   In planning, the practitioner devises a communications plan or strategy. The practitioner determines what communications tools will be used during the next three months and sets deadlines for each one. For example, dates for news releases to trade publications differ from those for statewide media. Magazines usually need copy two months before publication dates; broadcast media, online sites, and newspapers can print information within 24 hours of receiving it.

Communication. In the communication stage, the practitioner carries out the plan. Information is written and distributed via the communications tools: news releases, brochures, fact sheets, annual reports and other publications, Web sites, and speeches, just to name a few. Although writing is important in developing the plan, good skills are critical in the communication stage.

Evaluation. In evaluation, the practitioner uses qualitative and quantitative ways to evaluate the success of the communications plan and strategy and change in audience attitudes or behavior. For example, the bank can use focus groups of customers to determine how well they understood communication about the service. After the news release is distributed, the public relations staff can count how many times the news release information appeared in local media or the number of hits to the company's Web site link to the news release.

Public Relations Tools

Public relations practitioners often use the term "public relations tools" or "communications tools" to describe the techniques or methods they use to reach audiences. All require solid writing skills. Among the more common communications tools, which are usually online, are these:

News releases. Articles that describe newsworthy events and are sent to media outlets. They are written in a style ready to be used.

Feature releases. More in-depth, less timely articles about organization employees, projects, or services. These releases generally are targeted to a specific publication.

Media kits. Folders that contain relevant information on the organization or company or a special event. Included are fact sheets, photographs, reprints, biographies, and other material.

Direct mail letters.   Letters written to targeted publics, generally to solicit support for a project or event.

Brochures.   Booklets or folders that include general information or targeted information about an organization or a special project. These pieces are designed to be easily mailed or distributed at events or in racks.

Web sites.   Full-service Web sites that give information about an organization, invite the public to interact in a multitude of ways from e-mail to games, and link to other sites.

Face-to-face contact.   Speeches or appearances at meetings, conventions, or other programs.

Multimedia presentations.   Productions that incorporate text, audio, photography, graphics, and video to supplement information and to depict more visually an organization or its services. Such presentations can be posted online or distributed on CDs.

Specialized publications.   Newsletters, annual reports, and magazines produced for internal audiences, such as employees, or for external audiences, such as customers and the general public. In some corporate settings, annual reports are produced by the investor relations department, and the PR practitioner may help with some writing. Many specialized publications are online and linked to Web sites.

Video and audio news releases.   Actual film footage with or without sound, especially voiceover, to give radio and television stations ready-to-use material. Some organizations have broadcast footage or other images that can be downloaded from their Web sites.

Public service announcements (PSAs).   Short announcements, generally sent ready-to-read to radio stations or in video format for television use or posted on Web sites.

Blogs.   Short for Web logs. These online diaries are managed usually by one person, but companies are also using them for conversations among internal and external audiences.

Image advertising.   Attempts by an organization to improve an audience's perception of it. Such advertising is often done in conjunction with marketing departments.

Communications tools are incorporated into strategic plans that serve as guides for PR activities or campaigns. Corporate communications departments, for example, begin work in the fall on the next year's plan to support goals, specific actions, and target dates.

Of course, not all public relations is planned. A reporter might call the corporate communications department about a story idea, and the PR practitioner will respond or arrange for a company executive to reply. The practitioner might send the reporter a media kit that contains a mix of communications tools, often called collateral materials, such as a news release, a fact sheet, a CD with a multimedia show, and a brochure.

Considering Audiences or Publics

Just as in any other mass communication field, PR practitioners must consider their audiences, or what they call *publics*. The publics are the people who will be reading news releases or viewing video news releases. They may be employees, customers, other business people, town residents, lawmakers, reporters, or officials in local, state, or federal government agencies. Public relations practitioners must identify and know which publics are important to their organizations.

Imagine you are the public information director for a university system that is planning a capital campaign to raise funds for new buildings. The university administration has set a goal of $500 million. In planning a public relations campaign, you would have to consider the university's publics: alumni, faculty members, staff members, students, students' parents, potential students, donors, legislators (if the university is public or state supported), the general public, and the media. From that list, you might identify five key or important publics.

Practitioners use research, such as informal surveys or focus groups, to learn about their publics. Specifically, practitioners need to know how their publics get information. Then they can decide which media, or communications tools, are most effective in reaching them. And they can decide the tone and style of the messages.

As part of targeting publics, PR practitioners must be aware of the growing diversity of U.S. society and how to reach specific audiences. Specialized publications and Web sites are geared to individual interests, and

PR professionals should monitor a diverse array of media to stay up-to-date. For example, a range of news pertinent to African American audiences can be found on Black PR Wire at www.blackprwire.com and for Hispanics on Hispanic PR Wire at www.hispanicprwire.com. More on considering diverse audiences is discussed in Chapter 11.

The Media as a Public

An important public for any public relations practitioner is the media. The media learn about an organization through standard communications tools, such as news releases and media advisories. But they also use annual reports, Web sites, investor publications, executive speeches, brochures, and other means to find out information about companies. In turn, practitioners must know the media. They must know the media's audiences, formats, and content. They must convince the media to use PR information. Media are essential audiences because through newspapers, magazines, radio and television, specialty publications, online sites, and others, the practitioner reaches many other publics. Among the primary tools for PR practitioners to reach their publics through the media are news releases, fact sheets, brochures, and public service announcements, many posted on company Web sites.

News Releases

News releases provide timely information to media. They might announce a promotion or staff change; a service or product; new information, such as the effects of legislation or the results of a survey; financial earnings; an upcoming event; or community service, such as a new scholarship program. Some news releases, especially those concerning events, are presented in the form of media advisories, or short notices that tell media in advance about an event or issues and that focus on *who, what, when, where, how,* and *why.*

News releases must contain some of the news values discussed in Chapter 5: prominence, timeliness, proximity, impact, and magnitude. They may also include conflict, oddity, or emotional impact. The lead should summarize the relevant information. The rest of the release should be organized in the inverted pyramid style of writing discussed in Chapter 6 and follow Associated Press style, which most news outlets use.

The practitioner's goal in sending a news release is to get publicity. But the practitioner must remember that news releases are uncontrolled; the final story is up to the reporter's and editor's discretion. Reporters might use the release as a basis for an expanded story, or they might take the news release as is and even give the PR writer a byline. Reporters, editors, and producers need news releases that are complete, accurate, newsworthy, and appropriate for their audiences. They will favor news releases in a ready-to-use format.

News releases should contain the PR contact name, organization, organization address, organization phone number, fax number, e-mail address, and even the PR contact's home phone number. The information goes above the headline. (If the organization's address is readily visible on letterhead, it can be omitted.) The date and the headline follow, setting up the contents of the news release.

Often PR practitioners will include a contact name and telephone number within the text of the news release, usually at the end, to ensure that further information is available to interested publics if the news release is run verbatim. Online news releases, such as those posted on PR Newswire or other online news services, often contain a link so readers can give feedback on whether the information was useful and understandable.

Fact Sheets

Fact sheets generally are one page long—or the front and back of one sheet—and are designed to be read quickly. Information about the organization, a service, a product, or a special activity is highlighted in short segments.

An easy way to develop a fact sheet is to follow the news elements discussed in Chapter 5: *who, what, when, where, how,* and *why.* A statewide children's forum is planning its annual fund-raiser. The fact sheet would be organized:

Who:	The Children's Forum
What:	Annual fund-raiser—a black-tie dinner and dance
When:	June 14
Where:	Downtowner Hotel
How:	Ticket prices $75 per individual for the dance and $150 for dinner and dance through the institute offices at 444–1234
Why:	To raise money for administrative and program costs

Fact sheets should also contain the contact name, organization, and phone numbers if reporters and others want additional information. When fact sheets are produced or updated, the date should be placed at the bottom of the fact sheet to indicate how current the information is. Fact sheets are also uncontrolled. Media can use the information any way they wish.

Brochures

In writing and designing brochures, PR practitioners are limited only by their talent, creativity, and budget. With desktop publishing and multimedia technology, many more organizations can produce high-quality, good-looking brochures for little cost. They can also publish brochure content online. The more work that is done in-house, the more money saved. Here are some questions to answer when writing a brochure:

- Is the brochure persuasive or informative? If the brochure's primary role is to persuade, it will be written with emotional language, comparisons, and familiar concepts. If informative, material will be to the point and language straightforward.

- Who is the audience? Whether the audience is specialized or general will determine the level of language used.

- Will the brochure be read and thrown away or saved? Deciding how it will be used will affect the cost and design.

- Will the brochure be a stand-alone piece, such as those in a display rack at a state's welcome station, or a collateral piece in a media kit or with a related Web site? A stand-alone brochure must be complete because it cannot rely on information in other pieces or online links.

- What is the appropriate format? If the brochure is a self-mailer, it will need to have an address space. Information has to be arranged logically, and decisions have to be made on artwork, such as photographs, and on graphic elements and white space, the size, the number of folds or pages, and how the brochure will open. How will the brochure copy be formatted for a Web site?

Brochure copy should be short. Publics are looking for a quick read. Each panel should stand alone, and copy shouldn't jump from one panel to the next.

Brochures, whether printed or online, are appealing to PR practitioners because they are controlled messages. The practitioner has the final say on copy and design. No one can change the content or wording; the only uncontrolled aspect is placement—for example, whether brochures are left at a doctor's office to be displayed or given to volunteers to distribute. The concerns are visibility of the brochure rack and whether all brochures are handed out.

Public Service Announcements

Public service announcements, or PSAs, are generally short pieces that give information of value to a specific audience. Traditionally, media have accepted the briefs from nonprofit organizations or government agencies and run them for free. Most PSAs range from 30 to 60 seconds in length, though some produced by individuals and posted on YouTube or MySpace can run as long as the person thinks people will watch.

Public service announcements must get basic information into as few words as possible. When they include audio, writers must grab listener attention and write clearly so that the message is understood. Increasingly, the audio and transcripts of PSAs can be downloaded off Web sites, and running PSAs is part of broadcast outlets' community service programming.

You probably have seen numerous PSAs on television, online, or in print, pointing out the dangers of drinking. International advertising firm Saatchi & Saatchi did a series of posters using images of cars, bottles, and keychains to form a noose or a firearm with the simple message: "It's like killing yourself. Don't drink and drive."

Any online search can produce hundreds of PSAs on any topic, produced by anyone from individuals to government agencies and on topics ranging from healthy behaviors to public services. For example, other PSAs on drinking and driving use images from simulated accidents to the bar scene from *Star Wars Episode IV, A New Hope* to catch attention and drive home the message. PSAs are free for the taking because the creators want the message widely distributed.

Advertising's Role in Strategic Communication

Advertising is probably the first form of media writing that children notice. Kids respond to ads, often before they can talk. Toddlers excitedly point at Ronald McDonald and "read" the golden arches as a sign for food even before they know their ABCs. By combining color, sound, movement, symbols, and language, advertising creates some of the most powerful messages in our world today.

Like all media presentations, good advertising depends on good writing. "Good advertising writers are writers first. They are personal writers—people who bring their own feelings and reactions to the product," observes Professor John Sweeney, former creative director for a major U.S. advertising agency. "Good advertising slogans are some of the most effective communication available today. They have a concise, pithy, sensory quality that other writers would do well to study and adopt."

Volney Palmer is generally credited with being the first advertising "agent." In 1841, he began selling newspaper advertising space for a profit. Advertisers prepared their ads; Palmer and other agents placed the ads for them. Such advertising agents became concerned with copy and artwork for the ads several years later. In 1869, F. W. Ayer started N. W. Ayer & Son, an advertising agency that provided writing, art, and media placement to its clients.

Advertising agencies have changed throughout the years, but the seeds of the modern agency planted with N. W. Ayer & Son and other early agencies still exist today. Advertisers also have myriad ways to reach consumers, not just newspapers or billboards. A company might advertise in newspapers, on radio and television, and on the Internet. New media and the changing media habits of audiences allow advertisers to funnel product information directly to specific and special audiences.

The goals of ad writers, regardless of medium, have remained constant over the years:

- To communicate availability of products to audiences.
- To communicate product benefits to audiences.
- To provide accessible information about products in a few words.
- To communicate reasons why the product can deliver benefits.

Other goals include corporate image building, when a company wants consumers to view it as a good corporate citizen; response to a disaster, such as a utility company telling customers how soon power will be restored after massive hurricane damage; or public service messages, such as alerting audiences to the dangers of unprotected sex or the benefits of low-fat diets.

Some people think of advertising as propaganda—distorted information designed to lead, or mislead, its audience. Propaganda is manipulative, and so is advertising, some people say.

Unlike most other forms of published writing, advertising is one-sided by its very nature; no one wants to spend his or her advertising budget extolling the benefits of a competitor's product. But the absence of other products from ads does not have to mean that an ad is unfairly biased if the information presented is accurate.

Presenting your best to the public, Sweeney explains, is a core value of advertising culture. Advertising that is less than ethical is not advertising; it is propaganda or huckstering or manipulation. Professional advertising writing is an accepted form of argument—a fair argument—and it abides by an ethical code.

Advertisers are subject to many government rules and regulations. The Capital Council of Better Business Bureaus advises that all advertisers stay abreast of regulations through subscription services, such as Do's and Don'ts in Advertising or the National Advertising Case Reports. Such subscription services are quite expensive and typically are used by large agencies or companies. The industry has self-regulators, such as the National Advertising Review Council (NARC). The Federal Trade Commission has information on how advertisers should behave, whether advertising in print or online.

Advertising and Today's Audiences

The environment for advertising has changed tremendously in the past decade. New media and new products compete for audience attention, and advertisers may no longer assume that mere publicity will lead to success or consumers using services and buying products. Today's advertisers must understand how audiences think, feel, and behave. Only through selecting likely audiences and streamlining ads for those groups can advertisers reach consumers.

Ad production is seldom the work of just the writer. In most cases, the copywriter is part of a team. For an advertising agency, the team could include account planners, who determine audience interest and product competition; an account executive, who oversees the account and serves as the liaison with the client; the copywriter, who takes the research and theme and creates text; the art director, who designs ads and other collateral pieces for the client; the creative director, who oversees the concept and production; media planners, who develop strategy for placing ads; and the media buyer, who places ads. All members of the team must know the others' roles. The copywriter often works most closely with the art designer on aspects such as typeface, length of copy, size of the ad, and graphic elements.

Newspapers still design ads for advertisers who cannot afford to pay agencies to do the work. The newspaper ad staff could include an ad sales representative, art director, and copywriter—all working as a team to produce and place ads that appeal to audiences.

Advertising Strategy

When a copywriter and an art director sit down to design an ad, they are guided by a creative brief that presents the advertising strategy. The advertising strategy is made up of the media strategy (where the ads should be placed and when to place them) plus the creative strategy (what should be in the ads and how they should look). Generally, the ad strategy lists marketing or business goals, such as more sales or improved corporate image; target audience; positioning, or how consumers perceive the service or product vis-à-vis competitors; benefits; creative approach, such as tone of the advertising message; and appropriate media to reach audiences.

The plan will enable the copywriter to know what structure will have the greatest appeal to the target audience. The creative approach is affected by the goals—selling a product, providing general information about a company, positioning a product as superior among its competitors, or boosting a corporate image. Target audiences will determine the tone of language and whether the ad must be serious or can have humor. Even corporate image will affect how a copywriter pitches an ad.

One of the copywriter's first responsibilities to support the advertising strategy will be to come up with a theme or the "big idea." Philip Ward Burton notes in *Advertising Copywriting* that the theme "is the central idea—the imaginative spark plug—that will give your advertisements continuity, recall value, and thus, extra selling power. Your theme is the lifeline of your campaign."

Targeting Audiences

The process of identifying and communicating with specific audiences is often called *targeting*. Clinique might target girls aged 13 to 15 as a likely audience for messages about a new tinted lip gloss. With the target group in mind, Clinique's ad writers design messages that will appeal to young teens and place these ads in locations where teens go. Clinique, for example, might place an ad for its new lip gloss in *Teen People* magazine and between scenes on the TV show "The O. C."

Targeting is a necessity in an era of budget consciousness and the rise of cable TV and audience fragmentation that have limited advertisers' ability to reach mass audiences. To get maximum benefit from advertising dollars, advertisers select target audiences for specific products. Beer, tires, and trucks are advertised in sports sections and broadcasts; toys and sweet cereals are advertised with children's programming; and pain relievers, laxatives, and investments are sold with financial news.

Professional market research is used by major corporations to identify the best possible markets for particular ads. Cluster marketing attempts to impose some order on the new media-and-audience mix, dividing Americans into subgroups and predicting specific media behaviors, as well as products and services that each group is likely to use. Companies, such as Claritas, offer their clients detailed information about consumers. Through its Prizm feature, anyone— individual or business—can type in a zip code and learn what types of people live in an area. Advertisers can use the information to target audiences. For example, a community might be made up of "Boomtown Singles," "Up-and-Comers," and "Young Influentials." On its Web site, Claritas defines for each group characteristics, such as median income, housing type, and lifestyle traits.

Product Placement

You are watching television, and the scene moves to the kitchen. On the counter are cereal boxes, diet soda, and cans of spaghetti. All the product names are clearly visible. Having real products in movies and on TV shows is called *product placement.* The benefits of product placement seem obvious: product reinforcement and possible recall when consumers shop.

Product placement has been around for years and is a fairly well-accepted advertising tool. When product placement first came into vogue in movies, skeptical viewers wondered about the effects of certain products on younger viewers. For example, the war on tobacco and on smoking among teens included criticism of tobacco product use in movies.

Most product placements are the result of a business deal, and some companies make product placement their business. Popular television game shows, such as "The Price Is Right," award specific products to participants. The product names and logos are repeated during each broadcast. Companies have sponsored events, such as bicycle races, and have their products and logos included with promotional materials.

Advertisers use the word "integration" to describe incorporating specific products into movies, television shows, and elsewhere. Most agree that integration needs to make sense, that the product needs to fit with the show's theme or message. Product placement is less common in magazines or newspapers.

Whether product placement actually works is still debated. Research has shown that in some instances, cross-cultural differences prevent audiences from connecting with the products they see. As more and more products are included within television programming, some observers are concerned about consumers' reactions to their top picks becoming more commercial-laden. Most companies, however, like the idea of product placement as yet another way to create brand recognition. But researchers are still assessing whether product placement does increase brand recognition and sales. Seeing a product for a fleeting second on a movie screen or in the hands of a celebrity might not be enough to put it in a consumer's shopping cart.

Branding

Branding has become a primary factor in advertising strategies. Consumers are part of the branding process every day as they walk around with the apple on their MacBooks, Lexus logos on cars, Gap on baby overalls, Starbucks on coffee cups, and L.L. Bean on backpacks. Meaningful branding can inspire depths of customer loyalty, and companies rely on such loyalty to maintain sales and market share.

When a product is branded, it has a brand identity immediately recognizable to consumers. Part of the immediate recognition is an icon, a slogan, a jingle, and even colors that can trigger in consumers' minds the product—McDonald's golden arches, Nike's "Just Do It," or Ben & Jerry's black-and-white cow colors. Some slogans change, such as the U.S. Army's more recent slogan "Army Strong" instead of "An Army of One" used a few years ago. But the identity and association are still clear. Once consumers recognize the product, they ascribe certain feelings or values that create brand loyalty.

Companies have determined that brand loyalty is a combination of overall satisfaction and confidence or trust. Another component is emotional attachment. Think about brands you use and why you use them. You may use a certain deodorant soap because that's the one you always found in the shower's soapdish at home. Whoever did the grocery shopping in your family had a loyalty to that particular brand. Perhaps you prefer a certain type of fast-food pizza because of the crust, the toppings, the service, or the group of friends you usually eat pizza with. People develop a familiarity with a product, and they may oppose any changes to it. Companies bank on consumers and their ties to certain products.

When assessing what makes consumers become attached to a product, companies use criteria that represent loyalty factors. Looking at the soap example above, you may have loyalty to Soap X because it brings back good feelings about home—the emotional attachment—plus you like the way it cleans your skin. In the quest for determining customer loyalty, researchers have gone so far as to develop indexes that rate customer satisfaction. Gallup, known for its polling, has developed a measure of what it calls customer engagement. A list of questions measures customer loyalty as well as emotional attachment.

More and more in the last decade, companies have considered branding as a key to retaining customers and profits. Research has shown that the cost of attracting new customers is five times the cost of keeping current ones. As a result, companies are investing more research dollars into understanding what makes customers stick with certain products or brands. Businesses have adopted practices so they can determine which products and services customers buy and why. They can even track individual customers to find out more about their habits and needs. Such information is invaluable in focusing advertising—and in developing other areas that provide customer service.

Branding is important for anyone writing or designing ads. Armed with customer research, a copywriter might develop an ad that shows the product's character and appeal. Part of branding may be the slogan for the product, its name, or its logo that creates recognition and positive feelings. Consistency in the message across all media strengthens the brand identity. The brand elements add value and differentiate the product from similar products.

Another aspect may be choosing spokespeople to represent the brands. For example, at the 2008 Olympic Summer Games in Beijing, swimmer Michael Phelps surpassed his own 2004 Olympic medal total and that of Mark Spitz who won seven gold medals in 1976. Before competing in Beijing, Phelps already had done endorsements, particularly for Speedo. Others followed after his 2008 victories. His success evokes qualities of determination, stamina, down-homeness, and just an average American who wins big.

Tips for Ad Copy That Sells

No matter the medium, copywriters have to produce ads: strategic messages that move products and services. Advertising Professor Jim Plumb gave the following broad tips to both student and professional copywriters:

1. **Identify selling points.**   Focus on concrete reasons for purchase. An abstract reason to buy a Subaru wagon is safety, but a concrete selling point is that buying a Subaru keeps the driver from shoveling snow or paying a tow truck.

2. **List the benefits.**   Find and list the benefits of your product that are important to your audience. Build your ad writing around these benefits. Make sure they are unique from competitors' products. List them in the ad if you can, but be sure to mention them in some way. Don't forget to look for intangible benefits. Sometimes the most powerful benefits are intangibles, such as the mood a perfume creates or a feeling of belonging that comes from a health club. Again, the viewer or reader should experience the product.

3. **Identify the single greatest benefit of your product.**   Research should identify the quality of your product that is most meaningful to your intended audience. Then create a headline or slogan that will convey this benefit to your audience. With "Just Do It," Nike sells discipline, an intangible benefit, as its star quality. A slogan in ads for *The Washington Post* reads, "If you don't get it, you don't get it." That is, if you don't take the *Post* regularly, you'll be left out. By communicating benefits in a few words, ad writing has the power to modify attitudes and behaviors. The same technique, among others used by copywriters, can work in all forms of writing.

Other experts in the field remind copywriters of other specifics. In their book, *The New How to Advertise*, advertising executives Kenneth Roman and Jane Maas list elements of good advertising strategy. They note that a good ad will show solutions to a problem; effective ads will aim for target audiences; and every good ad projects the tone, manner, and personality of the product. Other experts also recommend that ad copy should note details; use well-chosen language; have strong, clear words; have one unifying idea or theme; contain a beginning, a middle, and an end; and, for the most part, use correct grammar.

But some contend if such rules are followed, the result will be well-produced but boring ads. Other techniques are needed for fun or zany, truly creative advertisements. George Felton in his book, *Advertising Concepts*, discusses reversal as an approach to writing ads. He notes:

> *All great ads employ reversal: Something significant has been put in, left out, inverted, photographed oddly, colored wrong, talked about differently, or in some way had violence done to its ordinariness. Otherwise, if our preconceptions have been fulfilled instead of violated, we'll be looking at clichés.*

He gives as an example the classic Volkswagen ad that took the maxim "Think big" and reversed it to "Think small." The print advertisement used exceptional white space and put a small Volkswagen near the upper left-hand corner. "The ad reversed our expectations twice: once as user of clichés and once as viewers of ads," Felton notes.

Strategic Communication Online

Since the mid-1990s, any organization that wants to reach audiences quickly and provide in-depth information has moved internal and external communications online. Corporate newsrooms on Web sites post the latest news releases as well as archives of past releases and visuals that can be downloaded. Inhouse Web sites, e-mail lists, and message boards help employees stay in touch, whether they are in the same building or scattered across the world. Established companies have found they can expand their marketing efforts through the Internet and even hook into the Federal Trade Commission's advice for advertising on the Internet found at http://www.ftc.gov/bcp/edu/pubs/business/ecommerce/bus28.shtm. Web sites also provide information about the company to potential investors and customers.

Public relations practitioners use online software to track how many people access information online. Instead of sorting through clips of print stories, a media manager can count clicks on Web links. Software can also help build media lists and generate more media coverage.

Companies that once relied on banner ads or pop-up ads on Web sites have moved into more innovative ways to reach customers, even though pop-ups are still a strong part of Internet advertising. Such innovation has been necessary to catch a visual audience with a short attention span and also to counteract software that can block advertising. Some companies advertise online by buying space next to editorial content on Web sites and using animation and video to attract attention—the more traditional advertising choice on the Internet. Or they have their own Web sites where they can advertise their products and offer troubleshooting advice.

As a result, e-commerce has prospered fairly well, allowing people to shop online. Shoppers can pick out products, change colors and styles, and buy online—then play virtual games. The shipment arrives on their doorsteps in a few days. Convenience sells products, and the more customers use credit cards securely to order online, the more willing they are to spend via the Internet. People who want to avoid having their e-commerce use tracked can install adware and spyware software to identify and quarantine cookies they might be downloading.

Any communicator must be creative and proactive in thinking about how the Internet can increase an organization's reach with its audience. Communication can be as targeted as podcasts and as broad as streaming video on a Web site. With the Internet, any company's information is available 24 hours a day. Web sites must be constantly monitored and updated, information has to be accurate and complete, and sites must be easily navigable.

For college students, the specifics that make up strategic communication online could be wildly different at graduation day from what you see in today's media landscape. Any changes are likely to offer more diverse career opportunities for those who have the skills to use words effectively and correctly and to add visually rich elements to online content.

Exercises

1. You are the public relations officer for the Campus Literacy Program. You want to recruit more volunteers to serve as readers to children in the community.

   a. Identify the audience(s) you are trying to reach as potential volunteers.
   b. Knowing your audience interests and media usage, identify three communications tools you would use to reach each audience.
   c. What information would your audience(s) need to make a decision whether to volunteer? Make a list.
   d. How could you evaluate the success of your communications effort?

2. You are the public relations director for Bicycle World Equipment Co. You are to write a news release for the local newspaper based on the following information:

> Bicycle World is planning to sponsor bicycle safety clinics in the public schools located in Wayne County, the company headquarters. The clinics will be held on two consecutive Saturdays from 10 a.m. to noon. Each of the county's six elementary schools will house the clinics. People who want to attend must call 555–3456 to register. The clinic is open to children 6–12 years of age. Each child must have a helmet.
>
> Bicycle World staff members will check each child's bicycle for safe operation and indicate on a check-off list any equipment that needs repair. Children will be advised of good bicycle safety, such as wearing helmets, riding in bike lanes, and using proper hand signals. Then each will be allowed to enter an obstacle course, which will test their riding proficiency. For example, as they ride down a "road," a dog may run out from between two cars. Children's reactions and reaction times will be monitored. After the road test, they will be briefed on what they did well and what they need to improve. At the end of the course, they will receive a certificate of accomplishment.
>
> "We believe bicycle safety is crucial for children," said company president Dennis Lester. "With just a little guidance, children can learn habits and rules that could save their lives. Those of us in the bicycle business want to ensure that children who use our products do so competently and safely. We want them to enjoy bicycling as a sport they can continue into adulthood."
>
> The clinics are free.
>
> Bicycle World is a three-year-old company that produces bike frames, components, bike helmets, clothing, and road guides to bicycle routes. Company President Dennis Lester is a master rider and formed the company to provide quality equipment to bicycle enthusiasts.

3. From the above information, write a one-page fact sheet based on the bicycle clinics sponsored by Bicycle World Equipment Co. You would be the contact, 555-2345. The company's address is 67 W. Lane Blvd., Your town, Your zip code.

4. President Dennis Lester at Bicycle World wants to implement a comprehensive advertising and public relations plan that will help sell more bicycles in your community. Develop a strategy that identifies target audiences and then include at least three types of advertising and PR activities that could reach each target audience.

5. Based on Exercise 4, you are to create an advertisement for Bicycle World to reach parents of children who ride bicycles. Make a list of the words that would appeal to parents looking for children's bikes, focusing on the prominent characteristics of bikes. Write at least three possible headlines for your ad, focusing on a characteristic in each.

6. Invite a professional who specializes in strategic communication to visit your class. Ask this person to talk briefly about advertising and public relations as part of strategic communication in today's competitive media environment. Have him or her talk about the importance of good writing and the influence of the Internet in strategic planning.

References

American Advertising Federation Web Site. Available at www.aaf.com.

"Auto Giants Push Harder for Magazine Product Placement," www.adage.com/news.cms? newsId545807, accessed August 19, 2005.

American Society of Newspaper Editors at www.magazine.org/Editorial/Guidelines/Editorial_and_Advertising_Pages/, accessed September 3, 2005.

Bruce Bendiger et al., *Advertising: The Business of Brands*. Chicago: The Copy Workshop, 1999.

Philip Ward Burton, *Advertising Copywriting, 6th ed.* Lincolnwood, IL: NTC Business Books, 1990.

Scott M. Cutlip, Allen H. Center, and Glen H. Broom, *Effective Public Relations, 7th ed.* Englewood Cliffs, NJ: Prentice-Hall, 1994.

George Felton, *Advertising Concepts and Copy.* Englewood Cliffs, NJ: Prentice-Hall, 1994.

Medialink Web Site. Available at www.medialink.com.

"Marketing beyond the Pop-Up," *Advertising Age*, March 10, 2003.

PR Newswire Web Site. Available at www.prnewswire.com.

Public Relations Society of America Web Site. Available at http://www.prsa.org.

Kenneth Roman and Jane Maas, *The New How to Advertise.* New York: St. Martin's Press, 1992.

Dennis L. Wilcox and Lawrence W. Nolte, *Public Relations Writing and Media Techniques, 2nd ed.* New York: HarperCollins College Publishers, 1995.

Appendix A

Keys to Grammar Quizzes

After years of working with these exercises, we recognize that no single answer exists for any exercise item. Each answer we provide is what we consider to be the best or preferred answer, rather than the only answer.

Grammar Slammer Diagnostic Quiz (pages 28–29)

1. Punctuation error. A comma replaces the semicolon because clauses on either side of a semicolon must be independent.
2. Subject–verb agreement error. The subject of the sentence is list, so the verb must agree. It is the LIST that HAS BEEN TRIMMED.
3. Punctuation error. A period or semicolon replaces the comma because commas may not separate independent clauses. Some would label this a comma splice; others, a run-on sentence.
4. Punctuation error. A comma is needed after OCTOBER 25 because commas follow all elements in a complete date and the phrase is a non-essential clause.
5. Sentence structure error. The modifying phrase, TRADITIONALLY EXPECTED TO BE IN CONTROL OF THEIR SURROUNDINGS is misplaced and needs to follow the word STUDENTS. In its present position, the phrase modifies THE INSECURITY.
6. Word use error. LIE instead of LAY when no action is taken.
7. Word use error. Modifying the word COUNCIL with the word HOPE-FULLY leaves the council filled with hope. It is preferable to say, "We hope the council...."

8. Punctuation error. Semicolons are used to separate all punctuated items in a list. A semicolon is needed after EASTERN.

9. Word use error. Use neither and nor as a matched pair. The same goes for either and or.

10. Pronoun error. Use the pronoun IT to agree with the noun COMPANY, a singular thing.

11. Punctuation error. Phrases that rename subjects (appositives) are non-essential and therefore set off by commas. Place a comma after COMMITTEE.

12. Subject–verb agreement error. LIVES is the verb that agrees with the true subject of the sentence, which is ONE.

13. Punctuation error. Commas follow both elements of a city and state combination that occurs in mid-sentence, even if the state abbreviation ends in a period.

14. Word use error. The past tense, USED, is correct usage in this idiom.

15. Sentence structure error. Including WILL PLAY in this list of parade items makes for faulty parallelism. Delete WILL PLAY.

16. Sentence structure error. This sentence is incomplete. It is a sentence fragment. Even though it is lengthy, it has no verb. Add the word CAME after SEVERAL PEOPLE.

17. Comma error. Semicolon or period needed after COOKIES.

18. The coordinate conjunction AND is used where a subordinate conjunction, such as BECAUSE or THAT, is needed and delete the comma.

19. Modifier problem. His muscles are not being a weight lifter.

20. Agreement. ITS SKIN.

1. Correct. Your princiPAL is your PAL. PrincipLES are LESSONS.

2. Correct. A waiver is a document of permission; a waver is a person who waves.

3. Incorrect. A bore is a dull person or event. A boar is a wild pig.

4. Incorrect. A navel is a belly button. Naval means pertaining to the navy.

5. Correct. StationERy is sold by stationERs.

6. Incorrect. A role is a part in a play. A roll is something rolled up, even a class list.

7. Correct. Note also bookkeeper and withholding.

8. Incorrect. Canvas is cloth. To canvaSS is to cover thoroughly, as in a canvass of the neighborhood.

9. Incorrect. Complement is a verb that means to complete. A compliment is a flattering statement.
10. Correct. Cite is correct in this case.

Slammer for Commas, Semicolons, and Colons (pages 34–35) (Rule numbers are noted before each answer)

1. Rule 4, comma after Bowl.
2. Rule 7, commas after Blimpo and man.
3. Rule 10, semicolon after strings; Rule 9, comma after basses.
4. Rule 2, comma after tall, after dark, after reading, and after fishing.
5. Rule 5, colon after concern; Rule 2, comma after 2 and 4; Rule 5, comma after 2009 and after yours.
6. Rule 8, comma after Dad.
7. Rule 10, semicolon after halftime; Rule 4, comma after however.
8. Rule 1, comma after bill.
9. Rule 7, comma after well.
10. Rule 10, semicolon after disappointment.
11. Rule 6, comma after 4, after 2008, after Baltimore, and after Md.
12. Rule 12, colon after semester; Rule 2, comma after journalism, after English, and after political science.

Slammer for Subject–Verb Agreement (pages 37–38)

1. include	9. exhibits	17. are
2. appear	10. are	18. are
3. gives	11. constitute	19. is
4. results	12. was	20. is
5. have	13. believes	21. teach
6. do	14. is	22. is
7. is	15. decides	23. consider
8. are	16. typifies	24. disagree

Slammer for Pronouns (page 40)

1. his or her	**6.** is	**11.** its
2. its	**7.** was	**12.** it
3. himself	**8.** was	**13.** are
4. its	**9.** their	**14.** himself or herself
5. its	**10.** is	**15.** his or her

Slammer for Who/Whom and That/Which (pages 42–43)

1. whom (everyone adored whom/him, the object of the sentence)
2. who (who/she was, the subject)
3. whom (Alvin avoided whom/them, the object)
4. who (who/she needed, the subject)
5. whose (not who's or who is health)

1. which, commas after gun and sale (the fact that the gun was on sale is additional, nonessential information)
2. which, comma after car (the mileage is additional, nonessential information)
3. that, no commas (the Jersey plates helped police identify the car, so essential information)
4. who, commas after Texans and drawl (Texans are people so who or whom; who is subject of spoke; how they spoke is nonessential information)
5. which, commas after gun and compartment (where she kept the gun is nonessential information)
6. who, no commas (again, person takes who or whom; who/he is subject of was; phrase tells which officer was shot so it is essential)
7. that, no commas (the lack of bullets allowed the officers to get the gun, so the phrase is essential)
8. which, comma after jail (the view from the jail cell is nonessential)

Slammer for Modifiers (pages 44–45)

1. The waiter served ice cream, which started melting immediately, in glass bowls.
2. Correct.
3. On the way to our hotel, we saw a herd of sheep.
4. Correct.
5. The house where Mrs. Rooks taught ballet is one of the oldest in Rockville.
6. Correct.
7. Without yelling, I could not convince the child to stop running into the street.
8. The critic said that after the first act of the play, Brooke's performance improves.
9. While we were watching the ball game, Sue's horse ran away.
10. Correct.
11. The bank approves loans of any size to reliable individuals.
12. After I was wheeled into the operating room, the nurse placed a mask over my face.
13. Correct.
14. Aunt Helen asked us to call on her before we left.

Appendix B

Key to Math Test

Slammer for Math (pages 51–53)

1. **a.** The ratio of men to women is 9:4. Subtract the number of women from the total to get the number of men.

   b. To get percentage, divide the difference by the base. In this case, 4 (the number of women) is divided by 13 for a percentage of 30.8 percent (the actual number is .3076 but is to be rounded to the nearest tenth for 30.8).

   c. The same process is used to figure the percentage of Hispanic men on the jury: Divide 1 by 13 for an answer of 7.7 percent.

   d. Again, divide the number of African American men (1) by the base of 13 and you get the same answer as 1c: 7.7 percent.

2. **a.** To get the cost for the center alone, multiply the number of square feet by the cost per square foot, or 15,000 by $85 for a cost of $1,275,000.

   b. The cost follows the same formula: Multiply 15,000 square feet by $25 for a cost of $375,000.

   c. To get the total cost, add the cost of the building to the cost of the furnishings for a total $1,650,000.

   d. To round off, remember that you round up after 5, 50, 500, 5,000, etc. So rounded to the nearest 100,000 would be $1.7 million.

3. **a.** To get the size, multiply 12 by 8 to get the size of one booth (96 square feet) then double it because each booth is two parking spaces. The answer is 192 square feet. Note: You can't double both measurements then multiply because the booth will grow only in width, not in depth. So the booth actually measures 16 by 12, which is 192 square feet.

   b. The company can rent 120 booths. Divide the number of spaces in the parking lot by 2 because each booth is two spaces.

    c. Multiply the number of booths (120) by $30 to get $3,600.

    d. Go back to 3a. One booth is 192 square feet. If you get two booths, you get 384 square feet.

4. a. First you have to calculate how many units per $100. So divide the house value of $175,000 by 100 and you get $1,750. Then multiply by the tax rate of 85 cents (.85) to get a tax bill of $1,487.50.

    b. Under the new tax rate of 88 cents, Sarah will pay 1,750 times .88 or $1,540.

    c. To calculate the increase in her tax bill, you need the difference between the old bill and the new bill. So subtract $1,487.50 from $1,540 to get $52.50. To find the percentage increase, remember difference divided by base or $52.50 divided by $1,487.50, or a 3.5 percent increase in value.

    d. To find out how much her property would increase, multiply $175,000 by 5 percent (0.05) to get $8,750. Add that amount to $175,000 to get the new value of $183,500. To find the tax bill, follow the steps in 4a. Remember to use the new tax rate of 88 cents per $100 to get the answer: $1,617.

5. a. The total female respondents was 275. Add the female counts of 107, 137, and 31.

    b. Total respondents is 627. (Add all the individual counts for male and female.) Divide the total number of women respondents, 275, by 627 and the percentage is 44.

    c. You cannot add rows of percentages to get this answer. You have to go back to your counts. Fifty-four respondents (male and female) supported Tucker. Divide by total 627 and the percentage is 8.6.

    d. The same rule for 5c applies here. A total of 274 supported Small, divided by the total respondents of 627, and you get 43.7 percent.

6. The key here is that if she has a 75 percent chance of band practice, she has only a 25 percent chance of going to the fair. Multiply the two probabilities, 50 percent (.5) and 25 percent (.25). The likelihood she will get to the fair is 12.5 percent.

7. The answer is C; $310. If he earns $7.50 an hour, 25 cents more means $7.75 an hour. Multiply by the number of hours, 40.

8. The answer is 61.29. You multiply the number of pounds by 0.454 to get the number of kilograms.

Index